FRAMING LATIN
AMERICAN CINEMA

Hispanic Issues

HISPANIC ISSUES
VOLUME 15

FRAMING LATIN
AMERICAN CINEMA
CONTEMPORARY CRITICAL
PERSPECTIVES

ANN MARIE STOCK
◆
EDITOR

FOREWORD BY AMBROSIO FORNET

UNIVERSITY OF MINNESOTA PRESS
MINNEAPOLIS   LONDON

The editors gratefully acknowledge assistance from the College of Liberal Arts and the Department of Spanish and Portuguese at the University of Minnesota. Chapter 11 is from *Sexual Textualities: Essays on Queer/ing Latin American Writing,* by David William Foster. Copyright 1997 by the University of Texas Press. Reprinted by permission of the publisher.

Published by the University of Minnesota Press
111 Third Avenue South, Suite 290, Minneapolis, MN 55401-2520
Printed in the United States of America on acid-free paper

Library of Congress Cataloging-in-Publication Data

Framing Latin American cinema : contemporary critical perspectives /
    Ann Marie Stock, editor ; foreword by Ambrosio Fornet.
        p.   cm. — (Hispanic issues ; v. 15)
    Includes bibliographical references and index.
        ISBN 0-8166-2972-2 (hc : alk. paper). — ISBN 0-8166-2973-0 (pb :
alk. paper)
        1. Motion pictures—Political aspects—Latin America.   2. Motion
pictures—Social aspects—Latin America.   3. Motion pictures—Latin
America.   I. Stock, Ann Marie.   II. Series: Hispanic issues ; 15.
PN1993.5.L3F73   1997
791.43'098—dc21   96-51570

For David

Contents

ix

Foreword

Ambrosio Fornet

(translated by Ann Marie Stock)

Thirty years ago, some of Latin America's most talented film-makers created a movement that would come to have continental dimensions: New Latin American Cinema. The "new" alluded to two factors, one of aesthetic character (the complete rejection of the "old" cinema, dominated by the commercialism of the large Brazilian, Argentine, and Mexican producers) and the other a sociopolitical characteristic (the fact that all its participants were young and believed in the viability of utopia). They believed, in effect, that after the triumph of the Cuban Revolution, nothing could stop the rest of Latin America from initiating a vast process of revolutionary transformation. Because cinema was considered a mouthpiece of utopia, those young filmmakers, having decided to set the example, began to dynamite the schemes of narrative cinema and propose, in their films, a serious reflection on reality and on cinematic language itself. It was the first time that this aspect of the problem — the filmic discourse, that of the very audiovisual language — acquired this importance: now the language would not only serve to "express" reality or to model the collective imaginary, but also to contribute to change the world, creating in the spectator the awareness of this necessity.

With goals so ambitious—and not always well defined—it is logical that along the way the successes would get mixed in with excesses, both in the theoretical and the practical terrain. In theory, with manifestos like the one containing Julio García Espinosa's lapidary statement: "Today a perfect cinema, technically and artistically achieved, is almost always a reactionary cinema." In practice—that is to say, in the images—with documentaries like those of Santiago Álvarez and Fernando Solanas/Octavio Getino, and with films like the following, selected at random: *Dios y el diablo en la tierra del sol,* by Brazilian Glauber Rocha, *El Chacal de Nahueltoro,* by Chilean Miguel Littín, *El coraje del pueblo,* by Bolivian Jorge Sanjinés, and *Lucía* and *Memorias del subdesarrollo,* by the Cubans Humberto Solás and Tomás Gutiérrez Alea, respectively. Similar credentials sufficed to give prestige to the movement in some European festivals, and it happened that in certain illustrious circles of Latin America—where regional cinema had always been underappreciated—some of these works were admitted to be true cultural achievements.

The notion that was imposed, however, was not so much cultural as political: for traditional criticism it was a cinema engagé, an engaged cinema based on concepts that had been defined by Rocha, in a challenging tone, as the aesthetic of violence, so that it was very easy to attribute to it the roots of simple propaganda. People began to talk—and not without a certain bitterness—of an international division in cinematographic work: that Hollywood administered entertainment, Europe art, and Latin America social conscience. (No one clarified what the function of such filmmakers as Akira Kurosawa in Japan, Satyajit Ray in India, or Ousmane Sembène in Senegal would be.) This means that the New Cinema was condemned to failure from the outset; between it and its public, beyond the problems of communication, arose also the implacable market logic. And to say cinematographic market in Latin America was to say Hollywood. The large transnationals of the medium dominate the region's screens—both the films exhibited in movie houses and those broadcast on television—and they exercise a permanent fascination over a good portion of the Latin American imaginary. Add to this an irrefutable dominion of commercial mechanisms. In the past decade an average of 240 films were produced in Latin America—two-thirds of them in Brazil and Mexico—but half of the films premiered in the region come from the United States. Fewer than ten distributors—almost all tied to U.S. transnationals—control, in great part, the circulation of films south of the Rio Grande. And tied to all of this is the dramatic problem of economics. North American cinema has at its disposal a world market that represents, at least in the West, 60 percent of screen time; Latin America constitutes only one of the sources of income, and not the most important one. The cinema of the region, in contrast, cannot rely solely on a local market. In the 1980s the average cost of producing a film was $250,000, and the price of a ticket at the box office was fifty cents, so that in order for a film to recover its production cost, it had to attract a minimum of half a million spectators, a number few films could manage in their respective markets. What to do, then, to try to get from the intruders a piece of the pie? How to conquer a part of this public, a public so near and yet so far, with the sparse and unstable domestic production? Convinced of the impossibility of either defeating Hollywood or ignoring it—of competing with its technology and its incredible financing, or of disregarding altogether its discursive strategies—the majority of Latin American cineasts divided in two groups: those who dedicated themselves, passively, to imitate consecrated models; and those who employed conventional narrative structures, but to tell *other* stories, conflicts, and peripeteias pulled from their own reality. In both cases the objective was engraved, although in a marginal manner, in what Debord called almost thirty years ago the society of the spectacle. "For aesthetic, moral and historic reasons," observed the Venezuelan director Carlos Rebolledo, "we cannot continue fooling ourselves with an alternative, sporadic, naively national cinema. Either we enter directly into the world of the spectacle, or we remain stragglers in the frivolous sainete of the past century."

The films that have accepted the challenge have almost unanimously earned critical acclaim and have demonstrated their effectiveness in communicating to diverse sectors of the public, both national and international. It is sufficient to cite a few of the most recent works: *La historia oficial* and *Un lugar en el mundo*, by the Argentines Luis Puenzo and Adolfo Aristaráin, respectively; *La ciudad y los perros*, by the Peruvian Francisco Lombardi; *Danzón*

and *Como agua para chocolate,* by Mexicans María Novaro and Alfonso Arau, respectively; *La estrategia del caracol,* by the Colombian Sergio Cabrera; *Fresa y chocolate,* codirected by the Cubans
Tomás Gutiérrez Alea and Juan Carlos Tabío. Are these authentic
achievements or simple concessions to prevailing taste? The sound
of the applause has not managed to drown out completely the
voices of alarm. Might these films reflect, on the structural and
linguistic plane, the shattering of the utopia that seems to have
been produced in the political terrain? Might these films not participate in the complex trajectory delineated by José Carlos Avellar in this very volume, as compromises, accommodations, and
rejections of the grand aspirations of the past? Do they not propose a return to the Aristotelian dramaturgy that, according to
Sanjinés, impedes us from understanding and re-creating the internal dynamic of our own reality? Be that as it may, under such
circumstances it would behoove filmmakers in Latin America not
to forget García Espinosa's insolent question of a quarter century ago; upon observing the repeated enthusiasm of European
critics, he asked, "Why are you applauding us?"

To assume such an attitude would, however, be to commit a
sin of excessive suspicion—and stubbornness. It is true that the
ways of telling determine the ways of perceiving—and, by extension, of imagining the world as something static or changing,
as something that can be transformed or as something that must
be accepted as it is—but it is not any less true that now, on the
eve of the new millennium, the priorities have changed. The
movement of New Latin American Cinema no longer exists as
such; if one were to wish to recover those postulates that are still
viable—like the most tenacious and polemic of all, that of cultural identity—they would have to be reformulated, taking into
account the specific roots of a situation characterized by its diversity and complexity. Consider the case of technology, for example. In his studies of the market, Octavio Getino affirms that
Latin American filmmakers are victims, and not beneficiaries, of
the technological revolution, but he insinuates that perhaps they
themselves are to blame for enclosing themselves in the world of
cinema instead of opening themselves to the universe of audiovisual communication. In effect, it is no longer possible to speak
of the production or circulation of images and sounds without

thinking of satellites, cable television, VCRs, compact discs...
But it so happens that this avalanche provokes an unsettling sensation among filmmakers of the vanguard. "There was a happy
time," said Mexican director Paul LeDuc ironically, "when cinema
was cinema and the world was the world. One went to the cinema
to dream and the world seemed transformable. Then the chips
arrived. And with them the TBC, the JVC and the VHS and NTSC,
and the very language became, if not incomprehensible, at least
strange and disagreeable." In this space, which some call tech-
notronic, it is not possible to continue tracing a sign of equality
between the schemes of enunciation and those of reception—as
if these last two were simple representations of the filmic discourse—because the very structure, as is known, also conditions the reading of the audiovisual text. The subject of national
cultures reappears time and time again, but now it is intricately
linked to coproductions: "It is necessary," warns Littín, "that our
films always have more than a nationality." Repeated attempts
have been made to establish cinema markets among diverse countries in the region. The "authors" who were the backbone of New
Latin American Cinema have gone on to become mere profes-
sionals in the medium from the moment they accepted commis-
sioned projects. Everyone learns English, even though the global
village is also immersed in French, Portuguese, Arabic, Spanish...
In brief, the present is not very different from the past—from
the periphery it is difficult to imagine postindustrial societies,
and at times even postcolonial ones, but it is obvious that, with
respect to cinema, the old categories of critical discourse do not
serve to make sense of the contemporary world, and are certainly inadequate for confronting the challenges it poses. The
Canadian critic Zuzana Pick defined the New Cinema as "a continental project"; today that goal—in whose origins lies the dream
of Bolívar, *la gran patria latinoamericana*—has suffered the same
misfortune as the other great narratives. It no longer seems viable. As a result, there are not any models; at best, there are *moda-
lidades*, peremptory and prosaic tactics, that serve to contend
with the new technologies and forms of production, the problems of economic yield, the necessity to elaborate a quotidian dramaturgy, which facilitates a cinema that is both economical and
attractive. And given that the majority of filmmakers and crit-

ics—often one and the same—of the New Cinema systematically put down the work of their predecessors, today the historians and critics have proposed to elaborate a vision of Latin
American cinema as a whole, in its first century, with the help of
contemporary theoretical paradigms. It is within this context
that the present volume acquires its real importance: its notable
effort to redefine critical priorities, subjecting to judgment many
of the assumptions and offering some keys for understanding
this *other* cinema—its symbolic connotations as well as its social
and cultural implications—with a renewed perspective.

Framing Latin American Cinema is the result of an indignation
that, like all legitimate searches throughout history, addresses
the question from its origins: "How has the notion of Latin American cinema been constructed through the years?" Keep in mind
that the very concept of "Latin America," coined by the French
in the nineteenth century, is extremely misguided, and it continues
to be controversial among Ibero-American historians. Professor
Ann Marie Stock, editor of this volume, has for a long time and
with a great deal of rigor been reflecting on the subject of inter-
rogating the intersections and the margins because it is there, in
the peripheral zones, where it becomes evident that traditional
critical discourse on Latin American cinema has been dominated
by conceptual schemes that "obfuscate rather than illuminate the
practices of the filmmakers." In most cases such practices deal
with abstractions and generalizations that dilute or erase altogether the specific, that which really characterizes each one of
the texts studied. For example, criticism has tended to become
entrenched in paradigms that are either geographic (national, regional), political (the metropolis-colony dichotomy), or cultural
(the division by dramatic genre), and because of this, argues Stock,
it tends to leave out all that does not correspond to these parameters. This becomes even more serious because the cancer of gen-
eralization tends toward metastasis in the weaving of the very
discourse; frequently the expressive or communicative efficacy
of a film is measured by its ability to employ this luck of filmic
Esperanto that Hollywood has imposed as a universal model of
language. In the space created by this contradictory artifice between that which is typical of a culture, for example, and the impersonal of the grammar, what becomes erased are the individ-

ual traits of the filmmaker and, along with them, those of the cinematic text. Arguments like these—among others the one that Stock has been developing in successive works—contribute to create a common platform for scholars of Latin American cinema, within and beyond Latin America, given that what some reject is not, in principle, this entelechy called Hollywood, but the incessant flow of filmic junk, technolotry, the infinite repetition of the trivial... Here, Stock has managed to bring together a group of collaborations that permit a testing of one of her boldest hypotheses: that Latin American cinema, from its origins, has been multinational and transcultural, and therefore all schemes that try to conform Latin American cinema to the Procrustean bed of traditional critical categories must be rejected. If researchers and critics wish to be faithful to their objects of study, they must instead examine the points of convergence among seemingly disparate elements, those zones where the diverse factors constituting cinema overlap and are articulated, as much in theory as in practice. It is possible, then, to discover unexplored links between production and consumption, national and international elements, literary and filmic expression, critical approaches and audiovisual discourse, cinema and television, fiction and sociocultural contexts. It has to do not only with renovating and enriching a field of study exhausted by indifference and routine but, above all, with opening new avenues for the understanding and appreciation of a phenomenon inseparable from Latin American popular culture.

Framing Latin American Cinema, moreover, has the merit of putting ideas into practice, as demonstrated by the diversity and multiplicity of the voices incorporated into this collective reflection. On the one hand, the project counts among its collaborators the two most important critics of Latin American cinema in their respective areas—José Carlos Avellar from Brazil, and Julianne Burton-Carvajal from the United States—as well as specialists like John Mraz, whose studies of the connections between Latin American cinema and its historical referents have become models of the genre, and Paulo Antonio Paranaguá, whose rigorous labor as a critic, editor, and festival organizer has contributed immeasurably to the awareness of Latin American cinema in Europe. On the other hand, the volume is enriched by the vision of specialists from other disciplines—as is the case with the cultural critic Néstor García Canclini—and the participation of young critics like Laura Podalsky and Patricia Santoro. All of this guarantees a variety of refreshing and distinct viewpoints. The set of ideas that the authors debate and propose constitutes a vigorous attempt to transcend the limitations of traditional critical discourse. Perhaps there is no better way to offer new alternatives to the study of Latin American cinema and, by extension, to the lesser-known cinematographies in other parts of the world.

Havana, summer 1995

Acknowledgments

This volume reflects the time and talents of many people. René Jara, Hamid Naficy, Fernando Pérez, Paula Rabinowitz, and Jenaro Talens expressed their enthusiasm for the project in its early stages. Ambrosio Fornet put me in touch with three of the contributors and was generous in sharing his half-century of editing experience. Lisa Grimes, Antonio Montero Campos, Mario Mora Quirós, Idia María Rodríguez, and Robert Schirmer helped me locate elusive information — in archives and libraries, from the Internet, and in the San José *páginas amarillas*. David Campagna, Kari Meyers de Riggioni, Jorge Ruffinelli, and an anonymous reviewer read parts of the volume as it evolved and offered provocative comments and valuable suggestions. The translations done by Tracy DeVine, Heather Reed, and Adriana Ximena Tatum enhanced the volume. At the University of Minnesota Press Mary Byers and Becky Manfredini saw the project through to its fruition, and David Thorstad carefully copyedited the manuscript. I am especially grateful to Nicholas Spadaccini, Hispanic Issues series editor, for his consistent and thoughtful guidance through every phase of this project. Several libraries and film centers provided up-to-date information, including the Margaret Herrick Library of the Academy of Motion Picture Arts and Sciences in Los Angeles, the Centro Costarricense de Producción Cinematográfica in San José (where director Rogelio Chacón has enthusiastically supported my research for this and other projects), and the Centro de Documentación of the Escuela Internacional de Cine y TV in San Antonio de los Baños, Cuba.

A number of programs and institutions offered financial support that made the project possible. At the College of William and Mary, a Faculty Summer Research Grant enabled me to dedicate several months to the project, and my travel to archives and festivals was subsidized in part by the Charles Center for Interdisciplinary Study, the Department of Modern Languages and Literatures, the Reves Center for International Study, and the Office of the Faculty of Arts and Sciences. Parts of this project were completed during the 1995–96 academic year, when I was the recipient of a Fulbright Lecture-Research Award to Costa Rica. The University of Minnesota supported my work in the planning stages; I am grateful to the Department of Cultural Studies and Comparative Literature, the Harold Leonard Film Memorial, and the MacArthur Program for Interdisciplinary Studies. Finally, grants from the Hispanic Issues Series at the University of Minnesota, and the Faculty Research Committee at the College of William and Mary made possible the publication of this volume.

Introduction

Through Other Worlds and Other Times: Critical Praxis and Latin American Cinema

Ann Marie Stock

> *The messenger... carries rolls of film from one cinema to another, so that people may walk without tripping through other worlds and other times and float high in the sky with a girl seated on a star.*
> Eduardo Galeano, *Century of the Wind*

> *What is cinema? It must be something important and beautiful because you're so interested in it.*
> *Por primera vez*

Documentary production in Latin America has been described by Paul Rotha as "simply a catalog of lacks." He goes on to note that "where there exists a will to use the film for public enlightenment, total absence of adequate sponsorship, equipment and skill makes impossible the development of any concerted programme equivalent to the documentary movements of Europe or North America" (341–43). For readers aware of the "boom" in film production in Latin America and of recent developments in the criticism of Other cultures, Rotha's 1952 remarks may indeed seem dated.

Yet, the critical tendency to characterize Latin American cinema in terms of absence—what it is not—still prevails. Even half a century after Rotha's contention, critical discourse often laments a perceived lack rather than embracing the profuse audiovisual activity south of the Rio Grande. That lack has less to do with the object of inquiry—Latin American cinema—than with critical paradigms intent on privileging cultural authenticity. In other words, the current critical praxis is, to a great extent, at odds with the production and consumption of films in present-day Latin America.

The essays in *Framing Latin American Cinema* foreground the tug of war between the critic and the object of inquiry, Latin American cinema. Rather than take Latin American cinema as a "natural" entity with fixed boundaries, the contributors to this volume address its construction. They do so by juxtaposing directors and films that support and challenge critical expectations of Latin American cinema, and by focusing on both production and reception. By embracing multiple modes of cultural analysis, this volume posits itself against the tendency to consider acceptable a single mode of criticism, one rooted in U.S. and European academic traditions. Such a practice effectively reduces Latin American films to illustrations of U.S. and European film and cultural studies paradigms, thereby perpetuating the center-periphery dichotomy. *Framing Latin American Cinema* challenges this privileging of "our" way of understanding "their" films; instead, it acknowledges and contemplates the ways in which critical discourse within and beyond Latin America frames cinema in the region.

Framing Latin American Cinema follows the lead of postmodern ethnographers who have shifted their focus from documenting "exotic natives" to reflecting on their encounters with the Other. Johannes Fabian's remarks, made within the context of anthropological inquiry, resonate for critics approaching Latin American cinema:

> In order to claim that primitive societies (or whatever replaces them now as the object of anthropology) are the reality and our conceptualizations the theory, one must keep anthropology standing on its head. If we can show that our theories of their societies are *our praxis* — the way in which we produce and reproduce knowledge of the Other for our societies — we may (paraphrasing Marx and Hegel) put anthropology back on its feet. Renewed interest in the history of our discipline and in disciplined inquiry into the history of confrontation between anthropology and its other are ... practical and realistic ... ways to meet the Other on the same ground, in the same time. (165)

Fabian's comments encourage us to acknowledge and scrutinize the "confrontation" between critical discourse on the one hand, and Latin American cinema on the other. By asking questions about how we make sense of those films and phenomena considered under the rubric of Latin American cinema, by recording the history of confrontation between film critics and their objects of inquiry, we concomitantly proffer alternative models for film criticism.

Cultural Authenticity in a Transnational Context

Néstor García Canclini contends that transnational migration and communication have led us to abandon "obsessions with the immaculate conception of authentic national...cultures" (11–12). Although cinema in Latin America has mediated the borders since its inception, critics have been hesitant to acknowledge and examine the ways in which filmmakers, films, and viewers cross territorial and cultural boundaries. Instead, the construction of Latin American cinema as a geopolitical entity prevails.

Critics have, for the most part, located their studies within geopolitical frameworks, treating the national cinemas of Argentina, Brazil, Cuba, or Mexico (e.g., David William Foster, Randall Johnson and Robert Stam, Michael Chanan, Charles Ramírez Berg, respectively); or they emphasize the regional, examining the New Latin American Cinema movement (e.g., Julianne Burton, Zuzana Pick). Such studies are tremendously valuable in documenting specific cultural traditions, recording as they do the trajectory of film production within the given territories. Yet, located as they are within geopolitical frameworks, they cannot adequately account for the ways in which cinema has participated in the ongoing construction of geopolitical identity within and beyond the region. Nor do they acknowledge the actual practices of making and viewing films that defy rather than reinforce national categories.

Coproduction is a common practice among the makers of *largometrajes* in Latin America. With limited budgets, devalued currencies, and soaring production costs, few filmmakers in Latin America enjoy the luxury of single-source local financing. Instead, they seek contributors from other parts of the region and beyond. Even established directors like the late Tomás Gutiérrez Alea, supported for decades from within Cuba's strong state-sponsored industry, now rely upon collaborative financing: Alea's highly successful film *Fresa y chocolate* (*Strawberry and Chocolate,*

1993) was coproduced with Mexico; *Guantanamera* (1995) was financed with Spanish currency. The prevalence of coproduction can be appreciated by considering the production credits for just a few of the films showcased during the 1994 International Festival of New Latin American Cinema in Havana: *El Acto en cuestión* (Argentina and Holland), *Angelito* (Chile and Australia), *Crucero/ Crossroads* (Canada and Colombia), *Me faz volar* (Brazil and Cuba), *Miss Ameriguá* (Paraguay and Sweden), *El silencio de Neto* (Guatemala and the United States), *Simeon* (Martinique and France), *Sin compasión* (Peru, Mexico, and France), and *De amor y sombras* (Argentina and the United States). These transnational productions illustrate the range of countries involved.

Despite the multicultural collaboration driving filmmaking in the region, critical discourse continues to privilege cultural authenticity. This tendency becomes apparent when considering, for example, the case of *Un lugar en el mundo* (*A Place in the World*, 1992). Adolfo Aristaráin's film, a contender for an Academy Award for best foreign-language film of 1993, was disqualified after a debate surrounding the film's national identity. The Academy suggested that the film, submitted as an Uruguayan entry, may actually be Argentine. After all, *Un lugar* had competed in festivals in Havana and San Sebastián as an Argentine entry and was registered in the same way for the Golden Globes. Moreover, Argentine collaborators far outnumbered the Uruguayan ones. *Un lugar* clearly did not find a place in the world of Hollywood's Academy. This controversy demonstrates the way in which cinema participates in the construction and negotiation of national identity on the one hand, and the critical insistence on cultural purity on the other. Within the context of Latin America, critical discourse appears to be at odds with the ways in which films are produced and consumed.

The *Amores difíciles* (*Difficult Loves*) films, a six-part series scripted by Gabriel García Márquez, provide another site from which to consider the tension between film theory and praxis. *Amores difíciles* conjoins filmmakers, screenplays, and themes from a variety of geopolitical contexts; works in the series include *Fábula de la bella palomera* (*Fable of the Beautiful Pigeon Fancier*, Ruy Guerra, 1987), *Milagro en Roma* (*Miracle in Rome*, Lisandro Duque Naranjo, 1988), *Cartas del parque* (*Letters from the Park*, Tomás

Gutiérrez Alea, 1988), *Yo soy él que tú buscas* (*I Am the One You Are Looking For*, Jaime Chávarri, 1988), *El verano de la señora Forbes* (*The Summer of Mrs. Forbes*, Jaime Humberto Hermosillo, 1988), and *Un domingo feliz* (*A Happy Sunday*, Olegario Barrera, 1988). Gabriel García Márquez perceives the potential of these works to "reaffirm the transnational possibilities of our identity" (Toledo, 649). Rather than highlighting the transnational features of a series involving directors from six different cultural traditions, one critic enumerates several problems with the series including its lack of "political specificity." B. Ruby Rich contends that in the six films "the qualities of individual national cinemas [are] subordinated to the creation of a homogeneous product" (23–24). The most successful film in the series, according to Rich, is *Milagro en Roma*. The critic ascribes *Milagro*'s success to director Lisandro Duque's talent and to the fact that, as "the only Colombian production in the series," it "benefit[s] from a grounding in the specificity of García Márquez's own culture" (27). Because the film can be identified as Colombian, *Milagro* satisfies the critical desire for national purity.

Guillermo del Toro, the young filmmaker who works in his native Mexico and in the United States, further illustrates both the increasing transculturation of cinema and the critical insistence on geopolitical paradigms. Del Toro distinguishes himself from other Mexican filmmakers who have relocated to southern California, stressing that he will always be a "round-trip ticket" filmmaker. "I am interested in making movies here in Los Angeles," he says, "but, of course, that's what airplanes are for. I always want to return home" (de Palma). His first feature-length film, *Cronos* (1992), produced by Mexico's Iguana Productions and Los Angeles-based Ventana Films, counts on the participation of Argentina's Federico Luppi, Hollywood's Ron Perlman, and Mexico's Tamara Shanath and Margarita Isabel. Moreover, it draws upon conventions from diverse traditions—vampire movies, love stories, family dramas, and black comedies. The innovative use of language in *Cronos* further underscores the film's hybridity. Spanish dialogues are interrupted by English and even Spanglish. Both the English and the Spanish utterances are subtitled in the film, a clever marketing strategy on the part of the filmmaker. "I know how lazy American audiences are to read subtitles," del

Toro has commented, "and this blending makes 'Cronos' almost an unsubtitled movie" (Harrington, G5). An all-Spanish version of *Cronos* exists as well, targeted primarily for Spanish-speaking audiences in the United States (Toumarkine, 8).

Neither del Toro nor *Cronos* is "obsessed" with authentic national culture. In fact, they flaunt their migrancy and hybridity. Nonetheless, García Canclini's claim that we have abandoned our "obsession" with "authentic national . . . cultures" appears overly optimistic. The elusive identity of *Cronos* indeed confounds critics, but they tend to agree on one adjective— "Mexican": "Guillermo del Toro Brings a *Mexican* Perspective to Horror Films" reads the headline for Adriana S. Pardo's article in the *Los Angeles Times*; Anthony de Palma finds in *Cronos* the "very *Mexicanness* of connecting decay and salvation—crossing horror with hope"; and David Overbey states that del Toro "gets to the heart of the eternal myth in *Mexican* style" (my emphasis). In the case of *Cronos*, it becomes clear that, to borrow the words of Paul Carter, the "genealogical rhetoric of blood, property and frontiers" prevails in spite of the combination of currencies, the hybridity of the text, the employment of multiple languages, and the marketing to diverse audiences.

I do not intend to suggest that cultural specificity has no place in critical discourse addressing cinema in Latin America, nor that claims for cultural authenticity be ignored. On the contrary, it is crucial to remember that these very parameters have been invoked by filmmakers throughout the region, most notably by cineasts in Cuba after the revolution and by adherents to the New Latin American Cinema movement. In both cases the strategy was to produce a politically engaged cinema appropriate for the revolutionary context, rejecting the theories and praxis of "old" cinema and developing a language of its own. What I do contend is that to evaluate cultural expression solely or primarily in terms of its geopolitical specificity—examining the extent to which it manifests its Cuban-ness, for example, or Latin American-ness—has serious implications; not only does it marginalize a great deal of contemporary expression, it overlooks those films that attest to culture's role in the construction of identity.

Consider, for example, the recent controversy surrounding *Frida and Diego*. When Luis Valdez cast the Italian-American actress

Laura San Giacomo in the role of Frida, Latino actors and actresses in Los Angeles protested the decision. They claimed that Valdez had "sold out," that he had been co-opted by Hollywood. Valdez defended his position, insisting that he had selected San Giacomo "not because she was an Anglo" but because of her talent and her resemblance to Frida. Valdez reminded protesters that Frida herself was "a child of America," the product of a "German Jewish immigrant father" and a "Spanish Indian (Mexican)" mother, as well as "an international citizen of the world." He admitted, too, that producers were looking for "star power" in order to market the film. These words only fueled the already heated debate. Not long thereafter, Valdez announced his decision to postpone the project, stating that "in the face of an unjust attack on my person, family, career and reputation, I can only vehemently declare that I am protesting in my own right that as a Chicano filmmaker, I have no artistic freedom in Hollywood" ("A Statement on Artistic Freedom," n.p.). The issues at stake are serious indeed: the limited options for Latinos in mainstream culture; the producers' and directors' power in hiring and casting decisions; the competing claims of artistic freedom; the connection between the U.S. Latino community and the Latin American population; and, as Valdez himself asks, the question of who determines authenticity. By framing the debate in terms of authenticity—focusing solely on Frida Kahlo's and/or Laura San Giacomo's ethnicity—one cannot address other issues such as those enumerated. To insist on viewing cultural phenomena exclusively through an authentic-inauthentic binary lens is to obliterate any space for engaging with the ways in which identities are constructed and negotiated.

Within the context of cinema in Latin America, this insistence on the national obfuscates rather than illuminates current filmmaking practices. Even though images are produced and consumed within complex transnational networks, critical discourse continues to privilege authenticity. This focus on strict geopolitical categories from the outset jettisons a range of issues related to the movement of films and filmmakers across national boundaries, the circulation of films and critics through multiple geopolitical and temporal spaces, and the links between cinema and other forms of cultural expression. To return to García Canclini's question, then, it seems that what remains when filmmakers and films constantly cross borders is, in fact, a critical nostalgia for cultural authenticity. Critical discourse remains fixed within geopolitical paradigms, while globalization increasingly impacts that body of work denominated Latin American cinema.

Flashing Back to the Future: A Century of Connections

Cinema in present-day Latin America mediates the boundaries perceived to separate geopolitical territories just as it did a century ago. Although the technology of filmmaking has indeed changed dramatically over the past century—spoken dialogue has replaced written intertitles; moving cameras have replaced stationary ones; intricate montage has lessened the reliance on single takes; colors brighten the previously black-and-white images; and special effects increasingly dazzle viewers—one important constant is the location of cinema on the borders. Moving pictures have conjoined local landscapes with distant environments; amusement parks, theaters, and other public spectacles with the filmic medium; literary texts with filmed images. The juxtaposition of cultural traditions and filmic conventions is not a new phenomenon; it did not "emerge" as a by-product of recent attention to globalization. From the outset, cinema in Latin America has effectively negotiated diverse geopolitical, cultural, and aesthetic frontiers.

Turn-of-the-century viewers greeted the new diversion with enthusiasm, pleased with the opportunity to "travel" to distant lands: "Every night the view changes," reported one Costa Rican journalist, "and what views, *mamita mía*, it's like traveling around the world" (Marranghello, 63–64). Moving pictures transported aficionados through multiple cultural contexts in quick succession. The images of distant lands enticed viewers to demand almost immediately that local surroundings also be filmed and projected. Thus, while Brazilian landscapes were projected in Havana, scenes of the island were captured on film and then carried off to the next port to be greeted by enthusiastic spectators. Images of various places in Latin America circulated among viewers in other parts of the region. As early as the first decade of this century, cinema linked the familiar and the faraway.

Early moving pictures participated in the cultural *mestizaje* not only in terms of reception—moving from one cultural context to another—but also through their production. Many of the notable "national firsts" flaunt their transnational makeup. In Argentina, the business of moving-picture production was in the hands of the Casa Lepage, a firm comprised of the Belgian merchant Henri Lepage, his Austrian assistant Max Glücksman, and the French photographer Eugène Py. The latter is credited with *La bandera argentina* (*The Argentine Flag*, 1897), the first moving picture filmed in Argentina. In Brazil, the Portuguese Antonio Leal filmed *De estranguladores* (1908), which has been termed "the first great success" in the country and "a model for the first genre of Brazilian cinematography" (Schumann, 83). In Costa Rica, Italian-born A. R. Bertoni, along with the Tico photographer Walter Bolandi, created the first feature-length film, *El Retorno* (1930). Early instances of transnational collaboration like these are complemented by examples of cultural cross-fertilization. In Mexico, Spanish culture inspired the work of many early filmmakers, including Mimí Derba and Cándida Beltrán Rendón; the former wrote her own scripts, drawing upon her experience as a *zarzuela* singer, and the latter secured the participation of Catalina Barcelá and other members of a Spanish theater company in *El secreto de la abuela* (1928). In Colombia, conventions of the Italian social melodrama popular at the time structured *La María* (1922), filmed by the Chilean Alfredo del Diestro and the Spaniard Máximo Calvo. From the time of the first projections and first productions, then, cinema in Latin America crisscrossed territorial and aesthetic boundaries. Even though critical discourse generally considers the present "globalization" of the media as an aberration—a recent and relatively unwelcome intruder—the production, consumption, and the texts themselves have been transnational from the onset. This is not to deny the grave implications of recent manifestations of globalization such as those addressed by Ambrosio Fornet, Néstor García Canclini, and José Carlos Avellar in this volume. Rather, it is to advocate a critical praxis capable of making sense of such phenomena rather than to disengage present-day cinema in the region from its past.

Toward a Critical Praxis for the Next Century

In approaching cinema in Latin America, we must move beyond the binary classification of authentic-inauthentic and the perceived separation of the present from the past. If critical discourse is to make sense of migrant culture, it must permit new questions: How does postnational culture promote a way of thinking that, in the words of Iain Chambers, "is neither fixed nor stable, but... open to the prospect of a continual return to events, to their re-elaboration and revision" (3)? Postnational practices of making and viewing films demand a postnational critical praxis, for a critical activity intent upon policing the borders of Latin American cinema is destined to marginalize current filmmaking practices. To insist upon cultural authenticity is to jettison a series of issues crucial to present-day and future film production and distribution practices related to Latin America: the experience of exile as articulated through cinema (e.g., Raúl Ruíz and Ariel Dorfman); the long tradition of exchange between Hollywood and Mexico City (e.g., Dolores del Río and Lupe Velez, Luis Buñuel and Orson Welles); the connection between Latin American and U.S. Latino audiences via Spanish-language news broadcasts and *telenovelas*; the role of transnational distribution channels (e.g., International Festival of New Latin American Cinema, Robert Redford's Sundance Institute, and the International Media Resource Exchange); the recent international popularity of "Latin American flavor" (e.g., *Como agua para chocolate* and *Fresa y chocolate*); the links among filmmakers working in Latin America and in India, Asia, and Africa (e.g., in La Escuela de Tres Mundos near Havana), and so on. To continue to define Latin American cinema narrowly, insisting upon the criterion of cultural authenticity, will only contribute to the demise of the critical object.

What is needed as Latin American cinema begins its second hundred years is a critical praxis responsive to migrant culture. More productive than lamenting the loss, or a perceived lack, is developing a method capable of accommodating those films and filmmakers who challenge the binary classification of authentic versus inauthentic. This volume reframes Latin American cinema in terms of presence rather than absence, insisting that only by embracing the border crossings of filmmakers, images and sounds, and audiences will we as critics be positioned to make sense of postnational cultural expression. Iain Chambers's observations of migrant culture are instructive; critical praxis, like the migrant culture it examines, must "abandon any pretense to a fixed site, as though it offered stable foundations...It is not solid in its surroundings, immutable in its co-ordinates. It is not a permanent mansion but is rather a provocation: a platform, a raft, from which we scan the horizon for signs while afloat in the agitated currents of the world" (Chambers, 7).

Framing Latin American Cinema is committed to foregrounding intersections and connections. The volume aims not to establish Latin American cinema as a unified body—a canon of titles or a list of characteristics or a directory of filmmakers—but to interrogate the convergence of national traditions, historical frameworks, and cultural forms. Although the essays in this volume are informed by a multitude of perspectives, they share a common interest in the intersections. The contributors interrogate the nexus of cinema and other discourses, especially history and literature, architecture and anthropology; the filmed object from the filming subject; the public from the private; film from television and video; Southern America from Northern America; and one theoretical paradigm—psychoanalysis, feminism, semiotics, historicism—from another. Moreover, all these analyses are contextualized in some way; films are not addressed as artifacts located in a generic theoretical space but as social/political/artistic expressions, affected by and effecting cultural transformation. Because virtually all the contributors to this volume have worked in archives and have interacted with filmmakers and audiences, their discussions complement the theoretical with the experiential. Dean MacCannell's comments in *Empty Meeting Grounds: The Tourist Papers* articulate the importance of the experiential: "Any discovery of a new critical subject necessarily begins and ends ethnographically, with observations of real people, events and relations. It cannot be contained in advance in philosophy, theory, or hypothesis, unless it is condemned to produce, or to fail to produce, only that which the investigator already knows" (9).

The first section examines cinema's relation to geopolitical configuration. Common to all of the essays in Part I is a conviction that cinema is crucial in constructing national identities.

Rather than treating filmic texts as purveyors or mere reflections of the national imaginary, these critics cast cinema as a central player in creating national culture. Laura Podalsky interrogates the intersection of urban spaces and cultural production within the context of 1960s Buenos Aires by relating three films—*La mano en trampa, Tres veces Ana,* and *Los de la mesa 10*—to material changes in Argentina. She articulates the dynamic intersections between the public and the private and the national and the transnational. In doing so, Podalsky illustrates cinema's participation in the construction of geopolitical paradigms. José Carlos Avellar focuses on the film production of Brazil two decades later. The turbulent 1980s were characterized by a dual glance, Avellar argues, with one eye looking back to the fleeting past and the other awaiting a glimpse of what was to come. Cinema was crucial in bidding farewell to a "national past" and heralding the arrival of a global future, a process attested to by the very films delineating the transitional period: *Bye Bye Brasil* and *Dias melhores virão.* Ilene S. Goldman also deals with the role of cinema in affecting and effecting cultural change; she locates her study in 1980s Colombia. Goldman argues that the *Violencia* or violent period in Colombia in 1948 is employed in the recent films *Confesión a Laura* and *Condores no entierren todos los días* as a parable for contemporary social and political turbulence. Her analysis underscores the power of cinema to recycle the past and to intervene in contemporary politics. Teresa Longo concludes the first section by turning her attention to a transcultural text, *When the Mountains Tremble.* In her analysis of the U.S.-funded depiction of Rigoberta Menchú, Longo rejects facile binary oppositions of dominance-resistance, Northern America-Southern America. Instead, she focuses on tension between the filming subject and the filmed object, thereby challenging theoretical paradigms that cast cultural texts as a priori national manifestations.

The mapping of geopolitical territory in the first section is followed by the plotting of the formal terrain in the second. Several critics address the ways in which cinema intersects with other cultural discourses and forms of expression including history, literature, and theater. Of primary interest once again is Latin American cinema's resistance to critical paradigms. These contributors examine the location of films and filmmakers in the interstices of various forms of cultural expression. John Mraz analyzes the ways in which three films by the legendary Mexican director Fernando de Fuentes engage with the history of the Mexican Revolution. In positing *Prisionero 13, El compadre Mendoza,* and *¡Vámonos con Pancho Villa!* alongside other historical narratives about the revolution, Mraz examines film's role in constructing or contradicting "official" histories. Patricia Santoro concerns herself with three versions — novel, drama, and film — of a single text, *Kiss of the Spider Woman.* She analyzes the varied forms of this complex work in terms of maternal discourse, and in doing so offers new strategies for engaging with issues of adaptation. Beat Borter examines the way in which Cuban filmmaker Fernando Pérez skillfully blends diverse cultural forms to create his films. Inspiration for Pérez's work ranges from Hemingway's *Old Man and the Sea* and songs by the Beatles to the films of Sergei Eisenstein and Steven Spielberg. Borter argues that, in synthesizing various forms and texts associated with distinct cultural contexts, Pérez's films challenge the critical insistence on cultural authenticity. Paulo Antonio Paranaguá traces the career of Román Chalbaud, a central figure in Venezuelan cinema and theater. Influenced by Mexican melodrama of the 1940s, Hollywood genre films, television programming, and theatrical conventions, Chalbaud's work, like that of Pérez, negotiates a number of cultural and aesthetic borders.

The final series of essays addresses film production, but the discursive event as well, the conjoining of the filmic text with the viewer/critic. Gilberto Gómez Ocampo's perspective as a Colombia-born resident of the United States enables him to reflect on his experiences as a film fan in both cultures. In considering ways in which moviegoing shaped him and others of his generation, he also comments on the shift in Colombia from Hollywood dominance to the political cinema of the 1960s and 1970s and on to television in the 1980s. Gómez's reflections offer readers a glimpse of a transcultural viewing experience. Julianne Burton-Carvajal considers melodrama and its discursive construction. After addressing the recent critical recuperation of melodrama, Burton-Carvajal argues for the employment of a new category of "melodrama of patriarchy." David William Foster analyzes the overdetermination of space in *Doña Herlinda y su hijo.* Jaime Humberto Hermosillo's film moves beyond the clichés of homosexual love, Foster argues, and cannot be dismissed as meaningful only for gay audiences. He contends that in examining such dichotomies as social obligation and personal need, the film postulates alternative clan arrangements, thereby subverting Mexican patriarchal structures. Néstor García Canclini concludes the volume with the question, "Will there be Latin American cinema in the year 2000?" García Canclini assesses audiovisual production and reception practices in Mexico, leading us to ask about the future of cinema in Latin America. His question has to do not only with the possibilities for producing films in the region, but also with the ways in which "Latin American" and "cinema" will be understood.

García Canclini's words invite us to reflect on our assumptions and practices. Our criticism, like the very migrant culture we critique, must, in the words of Chambers, inhabit "time and space not as though they were fixed and closed structures, but as providing the critical provocation of an opening whose questioning presence reverberates in the movement of the languages that constitute our sense of identity, place and belonging" (4). An examination of the gap between critical praxis and cultural expression — the desire for cultural authenticity on the one hand, and the transnational production and circulation of films on the other — constitutes just such a provocation. Certainly a critical praxis committed to embracing migrant culture yields more than one content to enumerate "a catalog of lacks."

Works Cited

Ansen, David. "Esperanto Epic." *Newsweek,* 11 April 1994: n.p.

Chambers, Iain. *Migrancy, Culture, Identity.* London and New York: Routledge, 1994.

De Palma, Anthony. "From a Mexican Grave Comes 'Cronos'." *New York Times,* 20 May 1994: n.p.

Fabian, Johannes. *Time and the Other: How Anthropology Makes Its Object.* New York: Columbia Univ. Press, 1983.

Galeano, Eduardo. "The Cinema: Havana 1910." In *Century of the Wind.* Trans. Cedric Belfrage. New York: Random House, 1988.

García Canclini, Néstor. *Culturas híbridas: Estrategias para entrar y salir de la modernidad.* Buenos Aires: Editorial Sudamericana, 1992.

Harrington, Richard. "A Monster Hit That's Not Out to Scare You." *Washington Post,* 22 May 1994: G5.

MacCannell, Dean. *Empty Meeting Grounds: The Tourist Papers.* New York: Routledge, 1992.

Marranghello, Daniel. *El cine en Costa Rica: 1903–1920.* San José: Cultura Cinematográfica, 1988.

Overbey, David. "Latin American Panorama." *Toronto Festival of Films,* 1993: n.p.

Pardo, Adrianna S. "True to His Frightful Visions: Guillermo del Toro Brings a Mexican Perspective to Horror Films." *Los Angeles Times,* 19 April 1994: F1, F8.

Rich, B. Ruby. "An/Other View of Latin American Cinema." *Iris* 13 (summer 1991): 5–28.

Rotha, Paul. *Documentary Film.* New York: Hastings House, 1952.

Schumann, Peter B. *Historia del cine latinoamericano.* Trans. Oscar Zambrano. Buenos Aires: Legasa, n.d.

Toledo, Teresa. *Diez años del nuevo cine latinoamericano.* Madrid: Societal Estatal Quinto Centenario, 1990.

Toumarkine, Doris. "October Strikes Deal for Cronos." *Hollywood Reporter,* 13 July 1993: 1, 8.

Valdez, Luis. "A Statement on Artistic Freedom." *El Teatro Campesino Newsletter* (September–October 1992): 2–3.

Chapter 1

High-Rise Apartments, Arcades, Cars, and *Hoteles de citas*: Urban Discourse and the Reconstruction of the Public/Private Divide in 1960s Buenos Aires[1]

Laura Podalsky

*The proud column was advancin' through the backed-up sewers or
the piles of garbage that mark the entrance to the capital.*[2]

Jorge Luis Borges and Adolfo Bioy Casares,
"La fiesta del monstruo"

"I had to close the hallway door. They've taken over the back part."[3]

Julio Cortázar, *Casa tomada*

Literary and filmic texts dealing with Buenos Aires proliferated in the late 1950s and early 1960s in Argentina: Beatriz Guido's short stories and novels; Osvaldo Dragún's theatrical work; Ernesto Sabato's *Sobre héroes y tumbas* (*On Heroes and Tombs*, 1961); Germán Rozenmacher's collection of short stories *Cabecitas negras* (1962); and Julio Cortázar's *Rayuela* (*Hopscotch*, 1963) among them. All of these works explore the interaction between characters and their urban environment and figure Buenos Aires as a site of alienation and disillusionment.[4] The preoccupation with the city was not isolated to literary texts but also inspired a series of works by young filmmakers such as Rodolfo Kuhn, David Kohon, Simón Feldman, and José Martínez Suárez who broke with the dominant Argentine studio system in the late 1950s and early 1960s. Known as the "generación del 60,"[5] these filmmakers formed their own production companies and were the first to systematically use location shooting for urban films.[6] Unlike the staid studio films shot on indoor sets, their films offered documentary-like depictions of the vibrant street society of young adults in Buenos Aires. Like their contemporary literary counterparts, the films often utilized recognizable urban spaces to examine the uncertain posi-

1

tion of their young protagonists in a changing social order. Thus, the city itself provided a mise-en-scène pregnant with associations recognizable to both filmmakers and audiences in Buenos Aires. An essential part of this collective imaginary of the city was the legacy of upheavals during the previous two decades. In addition to significant transformations of the physiognomy of Buenos Aires—most notably the construction of new government buildings and the growth of poor neighborhoods—urban denizens also began using the city in new and different ways.

Important physical changes occurred during the military government (1943–46) and the Peronist administration (1946–55). Commemorating Argentina's declaration of independence in May of 1810, the Plaza de Mayo as well as the surrounding buildings underwent immense transformation in the 1940s. The Banco de la Nación (1938–52), the Ministerio de Hacienda (1940), and the Banco Hipotecario Nacional (1947) located on the plaza itself, as well as the nearby Ministerio de Guerra (1938–42), were all built during this period, replacing other structures such as the old Congress building.[7] The imposing presence and neo-imperial design of these and other new financial and governmental institutions disturbed certain sectors of the populace. A distinguished architect and member of a prominent Buenos Aires family, Francisco Bullrich lamented their construction as well as the subsequent establishment of new building codes, saying "they finished off the remains of the Plaza de Mayo, which had yet to suffer the attack of municipal regulations designed to ensure that [the Plaza] was surrounded by other monstrosities identical to those that were supposedly so excellent" (470).[8] Bullrich's critique contains charged metaphors denouncing the way the new architectural order erased the remaining monuments to past glories. Thus, while spatial changes reflected social changes (specifically the displacement of the export oligarchy by new industrial and military elites), they also accentuated social tension, as is evident in Bullrich's comment.

The accelerated immigration of the 1940s, a response to both Argentina's stumbling agricultural economy and the growth of its industrial sector, also marked the city-text. Existing urban residences could not absorb the immigrants, nor did construction expand sufficiently to do so. The housing crunch forced immigrants to build their own homes. Some built temporary housing called *villas miserias* in areas between railroad lines and on the border between vacant state lands and residential neighborhoods. Other immigrants lived in old mansions that had been converted into individual apartments called *hotel-pensiones*. Traditional sectors of Buenos Aires society found the presence of the masses threatening as they transgressed or "played" with what Michel de Certeau calls the "literal meaning" of the city or the ordered and ordering "geometric space of city-planners and architects" ("Practices of Space," 136). Constructed with cast-off building materials, the *villas* had a patchwork appearance, exhibiting the qualities of bricolage. The *hotel-pensiones* were even more transgressive, signaling the fall of the oligarchic sectors as immigrants appropriated and partitioned the residences that had formerly embodied elite wealth. These constructions and reconstructions violated a vision of the city as the signifier of an ordered society.[9]

Other challenges to this vision arose from changing uses of public urban spaces. The distinguished Argentine historian Alberto Ciria discusses the importance of mass demonstrations in the Plaza de Mayo and along Avenida 9 de Julio in defining key moments in the Peronist administration: the initial mass support for the jailed Perón on 17 October 1945; the celebration of his inauguration on 4 June 1946; and the mourning of Evita's death on 26 July 1952.[10] These new appropriations of the Plaza de Mayo and the Avenida 9 de Julio, both significant as national landmarks, provoked violent counterresponses from anti-Peronist forces. Navy planes bombed Peronist demonstrators in the Plaza de Mayo on 16 June 1955 as a prelude to Perón's September ouster. After his overthrow, the Revolución Libertadora not only forbade the use of Perón's name in 1956 through Decreto 4161 but also prohibited mass public demonstrations (Ciria, 318). All these measures contributed to efforts to "retake" the city and to wrestle control from the provincial immigrants, considered by many to be the backbone of Peronism.

The upheavals within the city occasioned by the presence and political participation of new immigrants also provoked responses from literary circles. Published under the pseudonym Bustos Domecq, Borges and Bioy Casares's short story "La fiesta del monstruo" (cited in the epigraph) presented a scathing critique of pro-Peronist demonstrations by portraying their participants as barbarians invading the gates of the city to pillage and destroy civilization. Written in 1947 during the Peronist administration, "La fiesta" circulated among a small group of friends associated with the literary magazine *Sur* until 1955 when it appeared in the Uruguayan magazine *Marcha*. While Borges and Bioy Casares's "La fiesta del monstruo" attacked the Peronist masses' carnivalesque seizure of public streets, Julio Cortázar's story "Casa tomada" (from the 1951 short story collection *Bestiario*) imaginatively depicts how this faceless "other" infiltrates the private domain of an oligarchic family and forces its last members into the streets.[11]

Why was space such an important arena of social conflict? Edward Soja's *Postmodern Geographies* (1989) provides a key for understanding the relationship between spatial and social order.[12] Looking at the interrelations between the spatial, the social, and the economic in post–World War II Los Angeles, Soja suggests how changing residential and commercial patterns were a response to the new, post-Fordist stage of capitalism, which controls labor not through temporal relations (e.g., exacting surplus value and accumulating capital by manipulating the hours of the workday) but rather through spatial relations. His discussion points to the role of the local and national government in controlling spatial arrangements through regulation (e.g., zoning laws, building regulations, tax laws), investment (e.g., the allocation of funds for public housing, awarding of national defense contracts to specific companies), and policing, as well as to other forms of spatial control exercised by "private" or nonstate sectors (e.g., land development schemes, industrial development, architectural styles). One consequence of these tactics was to effectively create and isolate neighborhoods of cheap labor within the city limits to man low-skill manufacturing jobs (e.g., in the garment industry) as high-tech industry expanded on the outskirts of Los Angeles. Similarly, in Buenos Aires after 1946, the Peronist administration's reorientation of Argentina's capitalist system from agropastoral exportation to import-substitution industrialization was accompanied by spatial shifts.[13] The Peronist administration constructed numerous *monobloques* or multifamily residential units, instituted measures to benefit the working class (e.g., rent control), and expanded the scope of the Banco Hipotecario to grant more loans to lower-income families. These state-directed initiatives were an important mechanism for creating and maintaining spatially disciplined and easily mobilized working-class groups loyal to Perón.

After Perón's ouster and the ascension of a new administration favorably disposed toward middle-class interests (if not in deeds, certainly in its liberal rhetoric), a new configuration of spatial, social, and economic forces emerged. Among other concerns, the middle classes were intent on insulating themselves by fortifying the private domain from the public sphere, which had so recently been the site of roily disturbances. The growth of high-rise apartment buildings for the upper middle class; the initiation of arcade shopping in downtown areas; and the increased use of cars by the middle class are all examples of new formulations of the public/private divide: the high-rises by establishing private spaces removed from contact with the public streets; the arcades by providing shopping areas that were both protected from and adjacent to the street; and cars by substituting individual for mass transit. The films of the "generación del 60" represent yet another attempt to reconfigure the social imaginary in a similar fashion. First evident in the Borges/Bioy Casares and Cortázar texts, the public/private binary becomes a central issue in subsequent works like Beatriz Guido's short stories, Simón Feldman's 1960 filmic adaptation of Dragún's 1957 *Los de la mesa 10* (*Those at Table 10*), and David Kohon's 1961 feature film *Tres veces Ana* (*Three Times Ana*).

Although these texts all deal with the position of the middle class in the social order, they do not offer a single or unified model of society. This was a result, at least to some degree, of the divisions within the middle class, a problematic category itself. The late 1950s and early 1960s were a time of immense political instability; no single group could foster the consensus necessary to govern for any length of time.[14] The middle class was split over ideology and economic policy. Middle-class intellectuals of differing political persuasions who had united to denounce Perón quickly splintered after his fall (Terán, 1986: 197–215). Industrialists who had profited from the protectionist policies under the Peronist administration fought with other groups who pushed for the economic liberalization that occurred under the Revolución Libertadora and even more under the Frondizi administration.[15] Contemporary cultural representations registered these fault lines within the middle class as well as the unstable position of the middle class within the larger social order. The following discussion will map out some of these fractures and reformulations by relating cultural texts to the material changes occurring in Buenos Aires. By juxtaposing an analysis of texts about the city with a discussion of urban structures, my essay will identify the multidirectional forces linking the spatial, the social, and the economic. In addition, I will argue that the negotiation of the public/private divide in the city-text and in texts about the city was a way of relocating the place of the middle class in the social imaginary. Moreover, by dislocating films, buildings, stories, and cars from their traditional interpretive frameworks, the paper will seek out a more flexible and dynamic notion of culture.

High-Rise Apartments and Crumbling Mansions

The immense growth of high-rise apartment buildings was one effort by the middle classes to restructure their own living conditions in Buenos Aires. High-rise clusters appeared in both downtown (Barrio Norte) and outlying areas (Palermo, Belgrano).[16] Their towering presence solidified the association of these neighborhoods with the upper classes. In *Buenos Aires, vida cotidiana y alienación*, Juan José Sebreli argues that the high-rises in Barrio Norte separated the rich from the poor by placing land values and rents outside the means of those who were not well-to-do (34). This segregation was also accomplished through the architecture of the buildings. In Belgrano, the apartment buildings had imposing street-level facades that forcefully separated living spaces from the public thoroughfare. In addition, this type of construction limited the number of street-level shops, which thereby lessened interactions on the streets and added to the increasingly impersonalized atmosphere of the city (Gutman and Hardoy, 230). Finally, the new high-rise apartments also created a position from which to see the city from above. In the face of the "uncivilized hordes" who had invaded the streets, the apartments offered the upper middle classes a secluded retreat above the fray and a privileged and privileging overview of the city. In his article "Practices of Space," de Certeau describes the pleasure of standing atop the World Trade Center looking down on New York and "totalizing this vastest of human texts":

> The person who ascends to that height leaves behind the mass that takes and incorporates into itself any sense of being either an author or spectator... His altitude transforms him into a voyeur. It places him at a distance. It changes an enchanting world into a text. It allows him to read it; to become a solar Eye, a god's regard. (122–23)

In Buenos Aires, the high-rises offered a position from which to see society as a whole, a perspective impossible from the streets. While at once a response to changing economic conditions, the apartment buildings also effected changes in one's social and cultural outlook. In this case, the constructions made available a vision of an integrated city-text for those who could pay for it. If readable, the city might be controllable and less threatening.

Fashioning an overview of the city was a central concern of contemporary Argentine historians. In his 1976 book *Latinoamérica: las ciudades y las ideas*, Argentine scholar José Luis Romero wrote a comprehensive history of Latin American cities. Although the book is not solely about Buenos Aires, the Argentine city provides a key example of the trends he identifies.[17] As a historian, Romero's primary device for understanding the city is temporal, not spatial. He divides the history of the Latin American city into six periods, from the Spanish conquistadores' conception of the city as a civilized (and civilizing) outpost in an otherwise savage territory to a twentieth-century vision of cities as overpopulated and volatilely divided. Romero suggests that Latin American cities experienced immense changes after 1930 as the radical shifts in the world market forced Latin American countries to reorganize their economies based on industrialization. According to Romero, *ciudades burguesas* (the Latin American city from 1880 to 1930) ruled by middle-class sectors supported by foreign capital became industrializing *ciudades masificadas* or "massified cities" (the city from 1930 onward) split between the *sociedad normalizada* and the *sociedad anónima*. In his last chapter, titled "Ciudades masificadas," he explores how the *sociedad normalizada* and the *sociedad anónima* ("normalized society" and "chaotic society") vie for power and frequently characterizes their struggle as a conflict over space.

Romero tries to present a balanced commentary and is critical of both the complacency of the *sociedad normalizada* and of the naïveté of the masses. Despite his desire to maintain a critical distance from his objects of study, his analysis is peppered with spatial references that display an affinity with the perspective found in the stories of Borges/Bioy Casares and Cortázar. The social conflicts in the *ciudad masificada* are often described through the point of view of the *sociedad normalizada* as transgressions by the masses. Discussing the general urban trend toward "massification," Romero says: "even the upper classes became massified. Riches couldn't prevent their possessor from being pushed in the streets, or from having to stand in line for an elevator" (248).[18] Romero reiterates the same image of the harassed elite pedestrian later in the chapter: "a person who was in the habit of making way for others was confounded by those who pushed him aside to win a space" (365).[19] In fact, Romero takes up the perspective of the *sociedad normalizada* in many of his descriptions of nonelite sectors: "They were seen in the streets of Mexico City, Bogotá, or Buenos Aires in compact groups, ignorant of the rules of urban society, trampling the system that was already second nature for everybody else and taking over or destroying that of 'the others,' of the *sociedad normalizada*" (334).[20] His descriptions are often visual ("*se los vio en las calles de México*," "*Se veía que la ciudad se inundaba*"). Ostensibly acting as an objective observer of the immigrants' behavior, Romero periodically conflates his perspective with that of the *sociedad normalizada* that "*visualizó el conjunto inmigrante que se filtraba por sus grietas como un grupo uniforme* [visualized all immigrants that seeped through its chinks as a uniform group]" (323, 333). Speaking of the masses who squeezed through the cracks in normalized society, Romero again continually highlights the point of view of traditional groups: The *sociedad normalizada* "*la observó en ciertas calles céntricas los días de fiesta, acaso desde un balcón o desde un automóvil, y la vio como hidra de mil cabezas* [observed the *sociedad anómica* in certain downtown streets on special holidays, perhaps from a balcony or an automobile, and saw it as a hydra with a thousand heads]" (339). The last description could easily describe the crowd in Borges and Bioy Casares's "La fiesta del monstruo."[21] Like the high-rise apartment dwellers, Romero looks down on the *sociedad anómica* to read the city-text that is incomprehensible when experienced among jostling bodies on the street level. I do not wish to overstate the affinity between Romero's position and that of traditional sectors. Rather than seeing a thousand-headed monster as did Borges and Bioy Casares, Romero finds an unstable and factionalized social group reacting to changing economic conditions. However, in order to create a cohesive chronological master narrative about the Latin American city, Romero needed to trace lines of continuity and rupture. His metaphors characterizing the masses as floodwaters or crabgrass indicate his inability to see the actions of the immigrants as anything but a breach of the norms and consequently account for his reliance on the perspective of the *sociedad normalizada*.[22]

Fiction writers also wrote about the divided and divisive nature of Argentine society. However, few attempted a systematic overview of Buenos Aires.[23] Unlike Romero, who mapped out a comprehensible vision of society often focusing on spatial conflict in the public sphere, short stories many times explored the life of an isolated individual within the private sphere. Contemporary texts often used decaying mansions, apartment buildings, and various other smaller residential units as metaphors for changing social relations. By tracing the fall of the mansion and the rise of the apartment building, texts like Cortázar's "Casa tomada" and *La mano en la trampa* (both story and film) decried the increased fragmentation of urban society. Beatriz Guido's 1960 story "La mano en la trampa" and Leopoldo Torre Nilsson's 1961 film adaptation are chilling coming-of-age tales centered on the experiences of Laura Lavigne, the last in the line of an oligarchic family living in a town called San Nicolás between Rosario and Buenos Aires (12) founded by her ancestors. Set in the early 1950s during the Korean War (20), the characters' struggles can be read as an allegory for the final blow delivered to the oligarchy by the Peronist administration. On a holiday from boarding school, Laura returns to the huge family mansion where she lives with her mother, her aunt, and a crippled hunchback who was the bastard son of Laura's father. The illegitimate son lives in the attic, connected to the other inhabitants solely through the dumbwaiter. The Lavigne women support themselves by working as fine seamstresses for the women of the town. Similar to the siblings in Cortázar's

"Casa tomada," they mask their failing economic condition by maintaining an aristocratic facade, both in architectonic and personal terms. They cling to their ancestral home and steadfastly call their clients "visitors."

Both the story and the film portray the family's mansion as an entrapping space. Laura's move into adulthood is mapped onto her exploration of the house, specifically her gradual and horrifying discovery that her aunt Inés has lived in the mansion's attic under the guise of being the bastard son. Scorned by her fiancé Cristóbal Achával twenty years earlier, Inés and her sisters covered up the affront to their honor by hiding Inés while telling everyone in the town that she had moved away to marry a rich American. The ultimate sign of Inés's imprisonment is her weekly correspondence with an inmate of Alcatraz, the prison island in California (20, 44). Ironically, it is the convict's letters (ostensibly those of her American husband) that confirm the family's assertion that Inés has escaped San Nicolás (and her fiancé's betrayal) for a better life. Enclosure in the Lavigne household is self-imposed not only by Inés but by the entire family — with the exception of Laura. In the story's first-person narration, Laura disparages the way her mother and her other aunt "locked themselves up in the old shell [of the house]" (8). The story figures the family's behavior as a sign of social stagnation, a rejection of their changed social status after the family's *quinta* was sold off in lots (7), and suggests that it is the fragmentation of that oligarchic domain that prompted the women to retreat into an ever more constricted space.

Torre Nilsson's film version plays on the artifice of studio sets to represent the decay of oligarchic families; studio interiors highlight the mansion's claustrophobic atmosphere.[24] The film figures Laura's own growing sense of entrapment by shots that place her behind the gates that separate her home from the street and by others that frame her through terrace moldings and windowpanes. When Laura first meets Inés, the shot-reverse shot alternates between a high-angle shot of Laura through an opening in the terrace with a low-angle shot of Inés through a windowpane. Thus, in the initial moment of recognition, each sees the other trapped by parts of the house. The juxtaposition of these shots presents Laura and Inés as doubles, mirror images of one another.

The two are linked in other ways. When Laura enters Inés's room, the camera frames her through the windowpane in a medium close-up as Inés shuts a door in the background. The framing captures the claustrophobic atmosphere experienced by Laura, who is caught within windowpanes while the shot's deep focus emphasizes her affective distance from her aunt. Through these shots, the film effectively visualizes Laura's inability to escape the strictures placed on her by her family.

The Lavignes' inevitable destruction becomes apparent when Laura's fear leads her to contact Inés's former fiancé, Cristóbal Achával. Laura hopes that by confronting Inés, she will be able to free herself from her aunt's fate (21, 24, 27). Achával is a successful businessman who commutes between his family, home, and car dealership in San Nicolás and his apartment and racing career in Buenos Aires. As a member of the new bourgeoisie, Achával embodies the altered economic relations and lifestyles that emerged under Perón and signaled the downfall of the Argentine oligarchy. When Laura enters the attic with him, the ensuing confrontation dismantles the family's aristocratic facade and precipitates Inés's death.

However, Guido's story is not simply an indictment of Argentina's stagnant oligarchy; it also critiques the new social order. Rather than liberating Laura, Achával's "rescue" leads to new types of incarceration in the capital. After Inés's suicide, he takes Laura to his apartment located near La Recoleta in Buenos Aires. After Achával returns to San Nicolás, Laura leaves the apartment to walk down Santa Fe Avenue to Harrod's department store in the *microcentro* and then watches a film on Corrientes Avenue. Her brief tour of the city ends significantly at the Palermo zoo, a place of institutionalized entrapment that functions as a metaphor for Laura's current situation. When she returns to the apartment, Laura encounters her double in the numerous mirrors that line the walls:

> I returned at the end of the afternoon; I lay down on the bed, on the center of the bed. I turned on the nightstand light and sought my image in the mirror.
> Then I screamed. I screamed from dread, from terror: the mirror reflected Inés's room, with Inés on the bed; her live skeleton, between tulle and lace. (55)[25]

From Laura's point of view, the Buenos Aires apartment is a new type of cage where Cristóbal "keeps" her and employs a woman named Plácida to care for her. Like her aunt who claimed that the zoo animals were not as bad off as people said (42), Laura submits to Achával: "Dejé de llorar. Después de todo, tenía que acostumbrarme. Eran dos cuartos; quizá uno solo, donde él *nos* había encerrado" (55; my emphasis).[26] Laura's statement emphasizes the final elision of her identity with that of her aunt, which the film expresses through a subjective point-of-view shot. After a long shot of Cristóbal and Laura entering the apartment, the film cuts to a close-up of Laura reflected in the mirror with her aunt's bed located behind her. As she draws closer to the mirror, the sound of Inés's sewing machine becomes audible as the lighting gradually fades to isolate the reflection of Laura's face against a totally darkened backdrop.

By privileging Laura's subjective state of mind in the final moment, Guido's story and Torre Nilsson's film present a somewhat ambivalent perspective on the changes occurring within Argentina. The texts clearly critique the decrepit oligarchy, particularly its social suffocation of women. However, the story and film also suggest that the triumph of the new bourgeoisie does not change the situation of women. Laura's move to the city is not depicted as progress but rather as the continuation of the gendered division of space into public (male) and private (female) spheres. Both versions of *La mano en la trampa* unmask the repressive force of the separate sphere ideology. The texts argue that, rather than protecting women from harsh and uncertain life on the streets and in offices, the separate sphere ideology entraps women. They stop short of indicting the capitalist economy, which, I would argue, the separate sphere ideology both reflects and helps reproduce.[27] However, Guido and Torre Nilsson's critique appears even more radical placed against other efforts to refigure the urban text. Both the newly built high-rises and Romero's analysis offered overviews of Buenos Aires that recuperated the status of the city as an interlocking totality. In contrast, Guido's story and Torre Nilsson's film characterized urban life as hopelessly fragmented. The tensions they highlighted in the public/private binary would continue to be explored by other writers and filmmakers.

Arcades, Cars and *Hoteles de citas*:
Negotiating the Public/Private Divide

Certain contemporary urban innovations mediated the public/ private divide. Arcade shopping grew markedly during the 1950s as did the use of cars in the early 1960s. Like the high-rise apartment buildings, the two may be interpreted as responses to the "massification" of the street. Both provided a means of being simultaneously protected from yet thoroughly connected to common public thoroughfares, allowing the middle classes to enter the public sphere without mixing indiscriminately with the masses.

In 1945 the architectural firm Ashlan and Ezcurra remodeled the Bon Marché building on Calle Florida, a central street lined with shops in downtown Buenos Aires, as a commercial arcade with 130 shops facing inward. The walls were covered with frescoes by important contemporary artists such as Urruchúa, Berni, Colmeiro, Spilimbergo, Castagnino, and Torres Aguero (*Architecture*, 38). Named after the buildings' original owner, Ferrocarril Pacífico, Galería Pacífico was the first of many arcades designed by the firm. In subsequent years, other Ashlan and Ezcurra arcades appeared in the downtown area (Galería Santa Fe 1644 in 1954, Galería Florida 971 in 1957, Galería Florida 132 in 1959) as well as in Belgrano (Galería Cabildo 1749 in 1951 and Galería Cabildo 2272 in 1959). While not limited to the middle-class consumer, the arcades' locations and dates of establishment—during and after the demise of the Peronist government when the increased spending of working-class groups was curtailed—suggest that they were aimed at the middle-class consumer. The arcades were concentrated in the same middle-class areas where high-rise apartment buildings were built in the late 1950s. While the high-rises removed their residents from casual encounters with strangers on the street, the arcades offered passageways protected both from the weather and from hurrying pedestrians. For Walter Benjamin, "the relation between the arcade and the street was one of the relation between the interior and the exterior. The arcade offered a sheltered retreat from the chaos of the street and provided a public interior, a separate arena for public social life" (Frieburg, 74). Arcades provided liminal spaces, both private and public, for leisurely consumption. Often covered with murals by prestigious artists (*Architecture*, 50), the arcades gentrified commerce.

Cars offered another way to circulate in the public sphere while protected from unforeseen encounters. As suggested by Romero, automobiles as well as balconies served as platforms from which to view the masses. Even the Peronist administration was concerned about what middle-class car owners might see while driving. In the 1950s, it built walls to hide the *villas miserias* that had popped up along the newly constructed highways from Ezeiza International Airport ("La ciudad de masas," 220). Cars increasingly provided an alternative to a public transportation system dominated by the working classes. Immigrants, originally entering Buenos Aires from the interior on railroad lines (Romero, *Latinoamérica*, 332), continued to use trains, along with buses, as their primary means of transportation ("La ciudad de masas," 216). Meanwhile, the number of automobile owners increased. According to Sebreli, the number of cars in Argentina went up from 341,000 in 1955 to 400,000 in 1960 (153). This trend continued in the following decade when "the number of cars per 1,000 inhabitants rose from 23 in 1960 to around 75 by 1971" (Jenkins, 177). Both the extension and the cost of transportation were central to the differentiated dispersal of the Buenos Aires population according to class.[28] In the 1960s, the expanding highway system allowed certain sectors to move farther away from their place of work while the cost of automobiles tended to limit their use to the upper middle class. Cars were increasingly favored by those living in the upper-middle-class areas north of the city (Gutman and Hardoy, 225–26) who, after the mid-1960s when the government constructed the Acceso Norte channeling Routes 8 and 9 into Avenida General Paz, were able to move out to what had formerly been their summer houses (Chiozza, 440).[29] Contemporary literary and filmic texts consistently use cars and other types of transportation to symbolize the differences between their characters. In Guido's "La mano en la trampa" and in Torre Nilsson's film adaptation, the motor of Cristóbal Achával's car, which repeatedly penetrated the walls of Laura's decaying home, connotes the insistent presence of a new, more quickly paced lifestyle to which Laura finally accedes: "yo, en un coche de carrera, a 120 kilómetros por hora, lejos, muy lejos de mi casa" (36). In Simón

Feldman's *Los de la mesa 10* and the second episode of David Kohon's *Tres veces Ana*, modes of transportation mark differences between the characters' positions within the middle class itself; members of the upper middle class drive cars while those of more limited means ride public transportation.

The presence of cars in these films was part of a larger commentary on the position of young adults within the social order. The films figured this conflict in spatial terms, often showing their protagonists squeezed out of the sanctioned private space of the home and participating in new spatial arrangements that straddle public and private spheres. Cars provide individualized mobility for upper-middle-class characters seeking erotic encounters in weekend and summer retreats away from the prohibitive eye of their parents (e.g., the second episode of *Tres veces Ana* and Rodolfo Kuhn's 1961 *Los jóvenes viejos*). Those from the lower middle and working classes must act out their private relationships in public cafés, plazas, and bus stops. The films also deal with other liminal structures such as *hoteles de citas* (hotels of appointment or "no-tell motels"), which are public places for private sexual affairs. All these films focus on the inability of young adults to weave themselves into an urban loom hostile to their individual needs. On the level of urban landscape, the arcades, cars, and *hoteles de citas* offered new liminal spaces bridging the public/private divide and assuaging some of the more hostile aspects of public spaces for the middle class. On the level of cinematic discourse, the films suggested that attempts to negotiate this divide were not always entirely successful. Like *La mano en la trampa*, Feldman's *Los de la mesa 10* and Kohon's *Tres veces Ana* depict the private sphere as repressive and alienating for young adults rather than as a tranquil space for the middle-class family. Although both films link this use of space to the class structure, neither ultimately indicts the capitalist order.

Initially, *Los de la mesa 10* appears to critique the class structure that separates its young protagonists, José and María, who meet at a friend's graduation party and gradually fall in love.[30] José is a mechanic and María, a student hoping to complete a degree in architecture to follow in her father's footsteps. The film figures their class differences in spatial terms by contrasting their homes. María lives as an only child with her parents in a large two-story house spacious enough to include a study for her successful father, who is designing a building in Mar de Plata. But María's parents have a conflictual marriage and their home is fraught with tension. After María returns home from her first date with José, she overhears her parents arguing. A medium shot frames María lying among pillows on her bed listening to her parents' offscreen fight. The shot privileges María's experience of the house by isolating her in the corner of the room to simulate the suffocating effect of her parents' mutual hatred. Thus, *Los de la mesa 10* critiques her parents' use of their ample space, which clearly alienates their daughter. José's problem is not affective isolation but rather limited resources. José lives with his parents and younger brother in a cramped apartment in a building shared by other people. Readying himself for his date with María, José argues with his father over using the bathroom mirror to comb his hair. Later his family's needs constrict José's movements in more serious ways. When José and María decide to marry, his father angrily reminds him that the family cannot live without José's wages. While *Los de la mesa 10* differentiates between the two families' spatial resources, the film also highlights similar family pressures that drive both José and María out of their respective homes and onto the streets. In so doing, the film subordinates class differences to generational conflict.

As suggested by the nonspecificity of the film's title and the protagonists' names, José and María's dilemma symbolizes the problems of innummerable young people in Buenos Aires who remain anonymous among the urban crowds. This was the reading of contemporary critics like Tomás Eloy Martínez, who titled his review of the film "*Los de la mesa 10* y todos los demás" (*La Nación*, 2 October 1960). By exploring the way José and María traverse the public/private divide, *Los de la mesa 10* maps out the liminal position of young adults in the social order. Squeezed out of their family homes, José and María use public space (cafés, plazas, beaches, and subway stations) for their romantic encounters. They must negotiate their desire for privacy with the ever watchful eye of the law, which stands guard over the separate sphere ideology. After meeting in a café on Corrientes for their first date, José and María meander through a park where María accidentally discovers another couple kissing, an embrace that eroticizes the public space. When María and José first kiss at the base of a nearby tree, however, their action is censured. Caught in the illumination of a flashlight, the two awkwardly separate as a policeman barks, "Éste es un parque y no otra cosa." Under the harsh light of the law, which judges their actions inappropriate to that space, reminding them that this is a park and not something else, their kiss appears transgressive. Thus, the young couple is caught in limbo by the prohibitions imposed by parents and policemen over the use of home and street.

José and María's position becomes increasingly untenable. The couple initially responds to these prohibitions by looking for their own private space. Despite their families' objections, they decide to marry. Their search for their own apartment, however, becomes ever more difficult as they calculate the costs. When María cannot find a job and José quits his second job because of exhaustion, both realize they cannot overcome these obstacles. Their inability to negotiate public spaces or to financially handle a legitimate private space as a married couple leads José and María to an unsanctioned private space, an apartment of one of his male friends. The sequence portrays their awkward transgressions of social conventions in spatial terms. To enter the apartment, they must pass unobserved through public hallways. Positioned slightly above their heads and angled down at the corner of the corridor, the camera emphasizes the way the passageway boxes them in. Once inside the apartment, a series of jump cuts and canted frames mimic their distracted and frenetic embraces. The shots' spatial discontinuity de-eroticizes the sequence. Thus, the film depicts the apartment as a space that is part of, rather than separate from, social conventions. Overhearing a key scraping against a lock, María breaks apart from José, thinking that an intruder is about to discover them. Even after it becomes apparent that the "intruder" is really another tenant entering his/her apartment, María remains agitated and demands to leave. While the sequence contrasts the physical divide between private (apartment) and public (hallway) space, it also identifies their symbiosis, each shaping and informing the use of the other. The sequence suggests that there is no place — private or public — "outside" the rules of society.

While Feldman's film critiques the suffocating effect of this social ordering of space on young adults, it also shies away from indicting the bourgeois order that propagates the public/private division. By privileging the conflict between generations over one between classes, the film reasserts humanist values, a perspective evident in the final frame. María breaks off with José at their café table (*mesa* 10) where they've gone after their ill-fated liaison in the apartment. Walking out to Corrientes, she flags a cab whose driver asks her, "¿Adónde va?" Without responding, María slowly leaves the cab before it pulls away from the curb to stand outside the café window and peer down at José. The next shot frames them walking down Corrientes. As the camera tracks back, the two become indistinguishable from the other passersby. Thus, the ending suggests that their love withstands the societal pressures and tempers the inhumane anonymity of the city streets. Unable to find direction on her own (in the cab), María is able to move "forward" with José by her side. In so doing, Feldman's film reasserts the bourgeois values it initially tries to critique.[31]

David Kohon's 1961 *Tres veces Ana* presents a somewhat more severe critique. The film is split into three independent narratives involving women named Ana. Part I of Kohon's film focuses on the relationship of a young couple, Juan and Ana, who negotiate their way through a hostile urban environment, from entrapping family homes through public trolley stops and park benches to liminal *hoteles de citas*. Like *Los de la mesa 10*, *Tres veces Ana* explores the alienating effects of a couple's dislocation from the social order. However, Kohon's film offers no recuperative message. Its somewhat elliptical narrative highlights disjunction rather than continuity. The minimal dialogue places greater weight on incidental background noise and the expressive quality of the visual track to suggest that individuals are defined by their environment. Unlike Feldman's film, Kohon's work suggests that individual will is insufficient to overcome social and spatial conditions.

The suffocating family environment is not expressed through conflict but rather through silence. Two brief sequences show Juan eating with his parents and younger brother while exchanging only utilitarian comments like "¿La sal?" and "Toma." The overhead shot that opens the second sequence captures their affective isolation—emphasizing how each body is separate from the others. Parallel sequences with Ana and her mother demonstrate a slightly less oppressive yet equally alienating environment. Two of the three sequences begin with a medium shot from the street through the window into Ana's apartment. By framing Ana behind the crisscrossed grating, the shot effectively summarizes her feelings of entrapment. Juan and Ana find little freedom outside their homes. The public spaces where they encounter each other offer little privacy. On their first date, they rent a rowboat in a public park in Palermo. The slow track that follows the course of their boat in the background reveals other couples embracing on park benches in the foreground. A subsequent trip to Plaza San Martín situates their embrace in a similar context. A medium close-up frames their embrace from behind as they sit on a park bench and includes other couples who walk by arm in arm. These sequences place Juan and Ana's dilemma within a larger social field and problematize the separation of the public and the private. Public parks become places of romantic encounters and embraces formerly shared in the private sphere.

The film explores the couple's awkward use of these and other, more liminal spaces such as *hoteles de citas* that rent out private space.[32] References to the price of privacy are made on a number of occasions. On their first visit to the hotel, the manager asks for 200 pesos. When Juan and Ana go to the hotel for the second time, Juan must first check his wallet before they leave the bench in Plaza San Martín. The film also ties commerce to sanctioned sexual relationships like marriage. When Ana tells Juan she is pregnant in a café over the sounds of clattering coffee cups, traffic, and casual conversations about soccer games, Juan reminds her that they both help to support their families and cannot marry. Later, Juan expresses his fear of living in *piezas infernales*, hellish one-room apartments, like the unemployed men he sees on a daily basis when speaking to his doctor-uncle, who performs Ana's abortion. After the procedure, the uncle urges the two to marry and criticizes what he sees as the couple's irresponsible behavior. Juan responds, "la moral sale cara, sabes" (morality is expensive, you know). The couple's plight highlights the troubled division between the public and the private in contemporary Buenos Aires. *Tres veces Ana* suggests that the private (home) is no longer separate from but rather a product of the world of commerce, and that personal feelings are not unfettered from their material and social context. The abortion that precipitates the dissolution of Juan and Ana's relationship symbolizes the breakdown of the middle-class family.

Both *Los de la mesa 10* and *Tres veces Ana* represent the alienation of their young protagonists in spatial terms. However, their respective analyses of the contemporary situation are different. Feldman's film presents space as a reflection of social relations, thereby privileging the power of the individual to overcome spatial circumstance through reasserting the possibility of transcendental love. In contrast, Kohon's film represents spatial arrangements as implacable social forces that exceed the will of individuals. Although *Tres veces Ana* ends like *Los de la mesa 10* with the reunion of the young couple, Kohon's film characterizes their reconciliation as more troubled. In the final sequence, Juan approaches Ana while she waits in line for the trolley. As in the café where they discussed Ana's pregnancy, their conversation is permeated with the sounds and sights of the streets. High-angle shots from behind a tall iron fence lined with the books of a street vendor frame their exchange against the backdrop of the city. As Juan tries to convince Ana that they are better off together "sea como sea" (however that may be), and as she reminds him that they cannot start over at the same place, the voice of a man selling the latest newspaper and the sound of cars passing nearby filter through their words. Placing their reconciliation against a large advertising sign, the film situates their exchange as part of a larger process of negotiation in which love is not transcendental but rather contingent upon a myriad of everyday material conditions. In this and its other two episodes, *Tres veces Ana* decries the commodification of human relations as the source of alienation and, ultimately, social breakdown.

Negotiating Urban Spaces

As Buenos Aires changed, films and other texts about the city offered not simply reflections of the altered urban environment but also contestations to it, attempts to intervene and shape spatial and social life. Whereas Romero's history of the city was a literary corollary to the material changes promoted by middle-class sectors to recuperate their spatial control, films like *La mano en la trampa*, *Los de la mesa 10*, and *Tres veces Ana* unmasked the alienating effects of the city by critiquing the public/private divide that lay at the foundation of a bourgeois notion of the social order. Kohon's film, in particular, presented a pointed critique by revealing the commercial aspects of domestic life.

Nevertheless, the radical charge of the films was somewhat limited. The texts were not about people marginalized by the social formation and the economic order but about those—like middle-class women and young adults—who occupied liminal positions within the mainstream. The films made no references to the provincial immigrants present in the city. Nor did they mention the contemporaneous political climate of Arturo Frondizi's failing administration. Elected in 1958, Frondizi represented the last hope for promoting social cohesion through liberal principles. Even without direct referents, the films of the "generación del 60" registered traces of this liberalism. Structured around a limited number of characters, the films somewhat conventionally represented social conflict as a struggle between individuals. They did not deconstruct the public/private divide but rather lamented its hypocrisy. Like the increased use of cars, arcades, and *hoteles de citas*, the films were negotiations of the altered social landscape. While trying to make sense of the alienating cityscape, they actually exposed the regulation and commodification of private as well as public life. Although the films highlighted Argentine society's inability to reproduce a social-spatial order that could successfully integrate the next generation into the normative social fabric, they could not move beyond the concerns of middle-class sectors to reimagine the social formation.

Notes

1. I would like to thank John Crider, Daniel Balderston, and Ana M. López for their many helpful comments on this essay.

2. "La gallarda columna se infiltraba en las lagunas anegadizas, cuando no en las montañas de basura, que acusan el acceso a la capital" (translation cited from *Borges: A Reader,* ed. Emir Rodríguez Monegal and Alistair Reid [New York: E. P. Dutton, 1981], 207).

3. "Tuve que cerrar la puerta del pasillo. Han tomado la parte del fondo." The story appeared first in *Bestiano* in 1951. It was published alone in book form in 1969. All translations are those of the author unless otherwise noted.

4. The exploration of the urban environment and its denizens was also a central concern of the emergent field of sociology. Gino Germani, one of its earliest practitioners in Argentina, studied the phenomenon of urban migration by

comparing two neighborhoods in Buenos Aires. See "Inquiry into the Social Effects of Urbanization in a Working-Class Sector of Greater Buenos Aires," in *Urbanization in Latin America*, ed. Philip M. Hauser (New York: International Document Service, Columbia Univ. Press, 1961). While Germani explored the experiences of working-class immigrants, Juan José Sebreli's *Buenos Aires, vida cotidiana y alienación* (1964) was the first comprehensive study of the city's class structure. The book was amazingly popular, selling forty million copies between summer 1964 and October 1965 (*Primera Plana*, 26 October 1965: 39) and issuing its fifteenth edition in 1979.

5. Simón Feldman, *La generación del 60* (Buenos Aires: I.N.C./Editorial Legasa, 1990), provides an insider's perspective. For an overview of the period, see Ana López, "Argentina, 1955–1976: The Film Industry and Its Margins," in *Garden of the Forking Paths: Argentine Cinema*, ed. John King and Nissa Torrents (London: British Film Institute, 1987), and Mariano Calistro, "Aspectos del nuevo cine," in *Historia del cine argentino*, 2d ed. (Buenos Aires: Centro Editor, 1992).

6. With some important exceptions, the studios favored shooting their films on indoor sets until the 1950s. At that time, filmmakers began to use wide-screen or color stock to convey the majestic qualities of Argentina's landscape in films such as *Continente Blanco* (1957), *Los dioses ajenos* (1958), *Socios para la aventura* (1958), *Campo arado* (1959), *Salitre* (1959), *Zafra* (1959). Some studio directors, such as Leopoldo Torres Ríos, interspersed location and studio shooting in films set in Buenos Aires, such as *Edad difícil* (1956).

7. Originally built in 1863 on the south side of the Plaza de Mayo, the building became a repository of official archives in 1906 when a new Congress building was constructed at the western end of Avenida de Mayo. See James Scobie and Aurora Ravina de Luzzi, "El centro, los barrios y el suburbio," in *Buenos Aires, historia de cuatro siglos*, ed. José Luis Romero and Luis Alberto Romero (Buenos Aires: Editorial Abril, 1983), 174.

8. "se acabaron con los restos de la Plaza de Mayo, que aun tuvo que sufrir el ataque de una reglamentación municipal destinada a asegurar que fuese rodeada por otros monstruos idénticos a los que se reputaban excelentes" (470).

9. Angel Rama provides the most cogent discussion of the city as symbol of order in Latin America in *La ciudad letrada* (Hanover, N.H.: Ediciones Norte, 1984).

10. Ciria, 311, 314, 315, 318. See also Romero, 1983: 217 on the significance of Eva Perón's funeral in this spatial warfare.

11. This was not the first time that Buenos Aires exercised such a hold on the literary imaginary. Early twentieth-century Argentine literature registered the radical changes occurring in Buenos Aires, both in terms of the physical modernization of the city (e.g., the widening of major thoroughfares; the installation of a subway system) and of massive foreign immigration. Texts such as Raúl Scalabrini Ortiz's 1931 *Hombre que está solo y espera* and Ezequiel Martínez Estrada's 1940 *Cabeza de Goliat* dealt with the effects of those changes on middle-class sectors. See Beatriz Sarlo, *Una modernidad periférica: Buenos Aires 1920 y 1930* (Buenos Aires: Ediciones Nueva Visión, 1988).

12. Soja argues that space is a social construct and never simply "there" as an empty or natural container for human action. Rather, it both reflects social relations and reproduces them. Soja's work is informed by the theories of French Marxist Henri Lefebvre. Lefebvre argues that capitalism survived "from the competitive industrial form of Marx's time to the advanced, state-managed and oligopolistic

capitalism of today" by producing a space (i.e., an urbanized space) that, in turn, helps reproduce the dominant system of social relations (Soja, 91). See also Mike Davis, *City of Quartz: Excavating the Future in Los Angeles* (London: Verso, 1990), and David Harvey, *The Urban Experience* (Baltimore: Johns Hopkins Univ. Press, 1989).

13. For historical accounts of this period, see Daniel James, *Peronism and the Argentine Working Class, 1946–1976* (Cambridge: Cambridge Univ. Press, 1988), and Robert D. Crassweller, *Peron and the Enigmas of Argentina* (New York: W. W. Norton, 1987).

14. The Revolución Libertadora (1956–58) that toppled the Peronist government was followed by three other administrations (the presidency of Arturo Frondizi [1958–62]; the military interim under the puppet government of José María Guido [1962–63]; and the presidency of Arturo Illía [1963–66]) before another military government gained power in 1966 and governed for seven years.

15. In his article "Working Class Organization and Politics in Argentina," Torcuato Di Tella argues that World War II created "a deep division among the dominant classes" between "newly enriched entrepreneurs who faced disaster if, after the war, a radical policy of protection were not adopted, a thing not to be easily expected from the ruling conservatives" (*Latin American Research Review* 16.2 (1981): 47). For an overview of the economic history of this period, see Guido Di Tella and Rudiger Dornbusch, *The Political Economy of Argentina, 1946–83* (Pittsburgh: Univ. of Pittsburgh Press, 1989).

16. Gutman and Hardoy, 229–30; Ciria, 319; Yujnovsky, 462. By 1970 Barrio Norte had the highest population density in the city along with the area bordered by Callao/Pueyrredón and Córdoba/Rivadavia. Between 1960 and 1970, Barrio Norte experienced the highest annual growth rate within the federal capital. See Richard J. Walter, "The Socioeconomic Growth of Buenos Aires in the Twentieth Century" in *Buenos Aires: 400 Years,* ed. Stanley Ross and Thomas McGann (Austin: Univ. of Texas Press, 1982), 80, 85.

17. Romero's periodization of the development of the Latin American city became the basis of *Buenos Aires, historia de cuatro siglos,* the two-volume masterwork on Buenos Aires edited by Romero's son, Luis Alberto, and published posthumously in 1983 with Romero (father) appearing as coeditor.

18. "hasta las clases altas se masificaban. La fortuna no podía impedir que a su poseedor lo empujaron en las calles, ni que tuviera que hacer cola en los ascensores" (248).

19. "el que tenía el hábito de ceder el paso quedó azorado frente al que atropellaba para conquistar un lugar" (365).

20. "se los vio en las calles de México, Bogotá o Buenos Aires en grupos compactos, ajenos a las reglas de la urbanidad atropellando el sistema que para los demás era pactado y apoderándose o destruyendo lo que era de 'los otros', de la sociedad normalizada" (334).

21. Romero reveals his bias in other ways. He occasionally refers to the "sociedad normalizada" as "sociedad normal" (359, 362), switching emphasis from social construction to essence.

22. Romero finishes this last chapter with an extensive discussion of populism where he suggests that the masses were easily manipulated ("ciertamente la masa no sabía bien lo que quería," 340). Here Romero's epistemological model fails and his inability to understand is transferred onto the masses' irrationality.

23. Even Ernesto Sabato's lengthy 1961 novel *Sobre héroes y tumbas* questions the viability of totalizing narratives about the city and about Argentina in general. The one chapter in the otherwise highly fragmented narration that presents a comprehensive understanding of Buenos Aires is the diary of a paranoid.

24. The way that Torre Nilsson uses space expressively signals his transitional role within the film industry. Although schooled in studio conventions (his father was Leopoldo Torres Ríos), Torre Nilsson broke away to become recognized as the Argentine industry's first auteur.

25. "Regresé al final de la tarde; me recosté en la cama, en el centro de la cama. Encendí la luz del velador y busqué mi imagen en el espejo. / Entonces grité. Grité de espanto, de terror: la luna del espejo reflejaba el cuarto de Inés, con Inés en la cama; su esqueleto vivo, entre tules y encajes" (55).

26. "I stopped crying. After all, I had to get used to it. There were two rooms; perhaps only one, where he had confined *us*" (55; my emphasis).

27. According to Marx, the commodification of labor is the basis of the division between public and private spheres as well as the source of alienation. See Gerald Turkel, *Dividing Public and Private: Law, Politics, and Social Theory* (Westport, Conn.: Praeger, 1992), 43, 48–49. However, recent research in women's history and poststructuralist theory has challenged this traditional Marxist interpretation. See Dorothy O. Helly and Susan M. Reverby, eds., *Gendered Domains: Rethinking Public and Private in Women's History* (Ithaca, N.Y.: Cornell Univ. Press, 1992).

28. This was also the case in earlier periods. James Scobie demonstrates how clusters of residences for the upper middle class grew up along the recently opened *tranvía* lines running westward from the city in the 1870s. The daily fare was too high for skilled laborers, artisans, and small shopkeepers whose homes remained close to their downtown jobs (167). See *Buenos Aires: From Plaza to Suburb* (New York: Oxford Univ. Press, 1974).

29. Although the increased automobile traffic was to some degree a product of the opening of new highways, the demand continually exceeded the city's ability to absorb the cars on a daily basis. By the mid-1970s, the problem forced the military junta to limit certain streets such as Florida to pedestrian traffic and to build massive parking areas along 9 de Julio, both on and below street level.

30. Feldman originally wanted to make a film about "love in the city" composed of three episodes including the Dragún play and adaptations of two Roberto Arlt stories, "Noche terrible" and "Prueba de amor" (*La Nación*, 2 October 1960).

31. The Dragún play is much more formally experimental. It breaks realist conventions by using minimalist sets and by having actors play multiple roles. Nevertheless, the play ends with the same affirming sequence.

32. Beatriz Guido's story "Diez vueltas a la manzana" within the same collection of stories as "La mano en la trampa" also deals with a young couple's visit to a *hotel de citas*.

Works Cited

Architecture: Ashlan y Ezcurra, arquitectos, 1930–1980. Miami: Presse Internationale, 1981.

Borges, Jorge Luis, and Adolfo Bioy Casares (Bustos Domecq). "La fiesta del monstruo." *Nuevos cuentos de Bustos Domecq.* 2d ed. Buenos Aires: Ediciones Librería, 1977.

Bullrich, Francisco. "La arquitectura moderna." In *Buenos Aires, historia de cuatro siglos.* Ed. José Luis Romero and Luis Alberto Romero. Buenos Aires: Editorial Abril, 1983.

Ciria, Alberto. "Política Tradicional y Política de Masas." In *Buenos Aires, historia de cuatro siglos.* Ed. José Luis Romero and Luis Alberto Romero. Buenos Aires: Editorial Abril, 1983.

Chiozza, Elena. "La Integración del Gran Buenos Aires." In *Buenos Aires, historia de cuatro siglos.* Ed. José Luis Romero and Luis Alberto Romero. Buenos Aires: Editorial Abril, 1983.

Cortázar, Julio. *Casa tomada.* Buenos Aires: Ediciones Minotauro, 1969.

de Certeau, Michel. *Practices of Everyday Life.* Berkeley: Univ. of California Press, 1984.

———. "Practices of Space." In *On Signs.* Ed. Marshall Blonsky. Baltimore: Johns Hopkins Univ. Press, 1985.

Frieburg, Anne. *Window Shopping: Cinema and the Postmodern.* Berkeley: Univ. of California Press, 1993.

Guido, Beatriz. "La mano en la trampa." In *La mano en la trampa.* 4th ed. Buenos Aires: Losada, 1980.

Gutman, Margarita, and Jorge Enrique Hardoy. *Buenos Aires. Historia urbana del área metropolitana.* Madrid: Editorial Mapfre, 1992.

Jenkins, Rhys Owen. *Dependent Industrialization in Latin America: The Automotive Industry in Argentina, Chile, and Mexico.* New York: Praeger, 1977.

Romero, José Luis. "La ciudad de masas." In *Buenos Aires, historia de cuatro siglos.* Ed. José Luis Romero and Luis Alberto Romero. Buenos Aires: Editorial Abril, 1983.

———. *Latinoamérica: las ciudades y las ideas.* 2d ed. Mexico City: Siglo Veintiuno, 1976.

Sebreli, Juan José. *Buenos Aires, vida cotidiana y alienación.* 15th ed. Buenos Aires: Ediciones Siglo Veinte, 1979.

Soja, Edward. *Postmodern Geographies: The Reassertion of Space in Critical Social Theory.* London: Verso, 1989.

Terán, Oscar. *En busca de la ideología argentina.* Buenos Aires: Catálogos Editora, 1986.

———. *Nuestros años sesenta.* Buenos Aires: Puntosur Editores, 1991.

Yujnovsky, Oscar. "Del conventillo a la 'Villa miseria.'" In *Buenos Aires, historia de cuatro siglos.* Ed. José Luis Romero and Luis Alberto Romero. Buenos Aires: Editorial Abril, 1983.

Chapter 2

Backwards Blindness:
Brazilian Cinema of the 1980s

José Carlos Avellar

(translated by Heather Reed)

In September 1979, Carlos Diegues finished *Bye Bye Brasil*. Ten years later, in September of 1989, he finished *Dias melhores virão* (*Better Days Ahead*). By mere coincidence or unconscious plan, these two films, completed around Independence Day (7 September), propose a discussion of the country and an attempt to picture, in an immediately visible space, the future of the country, or what would become of the next decade.

Consider the two titles of the films as free images. They in fact work well this way. The titles are not reduced to just announcing the stories the films tell. They possess an independence similar to the images of cinema in general: they say something when considered alone and they say something more when integrated with the other images that make up the film. Set side by side, as words in a phrase, as levels of the same succession—*Bye Bye Brasil, Better Days Ahead*—the two titles form a picture of the feeling that, from the time of the premiere of the first film (1980, in cinema halls) to the appearance of the second (1990, on television), takes us to a road we can better understand, setting side by side the two stories just as we did with the two titles: to move from the experience of wandering artists pushed to the edge by television to the experience of the dubbers of American television movies.

Say good-bye to the country. Begin a journey inward. Travel through open country to the inside of a dubbing studio. In an intense manner, the cinema lived this desire that accounted for everyone—more precisely, for everyone who lived in the small part of the Brazilian society who could go to the movies whenever they wanted to. After suffering the pressure that began hitting harder with the AI-5 (the institutional act number 5 that in December 1968 closed the congress and opened the press censorship), after suffering the false image of "este é um país que vai pra frente" (this is a country that moves ahead) created to represent Brazil on TV, and after suffering the popular command "Brasil ame-o ou deixe-o" (Brazil, love it or leave it) (both image and command were woven into the cinema showings and interfered in regular intervals on the television), after embittering one thing after another, many people tried to leave the country any way they could, far away but still here, through an imaginary exit. Those who decided to stay, to resist the pressure with the critical vision offered by the cinema, also tried to leave the country, noticing that neither the *sertão* became the sea nor the sea the *sertão*, contrary to what was announced in 1964 in *Deus e o diabo na terra do sol* (*Black God, White Devil*), and that the Third World did not explode, contrary to what was predicted in 1968 in Rogerio Sganzerla's *O bandido da luz vermelha* (*The Red Light Bandit*). Abandon the country. Abandon the cinema. Abandon the drama supported by direct contact with reality. Abandon the cinema that was always concerned with remaining conscious of providing conscience.

In September 1979, in an introduction for *Bye Bye Brasil*, Diegues reflected on having made his film more cinematic. He admitted that he had grown weary of the rhetorical, discursive, and boring cinema that existed since the late 1950s; that he was removed from the literary tradition of that cinema, of its intentionalism and neurotic need to prove something; that he was interested in a radical cinema of action and emotion, an audiovisual spectacle that would not fear its own reflection, reality, but aware that it would enter through many doorways, windows, and slits, a cinema that would give pleasure and not only awareness, which is only an inevitable consequence of any film:

as it is necessary to say good-bye to a Brazil that no longer exists, to be able to arrange what remains, it is necessary to stop rationalizing like a romantic intellectual of the nineteenth century on the eve of the twenty-first century; it is also necessary to create a new cinema for the 1980s, to prepare for the arrival of the third millennium. And live out this adventure with neither maps nor biases. (Diegues, pressbook for *Bye Bye Brasil*)

The director's observations do not relate closely to the story told in the film. They refer only to what we receive upon the initial reading of the title. It is the start of the image, of the information, and of the sensation suggested by the title.

The text, a little more than one page, even states that the film is about a country that is coming to an end to make room for another that has just begun; about a backwards-moving population and the riches and the poverty in the country, about interpersonal relations, about the possibility of being happy with one another. The text is only an introduction, a way to encompass the vision of this particular film, not a program of action for films to carry out in the years to come. But the title, more so than the story told after it, is almost a manifesto; it expresses a desire confirmed in the following years and also in films of other creators likewise concerned with bidding the country good-bye. Diegues's observations can serve very well as an introduction to a great part of the cinema of the 1980s.

In September 1989, in an interview for the magazine *Tabu*, Diegues defines *Dias melhores virão* as a film of crisis, and speaks again of that which the viewer receives from the title—an image mainly connected to all that catches the viewer's eye before entering the theater. He claims that the general ideas are dead, and that what is important today is to make good films with no regard to any standard or to the language in which the film is made; no more attempt is made to create "a great movement, an unbelievable academy. There is even no attempt, I will risk saying, to construct the great utopia of a Brazilian cinema, but only to try to make good films. That utopia which was part of my generation, the construction of a great Brazilian cinema, is gone."

Bye Bye Brazil. The good-byes begin with the artists of the Caravana Rolidei in a small town in the desert. They make it snow in the exceedingly hot and dry Brazilian inland, the *sertão* — snow that tastes like grated coconut, in accordance with Dasdo, snow like that of Paris, New York, London, snow like that of a civilized world, in accordance with Lord Cigano. They set off on a random path, traveling among people who are too poor to be moved by the snow of civilization or by the animated shadows of Zé da Luz (he shows an ancient copy of *O ébrio* [*The Drunk*], a very popular film directed by Gilda Abreu in 1946, projected onto the wall); among people less poor but interested only in the television installed in a quasi altar in the town square; and among the Amazon Indians who, on the edge of the freeway that rips the forest, watch the plane that passes above in the sky and the television here below. On the road between the *sertão* and the Transamazonic, interrupted by "fish bones" — television antennas — stuck in the throats of the artists, the Caravana splits in two looking for better days: Lord Cigano and Salome become modernized, they learn to write "Rolidey" with a "y" and to use the "Brazil" of Frank Sinatra as a musical theme; Ciço and Dasdô open a *forró* theater in Brasília.[1]

Ten years later, the artists are shut inside a dubbing studio. They record in Portuguese the text of an American television serial. Something in the country has changed: the torturer has retired, and with nostalgia for the dictatorship, administers electric shocks to the pet cat. Something is not right in the country: the artists live trapped between the nightmares of the past and the dreams of a better future, waiting for some magical transformation of the tasteless present. They only have eyes for the television, which in this halftime is no longer a fish bone caught in their throats but a shark as in the American film, a huge monster that swallows everything from the throat down. Throughout the story, the dubbers pass by people being attacked, people arrested during a police raid, street kids throwing themselves at car windows to sell whatever they can while the light is red, beggars huddling on a corner — but they do not notice any of this, or at least they do not see any of it as their concern. Marialva and Dalila avert their gaze from the rough activity taking place on the street corner when they notice that it is only an assault. Marialva, paying attention only to her voice on the television, does not notice that the military police have ordered an inspection of "the Negroes

first." Contrary to the artists of the Caravana Rolidei, the dubbers, although in the margin of society, do not identify with others who, like themselves, occupy the margin. They only see the
center. They see the television. They live the lives of the serial
characters that they dub. They are not what they are. They are
not: they want to be.

> Look and don't see: make the discomfort of the real invisible or
> transparent: hasn't this strategy used by the majority of Brazilians
> to survive the daily violence worked well? In fact, this perverse
> mechanism of self-defense that makes people blind turns the
> whole country into a world closed to the cinema: here the cinema
> has come to exist only as a base for sound, the dubbing material.

This desire to be something else causes Marialva to tell the military police lieutenant, standing beside her at the bar A Buchada
da Odete, that she is in fact the Mary Shadow of television. She's
a young blonde American on television, and not the woman that
in fact she is. She is not the real Brazilian, black-haired and brown-
eyed, that in fact is there. Smiling, she points to the television,
insisting at his side that the woman speaking with him is not the
woman who is here but the one on the screen: "on the television:
that's me." The desire to leave the country in search of better
days is so overwhelming for Marialva that she denies her own
self. She leaves herself behind.

> Brazil, love it or leave it; Bye-bye, a farewell said in the
> American way

The films that clearly reflect this will to leave are those that
contain the likes of Molina of Hector Babenco's *Kiss of the Spider
Woman* (1984), a prisoner who lives not the prison life but the life
of the film characters that are etched in his mind. This will is also
reflected in films that contain the characters such as Molina's cell
mate, Valentín, who becomes interested in Molina's stories when
he realizes that it helps pass the time in prison. The films that
best express this desire represented by the dubbers of *Dias melhores virão* are those concerned with quoting, paying homage to,
or leaping into the fictitious universe of North American cinema
to escape the reality (or maybe only the cinema?) of a country
that appears as depressing as the imprisonment of Molina and
Valentín.

There is not that great a difference between the behavior of Molina and films like Eliana Fonseca and Cao Hamburger's *Frankenstein Punk* (1986), Guilherme de Almeida Prado's *A dama do cine Shanghai* (*The Lady of the Shanghai Cinema*, 1988), Cao Hamburger's *A garota das telas* (*The Girl on the Screen*, 1988), or Nelson Nadotti's *O escurinho do cinema* (*In the Darkness of the Cinema*, 1989). The films all attempt to poke fun at typical cinematic characters and situations produced for large-scale consumption by the huge industry: the dark and haunted castle of horror films, the bright and colorful city of the musical films, the expressionist light and ironic text of detective films, the heroes of the action films, and the stunts of the adventure films. The films may also play with the status of the viewer, with the moving image providing the illusion of reality. Like Molina, these films only have eyes for the cinema, or better yet, these films have eyes for what they see in the cinema, disregarding the cinema as a way of seeing. They are not interested in asking what the world has had to see, hear, and dream since the invention of cinematography, such as Caetano Veloso in *Cinema falado* (*Talkies*, 1986), but only to escape reality while remaining in it. *Ópera do malandro* (*Malandro's Opera*, 1986) by Rui Guerra, *Jorge, um brasileiro* (*Jorge, a Brazilian*, 1988) by Paulo Thiago, *Doida demais* (*Too Crazy*, 1989) by Sérgio Rezende, and *Faca de dois gumes* (*The Two-Edged Knife*, 1989) by Murilo Salles exemplify this. Exaggerating a bit by bringing to the foreground the dramatic structure that supports each one, it is possible to say that these films behave like Marialva, who sees herself reflected in Mary Shadow. They try to dub the images of the cinema made by the huge North American industry with conversations in Portuguese.

We should not, however, consider this trend of escaping while remaining as a mere imitation of North American constructs (like what clearly occurred among us in the early 1930s and 1950s). Just after making *Feliz ano velho* (*Happy Old Year*, 1987), Roberto Gerwitz observed that to leave the country was the best way to become immersed in its rich cultural diversity and to resist the cultural model imposed by the *política de integração nacional* promoted after the coup of 1964 "through a complex system of telecommunications that reached every corner of the country." With the military in power the large Brazilian cities adopted a growth model that "culturally is characterized by the internationalization of our production and our cultural codes." What occurred then was not a mere attempt of "assimilating to faithfully reproduce what was imposed upon us in one way or another. Many of the artists and intellectuals among us have already illustrated this process of reelaboration of other cultures to constitute this vague thing that we call Brazilian culture." We are an incredibly diverse country, continues Gerwitz,

> [and we need] to express this diversity. In this sense, a rock group from São Paulo or Recife is as Brazilian as a pifaro band from Caruaru or the Indian music of Alto Xingu. Every individual expresses all these realities in a certain form. Every one of them articulates the different spiritual states and moments of the Brazilian people. I don't see why all this should be integrated, besides the necessity to control by domination. I feel that as long as this continues to trouble us, we have to abandon our search to synthesize our country and our work. There were times when Brazilian artists fought to find a national culture and only managed to express parts of a whole that may be unattainable in a single piece of work. (Gerwitz, "La generación del 80")

The parallel established just now should not be understood as a value scale in which a certain film, cited as parodying or paying homage to North American cinema, would necessarily be less interesting, less accessible, less fulfilling. For example, to suggest that *Ópera do malandro* is a dubbing of the American musical, and to cut off the conversation at this point, gives a false idea of the film that actually provides, in a form familiar to the average viewer, a conversation and at the same time a critique of this way of conversing.

It is as if what we are calling here dubbing, parody or imitation of the classical model of the American industry, were to simultaneously show (something inside another, something reflecting the other) the spectacle as well as the art of construction that makes it a copy of the foreign model, the spectacle, and the double-dealing involved in making it an exact copy of a foreign-made musical. In the way that the image is composed, the film demonstrates an apparent cleverness and the real ingenuousness of a double-dealer, by imitating what is popular abroad and reaching us through the cinema in an attempt to take full advantage of its means.

After all, wasn't it in just that way that the *malandro* was sketched by North American cinema in the 1940s, like Zé Carioca, a parrot in a striped shirt and straw hat? There is a double meaning, a mocking intonation, an ironic manner that emphasizes the sketch in which Max, the *malandro* in Rui Guerra's film, delights in an American pen that writes but doesn't leak ink onto his white suit. The *malandro* look of fascination regarding the ballpoint pen appears today an almost childish reaction, because the film keeps the viewer half in and half out of the time in which the characters live. We see what was happening then, conscious of where we are now.

To say that certain films behave like Molina and others like Marialva does not explain everything, but it reveals the common motivation of different directors. It reveals the impulse that made them all say, in their own way, and like Diegues in the introduction of *Bye Bye Brasil,* that they were making a purely cinematographic film. Guilherme de Almeida Prado introduced *A dama do cine Shanghai* as "a Brazilian A-film about American B-films" (interview in *O Estado de São Paulo*), as a worldly film, "not only apart from its time but completely outside of spatial reality, with no obligation to reality," an adventure of "an actual character lost in a film noir of the forties and fifties" (information pamphlet). Sérgio Rezende affirmed that "the dream of Brazilian cinema, the dream of Cinema Novo, didn't work out" (Caderno 2), in introducing *Doida demais* as his best film ever made, "taking into account the aspect of cinematographic construction" (interview in *UH Revista*). Paulo Thiago defined *Jorge, um brasileiro* (1988) as a response to the "challenge to make Brazilian cinema universal, that tells of life in an inclusive way, so that it may be seen in Japan, for example, with colors less Brazilian." Rui Guerra introduced *Ópera do malandro* as "a film made to rediscover the pleasure of making films," as "a return to what aroused in him the passion for the cinema": the musical comedies of the Metro that he saw as a child; he still says that the hero of his infancy transformed into a villain when he became an adult and figured out how these films sold a certain image of North American society.

But even so, he cannot forget that the musicals hold all the charm of cinema.

A few years earlier, Arnaldo Jabor ended *Eu te amo* (*I Love You*, 1981) with the principal characters jumping into a Metro musical, dancing American-style—top hat, walking stick, brilliant costumes—and humming a few words in English and others in a half-swallowed Portuguese intended to sound like English. In the information pamphlet for his film, Jabor describes it as "a science-fiction ecstasy about love...in a continual magical mutation of lights, scenes, psychological situations in a spiral rhythm, *2001*, split mirrors, spaceships" in which a couple make and remake Bergman's *Scenes from a Marriage* in a rhythm of rock, bolero, or electronic music."

> *Break away from the cinema. To the other side of the world. To another age. To another time. Break away from the desire to make a Metro musical; a Hollywood B-film; a sci-fi film. Say "bye-bye" to the reality of the country. Break away from the desire to break away.*

This desire to break away to the outside has been expressed in other ways: the manner of constructing the narrative as a game of mirrors between the filmed action and the filming camera to situate the story in an unreal space and time—*Anjos da noite* (*Night Angels*, 1987) by Wilson de Barros; in the metaphoric construction that carries the viewer into the common condition of the foreigner (the Japanese, Italian, or Northeasterner migrant) on a São Paulo coffee plantation in the first half of the century—*Gaijin* (1980) by Tizuka Yamasaki; in the tense story of a son pulled out of boarding school by a father he hardly knows, and stuck in an empty apartment to await the moment to leave the country—*Nunca fomos tão felizes* (*Never So Happy*, 1984) by Murilo Salles; or, remembering the two other films made by Diegues in the 1980s, in the construction of a utopian Brazilian place far from here and yet right here—*Quilombo* (1984)—and in the portrait of the desire to leave the country right in the instant that the dream to leave, fed by the youngsters Vinicius and Dream, comes up against difficulties imposed by reality in *Um trem para as estrelas* (*Subway to the Stars*, 1987).

The desire to not be here was also expressed through a distanced vision, the most expressive examples of which are two documentaries made in 1989 about the misery and the marginalization in a large city: the concise *Ilha das Flores* (*Island of Flowers*) by Jorge Furtado, and the dislocated *Uma avenida chamada Brasil* (*Brazil Avenue*) by Octavio Bezerra. The first shows the absurdity of the good order of a society that saves a rotten tomato to feed the poor people; the second, the logic of the disorder that pushes part of the unemployed population toward a life of crime and at the same time represses criminal behavior with violence, generating more brutality, which demands more repression, which encourages criminal behavior, which in turn engenders more repression in a vicious cycle that never ends because it feeds off itself.

Ilha das Flores is organized like a speech (a speech exactly, as it is the narrating text that drives the documentary), incorporating in its style the apparent logic and good order of the society that created places like the Island of Flowers, a garbage island near the city of Porto Alegre. It explains the function that the social gear reserves for a rotten tomato that the farmer traded for a market owner's money and this for the money that the housewife exchanges for perfume. Rejected by the housewife to flavor the ham for dinner, thrown in the trash, and then rejected as food for the pigs raised by the garbageman to be exchanged for money later on, the rotten tomato becomes food for human beings equal to all others and at the same time different because they do not have money.

Uma avenida chamada Brasil breaks up like the bellow of one who does not know how to express oneself and, in the anxiety of telling about the violence in the margins of the big city, incorporates into the dialogue the brutality of the society that created places like Brazil Avenue, a major highway on the edge of Rio de Janeiro. The film is a collection of violent scenes — some taken from real life, others staged to appear as though taken from real life — all shown as trite: a stabbing attack, a conversation with a youngster who takes drugs to tolerate working as a prostitute, the shooting of a bandit by members of a death squad, a conversation with a young female victim of a sexual assault close to the hut in which she lives, the interrogation of two children imprisoned for stealing, an assassin's testimony of the pleasure he feels when killing, the youngsters' dance on the roof of a rapid train to avoid the high-tension wires, the transvestites attempting to outrun police cars. A confusing mechanism, a collage of things thrown one upon another to give to the viewer a sensation of unprepared material, a sensation of untouched reality.

The closeness of these two very different films reveals one of the most present feelings in this desire to get away: it does not seem possible that the society can be transformed by the actions of people (through the cinema, among other things). The two documentaries bitterly affirm that the country is not viable. To discuss the violence here does not mean to be combatively aligned with the victims, to share their point of view, and to behave in the way, for example, the militant cinema in the late sixties behaved. The filmmaker reconsiders — no longer sure of the possibility of changing the world, or at least the conscience of the people. Suffer sympathetically with the poor people in *Ilha das Flores* or, convinced of the impossibility of humankind's survival in that society, escape the suffering by mockery, by scandal, by indifference, as in *Uma avenida chamada Brasil*. The distancing that the camera maintains outside of the filmed situation does not seem to result in a desire to remain emotionally detached but to leave reason free to think in transformed action. Like the films of the sixties, they want to face up to the state of things, but this confrontation seems to result in the hope of a possible moving away from the confrontation, to face up to the state of things only with the tragic feeling that the problem has no solution. Brazil, love it or leave it. The only escape is to get out.

It is true that this impulse to get out did not drive all the films made between *Bye Bye Brasil* and *Dias melhores virão*. João Batista de Andrade, for example, returned to the present around the political opening and the first elections — *A próxima vítima* (*The Next Victim*, 1983) and *Céu aberto* (*Open Sky*, 1985) — or to the beginning of a past that took us to the dictatorship of 1964, *O país dos tenentes* (*The Lieutenants' Country*, 1987). In 1983 Walter Lima Jr. and Hermano Penna both addressed Brazilian authoritarianism, which was being exercised as something affectionate, civilized, protecting, *Inocência* (*Innocence*), and practiced without disguise, by brute force and the brutish *Sargento Getúlio* (*Sergeant Getulio*). Hector

Babenco and Leon Hirszman returned almost at the same time (in 1981) to the common scene of those living more or less at the margins of the industrialized city, *pivete* (a criminal child), *Pixote*, and the worker, *Eles não usam black tie* (*They Don't Wear Tuxedos*); Nelson Pereira dos Santos and Andre Klotzel returned to the imaginary farmer, in *Estrada da vida* (*On the Road of Life*, 1980) and *A marvada carne* (1985). Geraldo Sarno also came back to the farmer and the issue of land in two documentaries, *A terra queima* (*The Land Burns*, 1985), about the arid Northeast, and *Deus é um fogo* (*God Is a Fire*, 1987), about the faction of the Catholic church that gave the poor of Latin America their rights. Renato Tapajós posed a reflection on the popular struggles between the late sixties and the start of the eighties—more specifically, about the popular struggles and the cinema that placed itself alongside them in *Nada será como antes. Nada?* (*Nothing Will Be like Before. Nothing?* 1985). Oswaldo Caldeira reconstructed an episode of our recent history in *O bom burguês* (*The Good Bourgeois*, 1982). Sílvio Tendler brought together images of Juscelino Kubitschek and João Goulart in *Os anos JK* (*The JK Years*, 1980) and *Jango* (1984). Sérgio Rezende reconstructed the image of Tenorio Cavalcanti in *O homem da capa preta* (*The Man with the Black Coat*, 1985). Sylvio Back left in search of documents concerning the last-century war with Paraguay, *A guerra do Brasil* (*The Brazilian War*, 1987). Glauber Rocha, who dived deeply into the reality of the country and into the dream of transforming it into a more humane place, exploded in the desperate image of his last film, *A idade da terra* (*The Age of Earth*, 1980). Also in the country, in its daily routine or in the manner of representation inspired by him, other creators dived in order to compose a very personal manner of seeing (and living) life from both afar and right here: perhaps a better example of this is Joaquim Pedro, who made *O homem do pau-brasil* (*The Man of Pau-Brazil*, 1982), an adaptation of Oswald de Andrade, and dreamed of doing *Casa grande & senzala* from Gilberto Freye. Carlos Prates Correa (*Noites do sertão*, 1984, from Guimarães Rosa), Júlio Bressane (*Brás Cubas*, 1985, from Machado de Assis), and Lauro Escorel (*Sonho sem fim*, 1986, inspired by the life of Brazilian filmmaker Eduardo Abelim) are other examples.[2]

So as to avoid making the list too long and detouring the conversation toward a listing of directors and film titles, it is enough to remember that the most significant films made between *Bye Bye Brasil* and *Dias melhores virão* are specifically characterized by the concern to examine the country from the inside, from the viewpoint of those (Guimarães Rosa's phrase may better express this viewpoint) "with the devil in the street, in the middle of the whirlwind." The creator is inside the film appearing in the image, acting through a character, or speaking through the voice of the narrator in *Cabra marcado para morrer* (*Twenty Years Late*, 1984) by Eduardo Coutinho and *Memórias do cárcere* (*Memories of the Prison*, 1984) by Nelson Pereira dos Santos, two careful analyses of the imprisonment that has been imposed on a majority of Brazilians, from the intellectual to the laborer. The filmmaker is wrapped up in the search (through art) for the daily space lost in an image invented to escape/confront the aggressiveness of the real: *Imagens do inconsciente* (*Images from the Unconscious*, 1986) by Leon Hirszman.

But, besides the most significant, these films were at best only slight influences on the films that followed them. They are works—particularly the first two—that were inscribed in the tradition of considering the country's diversity starting from the 1920s, in the making of such works as *Raízes do Brasil* (*Roots of Brazil*) by Sérgio Buarque de Holanda; of *Casa grande & senzala* (*Mansion & Slave Quarters*) by Gilberto Freyre; of *Retrato do Brasil* (*Portrait of Brazil*) by Paulo Prado; and especially in the rendering by Mário de Andrade, *Macunaíma*, to think of "the Brazilian as a character who is lacking in character," and *Remate de males* (*End of Evil*), to consider the Brazilian as a broken unit: "I am three hundred, three hundred and fifty, but one day I will find myself at last." Recaptured, enlarged, debated, these ideas nourished the cinema from the late fifties. The films of Nelson, Coutinho, and Leon in some ways follow this path of the Semana de Arte Moderna (1922) until the Cinema Novo (1962), and possibly for this reason were taken as the closure of a cycle, a farewell, a rite of passage, another way to say bye-bye to one Brazil in order to make room for another. They passed by in plain sight like a cry of freedom, and were then forgotten. Almost nothing of the affectionate interest of seeing and hearing common people in motion, of putting oneself at their disposal, of learning with them, of opening one's eyes and leaving them open to reality just as it appears, directly (in the images of daily life) or indirectly (in the images of the unconscious)—almost nothing that characterized the films by Coutinho, Nelson, and Leon is found in the cinema that followed. In some ways these three films were hardly influential, but in other ways they were extremely influential: the fact that they existed at all freed those who had begun to make films; the new directors could put aside the reality discussed in these films and set off in search of better days.

Cabra, Memórias, Imagens showed up in the eyes of the new generation as the father appears to his son in *Nunca fomos tão felizes*. The story takes place in 1972. The son has been in the interior at a religious school for eight years, due to the death of his mother and the presumed imprisonment of his father. Suddenly, the father appears before the son who did not even know he was still alive. The father lives threatened by something the son does not understand. He struggles to survive, hiding from and confronting a persistent enemy unknown to the son. The father almost never speaks. He says that his silence guarantees the security of his son. It seems that he has become involved in the fight against the dictatorship. When the son asks his father if he is a terrorist, the man does not respond. Strictly speaking, the action is the conflict between the son who wants to know everything and the father who tells nothing. "During his internship at the school the son must have felt a lot of anger toward his father and the intense necessity to repress this anger," comments the filmmaker. Only when he is suffering does the father call his son by his name, Gabriel. And only after the father dies does the son take his picture and show it to a hot-dog vendor on the beach, saying, "meu pai" or "my father."

"For better or worse, the father returns to his life and leaves the son-character to figure out how to cope with the guilt and anger in the relationship with his father. In the tension produced by the father's reappearance, the son feels the need to put aside all feelings of anger. The film has a simple and predictable plot, but it appropriates other readings of a metaphorical level of the father-son relationship, be it about the optics of fondness or about its political content," explained Murilo Salles. For example, it is possible to see in a fragment of *Os inconfidentes* (*The Conspirators*, 1972) by Joaquim Pedro de Andrade, set in the middle of a scene, between the figures of the father and the son in *Nunca fomos tão felizes* who exchange silent glances (the son always waiting for the father's response), a poetic speech, a confession, a portrait of the character who hides behind the silence. We see between the faces of the father and son the moment in which Tirndentes—the main character of Joaquim Pedro's film—turns directly to the camera. Tiradentes at this point leaves the film reality where he is and, commenting on the scene he just finished living, speaks directly to the viewer, saying, "It then occurred to me, the independence that this country could have, and I began to want it and only later to worry about achieving it." The father represents the desire for independence. The son is one of the many things that we must care for in order to arrive at this independence. The story takes place in 1972, the year commemorating a century and a half of independence. The film was made ten years late, just as things began to return to a slightly more democratic state: characters like the father could then reappear and walk freely through the streets. The film considers what happened in the 1970s from a 1980s point of view, through a symbolic comparison of the father-son relationship with, as Salles has stated,

> [an] inability of the revolutionary left, which participated in the process of the armed struggle in Brazil, to communicate with the beloved object, because of security reasons and paranoia, producing the impossibility of the affection fundamental in any relationship. In my film I formulated a critique on the poetic level of the image, a critique symbolizing the armed struggle as it developed in Brazil. The father-character is a bit of a representation of this kind of militancy and the son-character is likened to the Brazilian middle class, sitting in front of the television watching soap operas and advertisements, singing rock, assuming an identity that was not ours. (Pressbook for *Nunca fomos tão felizes*)

Dedé Mamata (1988), by Rodolfo Brandão, recaptured the dialogue proposed by Murilo about the incommunication between the left and the large majority. Brandão observes that "the two films are cousins" but notes that "they are not very much alike." Like Gabriel, Dedé basically lives locked in an apartment with his grandfather. His father is one of the disappeared of the armed struggle against the dictatorship. His grandmother has recently died, and since then his grandfather ("the greatest anarchist of the modernist wing of '22," Dedé tells his friend Alpino) remains in a chair, without a gesture, without a word. In this way, motion-less, the grandfather resembles (as the memory of his father that appears here and there in Dedé's eyes) an image of the silent and soft pressure of a father over his son, of

> things that were imposed on Dedé; imposed — they are not the result of an education: the religious dedication to the Communist Party and the idea that what was most important just then was to save the country from ignorance and repression . . . The 60s generation didn't join the armed struggle because of familial pressure or out of a sense of duty; it was more of a free choice, a necessity for that generation that resolved to change the country and that, for good or bad, had access to the books in the university, to the student movements, to the things that stimulate young people to want to change and challenge. This was something they took from our generation. (Brandão, "A geração dos anos 70")

Five years after *Nunca fomos tão felizes*, in his second feature-length film, *Faca de dois gumes*, Murilo Salles narrates another conflict between father and son.[3] These two encounters are com-plementary. The second film inverts, at least in part, the situation shown in the first. The father is the one obligated to stay at home, threatened by something that, while familiar, cannot be precisely identified. He asks his son, Cuca (a popular Brazilian word for "head"), for help and tells him part of the mystery. He says little, however, so as not to endanger his son — another occasion when the son must trust in his father and not ask too many questions. The son tries to help his father, is kidnapped and killed. Taking this story line (which is composed by entwining various others with it), a question takes shape: does there exist, in these films, in the father figure, a little of the dream of a Cinema Brasileiro, the dream of Cinema Novo, that, as suggested by Diegues and rein-forced by Sérgio Rezende, did not work out? The father's char-acter would be an (unconscious) representation of Cinema Novo, revolutionary form persecuted by the censorship of the military and pressured by the lack of communication between the ex-hibitors and the public. And, along these lines, in the figure of the son, would there be the image of the desire of the 1980s, to make films with no commitment to reality, purely cinematographic constructions? Not in the foreground, not as the main theme, but there, diluted in the background of the scene, the films of Murilo Salles suggest that the boy-cinema, first represented in Gabriel and second in Cuca, feels rushed by the father-cinema into an adventure where, without any information, he ends up an orphan; the father dies as victim of the dictatorship; or he, the son, is assassinated for millions of dollars that were gambled away, unbeknownst to anyone. As Salles observed, "The orphaned feeling is something very alive in these films; they develop the idea that it is necessary to first be orphans in order to become adults" (interview, *Tabu*).

> *Leave the country, leave the fathers.* Cabra, Memórias, Imagens, *like the father's picture that the son shows to the hot-dog vendor.*

The films we have made in the past few years are closer to the son than the father in *Nunca fomos tão felizes*. It is an image closer to the desire to get out, which emerged around 1980, than to the desire of 1960 to enter into a sociopolitical discussion of the country as a reality transformable by human action (through film, among other things). The films that we have made in the past few years also have a lot in common with the youth who, taken by their father to an empty apartment, spend their time watching television and strumming an electric guitar. Cinema today is like "O estrangeiro," sung by Caetano Veloso on a record made in the middle of 1989: the backwards blind, who, as in dreams, only see what they want to see.

Cinema: to dream with open eyes, to stay awake with eyes closed to the rest of the world, a point of equilibrium between the reality we perceive when awake and the reality of our dreams. Following this, it may be possible to say that we have gone beyond the moment in which reality predominated in our films, almost as if dreams did not exist—the real thing was there in a dream, on the screen, almost just as it really is—to another moment in which we tended to see reality only as it was represented in our dreams, almost as if there was not a reality beyond the dream, as if the dream could be lived while we slept, while we were awake, and while we were in the cinema, dreaming with our eyes open—dreaming sweet dreams when a foreign film hit the screen.[4]

It is not entirely correct to say that we tended to see reality as it was represented in our dreams: what exists is a tendency to incorporate the dream that was dreamed by another as if it were our own; a tendency to reject our own image as it appears in our nightmares to see it as it appears in others' dreams. Perhaps it is necessary to rethink what Glauber wrote in his *Estética do sonho*—"the dream is the only right that cannot be prohibited"—to better examine the social mechanisms that condition the desire to dream as foreign, that inhibit free dreaming. Glauber does not refer to the portion of the population that makes and views films, but to the great majority without direct contact with the cinema. He refers to the dream of the hungry, remembering the "greatest self-destructive burden of each man," the poverty, and the division that it imposes on the poor, who are converted "into a two-headed animal, one head fatalistic and submissive to the reasoning that works it like a slave," and the other one mystical "in the way that the poor cannot explain the absurdness of their own poverty." The dream of hunger appears as a rebellion, "an impossibility of comprehending the dominant reasoning" that "denies and devours itself in front of this impossibility."

> *To dream as a foreigner, to incorporate the dream that is dreamed by another.*

Without extending the question to everyone, we cannot limit the power of this appeal to the sector of Brazilians who have the ability to produce, circulate, and consume cultural goods. The question is repeated each time more emphatically since the beginning of the 1980s. It is very possible that this desire to be a viewer and to dream the dream of another is spread throughout the whole country by television. It is very possible that all this started with the movies. In a certain way we all (not only all the Brazilians, we all) are used to dreaming another's dream in the cinema, just there, in the dark, in the screening room. Films invite us not exactly to dream, but more precisely to dream ourselves in others' dreams. Films invite us (let me make an exaggeration) to reject ourselves as individuals, as we are, to become what we are in the others' dreams, invite us to see ourselves through the others' eyes, feelings, and desires. To become a kind of not-yet-born. To live the lives of the ones in the screen. That is fine while we are in the screening room, but not so when we act outside the movie theater, as we do when watching a film: as a viewer. If some pressure in social life invites us to act as spectator, we can lose the possibility of inventing our lives and our dreams. It is possible that even dreams can be prohibited, induced, controlled. For example, Marialva sees herself as if she were a nightmare of television's Mary Shadow. Blind and backwards, she watches television but does not see the television: she daydreams, feeling awake, seeing a reflection. She dreams like the actress she is. She imagines herself there, on the show, not just a voice but a body and soul. She dreams like a viewer, underdeveloped and sentenced to be the spectator she is, imagining herself in that comfortable and colorful world rather than in the miserable reality that surrounds her. She dreams as if it were not a dream, as if the television were the reality.

Television's importance in the modern world was one of the impulses for the creation of *Dias melhores virão*. Carlos Diegues said: "The changes that we are seeing in Eastern Europe would not be possible if not for the worldly diffusion that television produces." Another impulse was "this fascinating element of the modern world in that people live the lives of others and not their own" (interview, *Correio Braziliense* 2).[5]

Likewise, the cinema of the 1980s lives the lives of others and not its own; it is a foreign cinema (it has not yet occurred to anyone in Brazil to call this radical feeling of the Brazilian cinema a foreign one). Foreign, as stated on Caetano's record, a foreigner more to the moment than the place. An issue that is not just ours: the status of living like a foreigner more to the times than to the place is common to those who live in large cities, pressured to live in the present, to disengage from history, to disengage from all other space and time.

A large part of the pressure comes from the television, suggests the German filmmaker Alexander Kluge in his films made in the 1980s, but it also comes from the cinema that, stated in the title of one of his works, gave the initiative to *Der Angriff der Gegenwart auf die übrige Zeit* (*The Blind Director*, 1985).[6] An issue that is not only ours, but one that we live in an intense manner; our way of being strangers more to the moment than the place seems determined by an attack of the future on the rest of time: we feel the present as if we lived in the past, behind the times; we feel the present and the past as empty (because, just as Stefan Zweig once stated, we are the country of the future). We do not have a history nor do we make one. We wait for the better days yet to come.

For this reason, in Lúcia Murat's documentary *Que bom te ver viva* (*How Good to See You Alive*, 1989), with eight political prisoners tortured during the military dictatorship, one interviewee, Estrela Bohadana, asks the filmmaker who would want to go to the cinema to see a film about torture. She asks as one who already knows the answer. She asks as one who knows that very few people will be interested in seeing a film about our recent history, about our worst days: "It is such an uncomfortable history that everyone thinks it best to forget...maybe to avoid contact with something so painful." The question is then changed to "Who is going to see the film besides us?" by the fictional character who edits the interviews. A personal image or testimony of the interviewer, she also was imprisoned during the dictatorship; a summary of the experiences of all the other interviewees, a reflection on the interviews, this fictional character thinks out loud: "Is it our wars that are smaller or our fear that is greater?" At the end of the documentary, another interview, that of Maria Luisa Rosa, raises a fact. She says that the cinema is good because people see a reality painted on the screen and from that they can fantasize. She says that life is dull and boring. In the cinema, however, life is varied. There she has the inspiration to go inside herself, to dream, to free her mind.

> *The way out as the only solution. There is only one exit: the way in. The exit inward as the only possible way out. Inside the cinema, inside the home, inside one's self.*

In the two films that Arnaldo Jabor made in the 1980s, the main characters exit to the inside to live a varied life, to free the mind. In *Eu te amo* (*I Love You*, 1981), Paulo locks himself inside his house and tells his friend Oliveira over the telephone that he is going to stay there, doing nothing, just being alone: locked up, because the factory went bankrupt, because his wife left him, because "the country is shit," because "we're so mediocre, so cowardly," and because "Brazil is an illusion. Only people exist. They live in shit but they live." In *Eu sei que vou te amar* (1985), only the octopus lives. Driven by the text, by the inner remarks and voices of a couple who are reunited in their home after a three-month separation, the film ends with a play on words, a joke of Corisco's final cry in *Deus e o diabo na terra do sol*, "mais fortes são os poderes do povo" (so strong is the power of the people). In Jabor's film, the man shatters an aquarium and almost steps on an octopus. The woman yells "olha o polvo! olha o polvo!" (careful of the octopus!). He misunderstands, and comments: "o povo!" (the people!). The woman is finally reminded of our people! The Brazilian people! She corrects him: "Not the people, idiot. The octopus!" He does not hear and continues solemnly, "Greater is the power of the people," which provokes another correction, "Not the people! the octopus!" In the last image the reconciled lovers, in one another's arms, are covered by a huge octopus, suggesting that the greater powers are indeed those of the octopus.

Already, in a film made just before those two, *Tudo bem* (*Everything's Fine*, 1978), Jabor situates the action inside a home undergoing modernization. Here the apartment functions, according to the filmmaker, as "a sort of island surrounded by Brazil. An island in the center of a country that tries to erect a fortress against the invasion of reality" (pressbook for *Tudo bem*). In *Eu te amo*, only the couple lives in the apartment. The home, now a renovated, modern fortress closed to reality, functions as a kind of image of the end of the Brazilian miracle: a shapeless and filthy mass appears in downtown Brasília ("the excrement of the nation has at last appeared," remarks Serginho, the janitor of the town hall), and Paulo, without a factory, without a wife, without a miracle, rejects the country as "an illusion" and locks himself in his home in search of liveliness. In *Eu sei que vou te amar* there is just the couple, who say bye-bye to the country and retreat into their inner selves, concerned with nothing else. A man and a woman, nameless, strangers to one another. In the middle of the discussion he protests: "I mean, that's enough! I can't take this anymore...Brazil owes a hundred billion dollars...The crowd outside is roaring with hunger! And you and I discussing a couple's problem! This is not important to human life! The world is coming to an end and here we are in this mediocrity, with a historic process out there!" She cuts in, "Damn the historic process! Damn international politics!"

The filmmaking of Jabor, the eye of the camera, of *Tudo bem* and *Eu sei que vou te amar* was, little by little, becoming seduced by its characters and also looking for an inner escape, an island, a fortress. As he observed in the introduction of *Eu te amo*:

> The artist who uses social denunciation in external contents in his life, in that he tried it on himself, he could be a good artist. But if he hasn't blended the denunciations and the criticism into the real that makes his life, if this doesn't become deep-rooted, if this real doesn't become hermaphroditically blended into the personal life, feelings, and affections, either the denunciation will be void of truth and sincerity or this artist will only be at the service of ideologies, creating a sort of social assistance through art. (Pressbook for *Eu te amo*)

Shutting one's self inside one's home as a way to open up to the strange. To better understand this strangeness, look past the cinema for an instant: to question whether the image in these escapist films has something in common with Macunaíma's letter written to Icamiabas, remembering the legend of the world's creation and destruction as noted by Curt Nimuendaju amid the Guarani.

Macunaíma, the Indian who was born black and becomes white and travels to the big city of São Paulo, writes about the "civilization of which today we are proud to be a part." He tells Icamiabas of "the main things of this Latin civilization" that he is learning, in order to initiate, when "returning to the Mato Virgem, a series of improvements that would aid our existence and also spread our civilized nation among the more cultured of the universe." Mário de Andrade, in letters to Manuel Bandeira, comments on the difference between the narrator's text in *Macunaíma* and that of the letter written by the hero. He "had resolved to force attention on Brazilianism, not only to closely examine the problem but to call attention to it." The hero, on the contrary, "had aims to write in standard Portuguese," to correctly adopt the language, and due to this, in this passage of the book, he adopts a "pretentious style, satirizing our Portuguese," quoting "entire phrases of Rui Barbosa, of Mário Barreto, of the colonial Portuguese chroniclers" (*Cartas a Manuel Bandeira*).[7] It may be possible to say that those who make films now have felt something similar to that which made Macunaíma write to Icamiabas in book-perfect Portuguese. After calling attention to Brazilianism, we experimented in filming by the book, a way to feel closer to civilization, to improve our existence, to make the region more cultured.

For the Guarani, the earth is supported in the West by two wooden stakes arranged in the shape of a cross — stakes that will one day fall, according to Curt Nimuendaju. Claps of thunder and flashes of lightning will be the first signs of this downfall, which will cause a flood and end the world. Salvation, the Guarani say, is in the East, beyond the sea, in a place without evil. For this, the constant migrations in the direction of the Atlantic and the rituals of song and dance at the seaside. The body should be light enough to cross the ocean and arrive at the place of no evil; this explains the constant destructuring of society among the Guarani, the temporary villages: the society cannot organize. In other words, the society organizes itself to leave itself, because the idea of good order, well-being, and happiness that commands it is out there, in the place that once belonged to the Guarani. Those who lived now in the South and Southwest of the country, all those who make films in this area, are influenced by the Guarani's worldview without knowing it, live a provisional life, ready to travel, preparing for the moment to leave, constantly saying goodbye, dreaming of better days.

It is not really about escaping to a definite place but of living the dream to leave for a no-man's-land, a paradise where one is a friend of the king, as Manuel Bandeira sang in his poem "Vou-me embora pra Pasargada." The search for a place without evil is the dominant preoccupation of the characters who emerge halfway on the path that connects *Bye Bye Brasil* to *Dias melhores virão*. They are young people who are trying to understand who they are and what to make of the world around them. They live a crisis of identity. They are portraits of an uneasiness found in every instant outside of films. They are like the directors of first films who search to define their identity and film in their own style, in the correct cinema.

Paulo, of *A cor do seu destino* (*The Color of Destiny*, 1986) by Jorge Duran; Eliane, of *Com licença, eu vou à luta* (*Excuse Me, I Will Fight Alone*, 1985) by Lui Farias; Bauer, of *Vera* (1986) by Sérgio Toledo; Mário, of *Feliz ano velho* (1987) by Roberto Gerwitz; and Dedé, of *Dedé Mamata* (1988) by Rodolfo Brandão are either individuals equally pressured by a social context that does not give them room to show themselves, or part of a family that likewise represses the liberty of their children. They are different facets of the same undefined individual, partly ready to affirm themselves, fighting to transform their condition, and partly immobilized, inhibited, awkward, not knowing how to change life. Each one of them is a stranger to the other. Each one of them is a stranger to the self. They all behave like the two central figures in *A hora da estrela* (*The Hour of the Star*, 1985) by Suzana Amaral: now as Macabea, migrant Northeasterner who does not even imagine himself equal to the people of São Paulo; now as Olímpico de Jesus Moreira Chaves, also a migrant Northeasterner, who, to feel like a real person, escapes reality and dreams of becoming the deputy general of Brazil. Macabea and Olímpico are like the two halves of Paulo, of Eliane, of Bauer, and of Mário. And all of them—Macabea, Olímpico, and the others—steprelatives of Gabriel in *Nunca fomos tão felizes*.

Paulo fights with his mother (who is Brazilian) and his father (who is Chilean) because he suddenly decided to return to Chile (his brother died there, a victim of the repression). He fights because he does not care about politics, because his girlfriend also dates the professor, because he feels like attacking the whole world, and because, as he says at a certain point, he is going crazy. Eliane fights with her parents because she does not want to be the way they want her to be, because she wants to marry Otavio, who is older and legally separated, and because, even without really knowing how, she wants to fight alone. Vera Bauer, an orphan who learns to fight in the reformatory and to be strong to survive, struggles at work because she does not want to be what everyone insists that she is, a woman. What Vera wants to be and dreams of being is a man, Bauer. Dedé, lost between his paralyzed grandfather and his unstable, swerving friend, between the drug underground and partisan militancy, struggles silently with himself; the filmmaker describes him as "a character with a very complex psychological profile, a fragile youth who has created an autodefensive shield. He hardly speaks" (Brandão, "A geração dos anos 70 vista sem maniqueismo"). And Mário, paralyzed after a diving accident, is the most patient stranger of them all: he feels as if everything that moves belongs to a world foreign to him. It is an image of immobility, of the impossibility of fighting. "That such a young person, twenty years old, couldn't walk," says Gerwitz, "symbolized and synthesized the time that I had passed through, a time of withdrawal, of the fear of being paralyzed for the rest of my life" (Gerwitz, "Un movimento pesoal").

The stories and the characters' attributes summarized here only explain part of the issue. The images, the figures of these youths are really much more important than the plots they live; they better define the impossibly strange condition of behaving as every one of them does. Little is needed to perceive the common point that we are interested in emphasizing here; it is enough to think of the uncomfortable and nervous gestures of Paulo, Eliane, Dedé, Vera, and Mário—the way of moving from side to side like someone wanting to push away something invisible that squeezes them, that is stuck to them; or the stifled gesture of someone who is pressured by such heavy air that they cannot move. And it is very probable that this tension has resulted as much from the effort of the directors of these films as from a spontaneous gesture of the interpreters, who, young themselves, amid a society that pressures and pushes them out, imbue the characters so like themselves with a few of their own natural gestures. Guilherme Fontes gives Paulo of *A cor do seu destino* quivering movements and voice, a cringing that every now and then gives way to a distorted cry difficult to understand, because the emotion swallows part of the words, or to a false gesture that does not destroy but destabilizes the balance. It is this quivering voice and gesture that he lends to *Dedé Mamata* (and extends to Vinicius of *Um trem para as estrelas* by Diegues). Fernanda Torres gives Eliane of *Com licença, eu vou à luta* sudden movements, as if she were to burst of unhappiness. The viewer knows nothing of her in the beginning of the film, but soon senses her discomfort with her surroundings; she is irritated by the heat, by the closed window of the bus, by the passenger behind her, by the hard-to-breathe air—by everything in life. Ana Beatriz Nogueira appears in *Vera* with hard and controlled gestures, as if imprisoned, determined by reason, steady and decided, an excellent masculine attitude, artificial masculinity, like the Bauer that Vera has in her mind. Marcos Breda as Mário in *Feliz ano velho* is almost devoid of gestures, with a shrunken voice as if it, too, were imprisoned in the wheelchair.

None of these characters feel as they would like to, and to not feel as they would like in this world is what characterizes them. All of them, even those who do move with big gestures, are like the paralyzed Mário, confined to a wheelchair, victim of an accident. All of them, those who speak a lot and those who do not say a word, resemble the dubbers of the Diegues film, positioned to better adjust their eyes to what happens on the television.

In these films where nobody is comfortable, only the television is free, its own mistress, guiding its own action and inhibiting the movement of others. It is a constant presence—from a fish bone in the throat of the artists of the Caravana Rolidei in 1980, to the intermediary of Paulo and Barbara's relationship in *Eu te amo* in 1981. Paulo first appears as a TV image, pretending to be the announcer of the *Jornal Nacional*, only to be in a film as a real person, in an apartment, surrounded by televisions and video cameras. Then, soon after, he returns to being the TV image to converse with Barbara. She is right there at his side, but Paulo speaks with her through the television. He sticks his lips out to the camera, she kisses his image on the screen. Later, it is the television that opens the story of another Paulo, the Chilean youth who lives in Brazil in *A cor de seu destino*. Then it opens Vera's story, passes on to Macabea's story, and that of Eliane, to emphasize and conclude Dedé's story and then to anticipate and comment on Gabriel's meeting with his father in a short quotation from *East of Eden*[8] in *Nunca fomos tão felizes*.

Another dimension of not being as one would like to be can be perceived in the son-character. The father who he had thought was dead appears one day at school to pick him up. He takes the son to an empty apartment where he will await the upcoming trip abroad. Until then he is to stay inside, without questioning (his father said he cannot answer), without going out, without being seen (his father said it was dangerous). Outside, in the street, in the city, in the country, there is some threat that scares the father and makes the son feel more confined than at the boarding school. He does not know his father, the stranger who took him out of school. He does not know the outside world, either. He is not even sure he knows himself. The young students of *Verdes anos* (*Green Times*, 1983) by Giba Assis Brasil also live part of this experience. They are in a sort of open boarding school, in a southern city of the country at the beginning of the 1970s, the same time that Gabriel is taken by his father to the empty apartment. Without realizing what happens in a large city, without perceiving the tension that interferes in the lives of their parents and professors, the young people feel comfortable; they live the moment that precedes maturity confident that even better days are yet to come. Gabriel, paralyzed, uneasy, with a passport and a plane ticket, does not feel comfortable anywhere. He is a stranger in his own home.

> *It's not right the way so many people among us feel today?*
> *Stuck in the country, with a passport and a plane ticket in hand,*
> *but unable to travel, unable to leave home?*

Another dimension of feeling like a stranger can be noted in Macabea of *A hora da estrela*: she is the extreme sensation of isolation and discomfort common in the other characters, herself and her double, Olímpico de Jesus. At a certain time in their stories, Paulo, Eliane, Vera, Mario, Gabriel, and Dedé feel embarrassed by something they have done, of being as they are. Macabea feels this way all the time. She asks for forgiveness, walking with back hunched and head lowered. She lives unhappily, taking aspirin regularly because she hurts inside. In her book, which inspired the film, Clarice Lispector states that if Macabea were a creature who could express herself, she would say "the world is outside of me, I am outside of myself." As Suzana Amaral shows in the images of the film, when Macabea looks at herself in a mirror she chooses the darkest, dirtiest, most scratched and broken of all, as if only something such as this could show her disgraceful face. Macabea, who likes horror films and musicals, states Clarice, who wants to be a film artist, who likes to listen to the radio because only the radio converses with her, as shown by Suzana — Macabea is really much more than the sum of these other strange characters. She is the image of the Brazilian, and of Brazilian cinema between the bye-bye and the hope for better days. It is diffi-cult to say whether the feeling is stronger on the screen than in the eyes of the viewer: our films suffer something close to the infe-riority that dominates Macabea. Or, in order to not feel like Maca-bea, who does not even feel, in order to not feel cinema that is not real cinema, our films try to behave like Olímpico de Jesus in the scene where he buys a huge stuffed animal with pink hair and appears very handsome with the present to win over Gloria, Macabea's coworker.[9]

This is not an issue only encountered in the cinema. Today everything Brazilian seems as awkward as the invented gestures of Marcelia Cartaxo and José Dumont to give life to Macabea and Olímpico. It does not happen only in cinema, but in cinema it is much sharper, maybe because the moving television image can-not support all the fantasy necessary to cover the reality and stim-ulate a strange feeling that eliminates the risk of seeing ourselves (this is really how we are if we look) out of order, awkward, un-derdeveloped, inferior people of the Third World. To feel strange, to be a stranger even to oneself, to jump outside of one's own skin, to live not one's own life but that of others seems the only way to be real people. That is the dream of those who live condi-tioned to behave outside of the cinema as spectators of a world in motion, unable to act effectively in the day-by-day; this is also the behavior of a good part of our cinema. This common desire to be foreign does not itself contribute to a simplified relationship between viewers and films. They see them as strangers, they try to converse through gestures. They do not speak the same lan-guage, they do not pertain to the same culture, they do not speak with the help of a translator, they dream of a dubber.

Even the films without the urge to break away from the country were seen as strange. Possibly stranger than the others, because they run backwards, blind to the desire to escape to someplace far away while still remaining here.

Dias melhores virão follows this conversation given in a foreign language without translation. Its central figure is a character who poses as the mediator, as the interpreter of the foreign Brazilian, the dubber. The dubber learns to speak in a foreign tone of voice, hoping to leave behind the worst days, consciously learning to speak as if speaking were not an expression of personal feelings, not an expression of daily experiences but only a technique, a way to adjust sound to translate the correct, modern, developed feeling felt over there. Marialva is sometimes betrayed by the unconscious in the middle of the dubbing and a phrase in English is repeated in place of the Portuguese text. "I'm so happy" sounds so much better in English, she explains—and everyone agrees because no one is really happy in Portuguese. Here, Marialva does what a good part of our cinema has done to become modernized. In the same way that the Mary Shadow program can be seen as a possible representation of American cinema made to be exported, Marialva and the other dubbers can be seen as a representation of the Brazilian, of the spectator and the film, in the 1980s.[10]

In this cinema that acts as a dubber, there is a greater preoccupation with the technique of filming. We had mainly experiences of showing—showing here understood as something of an academic exercise, like the sophistication of speech, like a technique of talking more or less disconnected from what is planned to be said, like a formula to be applied with professional precision—a well-done dubbing: Portuguese spoken in the rhythm of English, Portuguese thought in English. What we had was a particular condition of strangeness: strange not because it appeared as any other cinema made abroad, but because it is strange as is the condition of existence, strange in a very Brazilian way. In closing its eyes to the surrounding reality, the cinema was not exactly turning its back on the country, but on the contrary, diving deep into the sentiment of its most industrialized part, the South, the Southeast. It was attempting an impossible dialogue with people who speak languages foreign even to themselves, who need to dub even the inner conversation. For those who suffered the pressure of "este é um país que vai pra frente" and of "Brazil, love it or leave it," maybe there was no better way to be Brazilian. And for Marialva, the dubber who finds better days—direct heiress of Paulo, Eliane, Vera, Mário, Dedé, Olímpico, Gabriel, and all the others—it is a perfect expression of renunciation of living another life on behalf of living the life of another. In fact, Marialva seems like Macabea, who encountered her fame and went off to be a stranger abroad.

Notes

1. *Forró* is a popular music and dance and by extension the place where this music is listened and danced to. The word apparently comes from the English "for all."

2. A few more good examples are Denoy Oliveira (*O baiano fantasma*, 1984), Ana Carolina (*Das tripas coração*, 1982; *Sonho de valsa* [*Dream of a Waltz*], 1987), Vladimir Carvalho (*O evangelho segundo Teotônio*, 1984), Eduardo Escorel (*Ato de violencia*, 1980), Carlos Reichembach (*Anjos do arrabalde*, 1987), Giba Assis Brasil (*Verdes anos*, 1983), Sérgio Bianchi (*Romance*, 1988), Paulo César Saraceni (*Natal da Portela*, 1988). Joel Pizzini, who searched in the poetry of Manoel de Barros for the starting point for *Caramujo flor* (*Snail Flower*, 1989), is another good example.

3. Murilo Salles states: "Cinema Novo was fundamental in why I am making films today, so that there is cinema in Brazil, but this is a heavy burden, like a father's burden" (*Tabu* 41 [September 1989]).

4. "How is it that the idiot inside a Mercedes-Benz is a reality and a poor wretch who dreams of a Mercedes is a fantasy?" Arnaldo Jabor asks in the pressbook for *Tudo bem*. He then explains: "These things arise from the same point. In this, dreaming is economic, delirium is the social situation, and the social situation is delirium. Or: the unconscious is a production and output is the unconscious."

5. In September 1993, in "O futuro passou," in the book *Reflexões para o futuro,* distributed with the twenty-fifth year commemorative edition of the magazine *Veja,* Diegues expands on living another's life: "At best, we've turned into a kind of dubbing culture, we've put our voices to their fascinating images, our spirits into their music, our hearts into everything that they invent for our pleasure. We try to produce, at best we reproduce."

6. The German title, literally translated into English, is "the attack of the present against all the rest of time."

7. In the critical edition of *Macunaíma* coordinated by Tele Porto Ancona Lopez for the Coleção Arquivos, and edited in 1988 under the auspices of Unesco, two texts extensively discuss the character from the viewpoint cited here: in *Situação de Macunaíma* Alfredo Bosi deals with the hero's problem of not feeling comfortable in the Amazon world ("the metaphor for the Brazil that lives outside of modern civilization") nor in the city: "a Brazilian would be a man who is not in sync with himself. Not being able to find his own place either in the jungle or the city, either in Uraricoera or in Pauliceia, he suffers in both. It is not by accident that Macunaíma detests living in this place. But escape to where?" In "A carta pras Icamiabas," Maria Augusta Fonseca discusses the issue inherent in the hero's text: "For a people without cultural (and therefore linguistic) identity, would it be possible to express their own fears and fantasies, free themselves, or purge themselves, of them? In choosing a pure Portuguese to capture his fascination with the city, the hero goes along embellishing the Portuguese language and the cultural tradition of the West, dishonoring one as much as the other. The illustrated desire to incorporate an alien culture, the opposite of searching for support in its own roots, can be found in insecurity."

8. *East of Eden,* an Elia Kazan film, USA, 1955, with James Dean, Julie Harris, Jo van Fleet, Burl Ives. The quoted passage shows the son seated by the bed of his suffering father.

9. "I believe that we've succeeded in making a Brazilian film of which I am proud," stated Murilo Salles in an interview in the pressbook for *Faca de dois gumes*. "I'm embarrassed by Brazilian cinema in general; I think it's half catastrophe, excluding the emerging generation of youths. This cinematographic inheritance, which was good during the Cinema Novo, is now a catastrophe. Fortunately, about ten filmmakers are now emerging."

10. "I remember a time when it was said that a Brazilian cinema wasn't possible because our idiom didn't have the English 'I love you,'" comments Arnaldo Jabor in explaining the choice of his film's title, *Eu te amo*, in the pressbook edited by Embrafilme. "People in general don't say this," he continues, "perhaps because of linguistic shyness, but also because of the real impossibility of it."

Works Cited

Brandão, Rodolfo. "A geração dos anos 70 vista sem maniqueismo." *Filme Cultura* 48 (November 1988).

de Almeida Prado, Guilherme. Interview, Caderno 2 of *O Estado de São Paulo*, 13 December 1986.

———. Pressbook for *A dama do cine Shanghai*.

de Andrade, Mario. *Cartas a Manuel Bandeira*. Rio de Janeiro: Organizations Simões, 1958.

Diegues, Carlos. Interview, *Correio Braziliense* 2 (7 January 1990).

———. Interview, *Tabu* 41 (September 1989).

———. "O futuro passou." *Reflexões para o futuro* (special book published for the twenty-fifth anniversary of the weekly magazine *Veja*, São Paulo, Editora Abril, September 1993).

———. Pressbook for *Bye Bye Brasil*.

Gerwitz, Roberto. "Um movimento pesoal contra a imobilidade." *Filme Cultura* 48 (November 1988).

Gerwitz, Sérgio. "La generación del 80: Festival de Havana." *Memoria del X Festival*. Mexico City: Univ. Nacional Autónoma de México, 1989.

Guerra, Rui. Pressbook for *Opera do malandro*, Cannes Festival, 1986.

Jabor, Arnaldo. Pressbook for *Eu te amo*, Embrafilme, 1980.

———. Pressbook for *Tudo bem*, Embrafilme, 1978.

Nimuendaju, Curt. *Die Sagen von der Erschaffung und Vernichtung der Welt als Grundlagen der Religion der Apapocuva-Guarani* (The legend of the creation and destruction of the world fundamental in the Apapocuva-Guarani religion). Originally published in *Zeitschrift für Ethnologie* 46, Berlin, 1914.

Rezende, Sérgio. Interview, Caderno 2 of *O Estado de São Paulo*, 19 December 1988.

———. Interview, *UH Revista de Ultima Hora*, 28 September 1989.

Rocha, Glauber. "Estética do sonho." *Revolução do Cinema Novo*, Alhambra/Embrafilme, 1981.

Salles, Murilo. Interview, *Tabu* 41 (September 1989).

———. Pressbook for *Faca de dois gumes*.

———. Pressbook for *Nunca fomos tão felizes*, Embrafilme, 1984.

Thiago, Paulo. Interview, *Diario da Tarde*, Belo Horizonte, 1 February 1989.

Chapter 3
Recent Colombian Cinema: Public Histories and Private Stories

Ilene S. Goldman

Colombian Cinema and Latin American Film Criticism

Recent Latin American film scholarship has all but ignored films made in Colombia. Perhaps because Colombian films receive limited distribution at home and abroad, scholarship has tended to collapse Colombian cinema into discussions of "the Andean region," typically little more than an aside in Latin American film studies, or to discussions of the role of the state in film production.[1] Two exceptions to this rule are fiction filmmaker Víctor Gaviria and the documentary team of Marta Rodríguez and Jorge Silva. Recently, Gaviria's 1991 film *Rodrigo D.—No Futuro* (*Rodrigo D., No Future*) was exhibited across the United States with limited success in art houses. A fictional representation of the violence arising out of Medellín's drug culture, *Rodrigo D.* most likely found an audience because it portrays Colombian society as North Americans expect it to be—violent, drug-infested, and corrupt. Rodríguez and Silva were part of the generation of young filmmakers who advanced the New Latin American Cinema through their films and writings despite Colombia's marginal participation in the movement.[2] They achieved a certain amount of international recognition for their 1968–72 film *Chircales* (*The Brickmak-*

ers), which documented and exposed the exploitation of brickmakers in the outskirts of Bogotá. Rodríguez and Silva's subsequent projects continued to use the cinematic medium to depict the reality of Colombia's poor. As a body of work *Chircales, Planas: testimonio de un etnocidio* (*Planas: Testimonies of an Ethnocide*, 1972), *Amor, mujeres y flores* (*Love, Women, and Flowers*, 1986), and *Nacer de nuevo* (*To Be Born Again*, 1985) constitute Colombia's best-known contributions to Latin American cinema. These films combine politics with art, urging viewers to think and act. All were produced independently.

That the scholarly community has not discovered Colombia's cinematic output—its prolific production of short films in the late 1970s and 1980s, its national *telenovelas*, and its feature-length fiction films—reflects, in part, Colombia's marginal position in Latin American studies in general. As David Bushnell, the foremost Colombian historian in the United States, has written:

> Colombia is today the least studied of the major Latin American countries, and probably the least understood. It has attracted the attention of specialists in Latin American literature, in good part thanks to its Nobel prize-winning novelist, Gabriel García Márquez; economists have taken note of its slow but steady economic growth, in a region better known for sharp fluctuations; and a number of political scientists have been intrigued by the peculiarities of its traditional two-party system. Meanwhile, at the level of popular impressions in the United States and Western Europe the name *Colombia* suggests mainly drug trafficking and endemic violence. If anything more positive comes to mind, it is the familiar Juan Valdez of the Colombian coffee growers' advertising, whose image is really that of a stereotypical Latin American peasant farmer. (vii)

Bushnell asserts that "Colombia deserves better than this, if only for reasons of size."

In film studies, Colombia may deserve more attention because its state-supported film industry, while now defunct, was one of the most successful programs of its kind outside of Cuba in the past fifteen years. Although feature-length filmmaking stagnated in the seventies, in the first ten years of screen quotas for national films and of financial support for the production of short films, more than six hundred short and medium-length films were produced (Alvarez, preface). In the 1980s, state support for filmmaking boosted production to an annual average of four *largometrajes* or feature-length films. Since 1960, Colombia has hosted the Cartagena International Film Festival and the nation's capital, Bogotá, also hosts an annual festival. Colombia's position as the third most populous country in Latin America gives it a substantial film audience. More than 48 million Colombians went to the movies in 1987 (Arbeláez, 42). Filmgoing has long been a primary source of entertainment for any Colombian with leisure time and extra cash. Along with state support for filmmaking, this audience would seem to add to Colombia's merits for serious study.

However, the elision of Colombian films by critics results from the fact that, despite the potential indicated earlier, Colombia has been unable to support a film industry or to foster a consistent filmmaking tradition. The frustrations thwarting the growth of a true Colombian film industry are the same as those impeding the growth of many industries in developing and dependent countries. Foreign—especially Hollywood—products inundate Colombian theaters and audiences have learned to prefer this foreign fare. Like viewers in neighboring countries, Colombians have grown accustomed to the production values of American and European cinemas. "Latin American cinema has found itself in a double bind. On the one hand, it has not had the economic wherewithal to equal the technical achievements of advanced industrial countries, and on the other, it has often lacked audience support for introducing different modes of filmmaking" (Johnson, 208). Colombian features also suffer from poor distribution and fleeting exhibition: even the best films remain virtually unknown in their own country. Fewer than 1 percent of the 48 million filmgoers in 1987 saw a Colombian film. Furthermore, Colombia has never established an export market for its films, so, despite festival awards and international critical acclaim, its filmmakers cannot hope for international distribution or exhibition.

Thus, despite the production of feature films and the abundant output of *telenovelas* and documentary film and television, we cannot yet speak of either a "Colombian film industry" or a "national cinema." Agosto Bernal, one of Colombia's leading film historians and director of Bogotá's Cinemateca Disitral, believes that the difficulties in establishing a filmmaking tradition arise from a lack of "cultural formation."[3] Bernal asserts that although Colombia has a rich folk culture and oral history, in which Colombian literature finds its identity, visual culture has not evolved as it has in other Latin American countries. Because Colombia does not have a tradition of painting, then, it is difficult to pass from the oral histories to visual culture. Bernal continues, "We cannot speak of a Colombian culture; the continual violence and civil wars have not permitted us to find our identity, not in theater, not in television, and not in cinema." Bushnell also comments on this phenomenon:

> The problem of Colombia's image as a nation is compounded by ambivalent characteristics of the Colombians themselves . . . they continue to exhibit major differences along the lines of class, region, and in some cases ethnicity. It is thus a commonplace to say (with Colombians often saying first and loudest) that the country lacks a true national identity or a proper spirit of nationalism, at least as compared to most of its Latin American neighbors. (viii)

Interestingly, this country with "no true national identity" has recently produced a number of films dealing with the particularly Colombian theme of violence and its pervasive effects on Colombian life. Do these films signal the existence of a national identity, the beginnings, at long last, of a "national cinema"? Or are they singular ruminations on the phenomenon of violence that continually transforms Colombian politics, economics, and culture?

Historical Memory and Remembered Stories of Violence

Two films in particular address the bloodiest moment of contemporary Colombian history, the period known as the Violencia. The Violencia, or the Violence, refers to the period of virtual civil war that broke out following the assassination of Colombia's popular liberal leader Jorge Eliécer Gaitán on 9 April 1948. This essay compares *Condores no entierren todos los días* (*Condors Are Not Buried Every Day*, Francisco Norden, 1984) and *Confesión a Laura* (*Confession to Laura*, Jaime Osorio, 1990),[4] investigating how the

Violencia changed the course of people's lives by impacting the power structures in specific gendered spaces. In addition, it explores the ways in which narrative investigations of the Violencia play an integral role in the search to understand how contemporary violence is continually transforming life in Colombia. Finally, the essay asks whether we can today begin to recognize a Colombian cinema, defined by its concern with the relationship of today's Colombia to the country's tortured past.

Colombia's socioeconomic and political problems preoccupy its filmmakers. For a country with no substantial film industry and an erratic history of filmmaking, Colombia's feature fiction films in the 1980s and early 1990s demonstrate remarkable consistency in situating narratives in moments of historic social violence. In the first of these films, Dunav Kuzmanich's *Canaguaro* (1981), the title character narrates the story of bloodshed in the eastern plains in the years following the assassination of Gaitán. Gaitán's death and the ensuing violence became a defining point in Colombian history and the two films under investigation here explore the social transformations instigated with that single shot in downtown Bogotá. *María Cano* (Camila Loboguerrero, 1989) recovers the life of the eponymous labor leader whose struggles included violent labor strikes in the early part of this century. *Rodrigo D.—No Futuro* investigates violence arising out of the Medellín drug culture. Screenwriter Alexandra Cardona Restrepo has written a screenplay that takes place during the events surrounding the massacre of striking United Fruit Company workers on 6 December 1928 in Ciénaga, an event unknown to many Colombians.

This group of films demonstrates that the very elements that Bernal believes have thwarted Colombian cinema — violence and fear — connect Colombia's most recent films thematically and sensibly. As Isabel Sánchez writes, "It cannot be coincidental that all of the scripts that have won prizes in this country relate to violence. It is precisely because their authors have wanted to shape the most everyday in our lives, and in approaching their characters they have found none who escape the leit motiv in our history" (14).[5] Violence has plagued the country throughout its history as a republic, with the drug-related strife of the 1980s prolonging the effort to establish domestic peace. Gonzalo Sánchez notes that, in studying Colombian history, "what is immediately apparent in contrast to [Colombia's] established view of democracy is that Colombia has been a country of *permanent* and *endemic warfare*" ("La Violencia in Colombia," 789). Not surprisingly, Colombia's most recent films have incorporated the most violent moments of social history in an attempt to communicate shared concerns about the country's present with contemporary audiences.

In the cinematic narrativization of their violent past, Colombians recognize the problems of their violent present ("the represented future"), a present too real and too frightening to talk about. Subjectively, viewers might identify with characters acting and reacting within a recognizable or remembered historical situation. Colombians can remember political violence forcing them to remain inside, whether from their experience during the Violencia or because of more recent acts of narcoterrorism. Contemporary Colombians perceive connections between today's violence and the violence of the recent past. Yet, the events following Gaitán's assassination in 1948 are more easily examined than today's complex layering of guerrilla actions, drug-related terrorism, and paramilitary violence. The discourse of narrative cinema interacts with the identity of historiographic and political analyses, with ideological practice and claims of knowledge (Rosen, 31). Films like *Confesión* and *Condores* stretch the hypotheses of the *violentólogos*,[6] using popular media to explore how the two decades of the Violencia contributed to later insurgent movements by providing the "historical memory" of collective experience for new or reborn guerrilla organizations (Peñaranda, 307).

Michel de Certeau, in discussing historical writing, has noted that "Historical discourse makes a social identity explicit, not so much in the way it is 'given' or held as stable, as in the ways it is differentiated from a former period or another society. It presupposes the rupture that changes a tradition into a past object" (45). This rupture and its implicit connection to the past permit viewers to focus on "how the 'I' becomes 'we' or 'us'" (Rowe and Schelling, 162). As Isabel Sánchez writes:

> The films produced [in the 1980s] permit us to recognize ourselves in them, and at the same time we are able to observe details that frequently escape social scientists such as the behavior of individuals, the different reactions of

those who have been subjected permanently to all types of violence, the impact on a human being of national and global events, which s/he might never have imagined would in any way affect his or her existence. (11)

Private Lives Transformed by Public Events: *Condores* and *Confesión*

Violence has shaped Colombia's history since the days of the Spanish conquest and the imposition of colonial rule, but the Violencia "represents one of the most important and traumatic social processes in the nation's history" (Osquist, 12). Although Colombia had experienced violence stemming from the clash between the Liberal and Conservative political parties for decades, Gaitán's death unleashed unprecedented brutality. Bogotá's streets, threatened by rooftop snipers, were littered with dead bodies and debris from looting. The riots in the country's capital came to be known as the Bogotazo, signaling the ferocity of the urban uprisings. Although the Bogotazo was quelled after one day by the Liberal party agreement to reenter a coalition government with the Conservatives (Bushnell, 204), elsewhere the clashes between Liberals and Conservatives continued. Gonzalo Sánchez notes in "The Violence" that

during the two weeks following Gaitán's assassination, countless Colombian towns and rural districts lived under a formidable inversion of the constitutional order. Police were "at the service of the Revolution" as they put it in the provinces. It was as if the character of social and political development prior to April 9 had been dislocated, and it was no longer the city but the most remote provinces that displayed their full revolutionary potential. (83)

Despite the brief respite following the calming of the Bogotazo, the atmosphere of terror continued throughout the country for nearly two decades. Between 1948 and 1966 at least two hundred thousand Colombians died due to social violence, 112,000 in the first two years (Osquist, xi). "No part of the country was wholly spared although the phenomenon was primarily rural, not urban (with the notable exception of *el nueve de abril* itself)" (Bushnell, 205). *Pájaros,* or paid assassins, committed politically motivated murders for the highest bidder. Symbolic of the bloodiest moments of the Violencia, *pájaros* did not kill because of particular affiliations. Rather, they assassinated innocent victims for the sake of violence itself (Gerdes, 24).

This painful episode in Colombian history provides the backdrop for *Confesión a Laura* and *Condores no entierren todos los días*. *Confesión*, a fictional melodrama, narrates the private lives and social changes of three middle-aged characters, Josefina, Santiago, and Laura, living through the Bogotazo. The riots of 9 April confine the film's action almost exclusively to the domestic private space of two women's apartments. Each apartment takes on the personality of the woman who lives in it. Santiago moves, literally and figuratively, between the two spaces. *Condores*, on the other hand, takes place in an unidentified village near the capital. The story is loosely based on the life of a legendary historical figure Don León María Lozano and his transformation from a seemingly mild-mannered bookstore clerk into one of the era's most feared assassins. Much of the action occurs in the streets and public places of the village—spaces controlled mostly by men from which women are absent. *Confesión* and *Condores* explore the public and private transformations of behavior and relationships motivated by the events following Gaitán's assassination.

Confesión begins moments after the assassination of Gaitán and ends the following morning. Josefina sends her husband Santiago across the street with a birthday cake for their neighbor, the unmarried schoolteacher Laura. Bogotá's streets are already becoming dangerous and all stores are closed. Santiago reluctantly carries the cake to Laura but cannot return because a curfew is announced, prohibiting any civilian from being in the streets. Laura and Santiago, thus trapped in her apartment, begin to learn about one another and Santiago discovers that Laura is much more sympathetic than his wife to his beliefs and dreams. During the course of the day and evening they grow closer. Josefina observes this growing intimacy jealously from her drawing-room window, constantly interrupting Santiago and Laura with telephone calls, ultimately insisting that they light every candle in the apartment so she can see what they are doing. Finally, Josefina's jealousy and impatience lead her to demand that Santiago return immediately, even though they have been warned that anyone who ventures into the street will be shot. Laura protests, but Santiago, always governed by his wife's demands, puts on his overcoat and hat and leaves. A man crosses the street and is shot. Josefina, believing it is Santiago, is prevented by a sniper from running into the street while a mule-drawn cart removes the body.

On opposite sides of the street, alone in their apartments, Laura and Josefina mourn the man they loved and believe dead. Someone knocks on Laura's door. She opens it to discover Santiago, who explains that he was about to go into the street when the other man appeared and was shot. They fall into each other's arms, relieved. When morning comes, Laura convinces Santiago to use his "death" as an opportunity to start over, to live the life he has dreamed of. As day breaks, Bogotá's streets return to some semblance of normalcy and Josefina appears at Laura's door seeking comfort as she mourns the husband whose death she feels she has caused. In the film's final moments Santiago joins the morning pedestrians, arranges his hat at a jaunty angle, and lights a cigarette.

Condores opens with a panorama of a Colombian savanna, a breathtakingly beautiful shot of lush plains and mountain ranges over which an introductory text is scrolled. This title sets the historical context of social violence in Colombia and then introduces the era of the Violencia. It specifically mentions the ordinary men who became assassins and the most feared of them all, Don León María Lozano. The following sequence shows an unidentified car approaching a farm and alludes to the fact that the car's occupants murder the rural family in cold blood. Ambient street sounds connect these first images to a village in which a clerk is awakened from a nap at his desk by horses and screams. He goes outside in time to witness a horse-drawn cart pass, bearing bodies being burned alive. The rest of the film takes place in and around this rural village as tensions between the Conservatives and the Liberals build. The narrative revolves around Don León María, the bookstore clerk seen in the second sequence and an avowed Conservative, whose actions on the evening of 9 April 1948 change the course of his life.

In the first few minutes of the film, Don León María approaches Doña Gertrudis Potes after Mass to ask her help in finding a new job because the bookstore can no longer afford to employ him.

Although she is one of the town's Liberal leaders, she arranges a position for León María as a cheese broker in the marketplace. This and the preceding mass scene establish that although there is rivalry between the two parties, in this town they coexist peacefully.

Shortly thereafter Gaitán is assassinated. As town criers relay the radio reports, hysteria mounts. Villagers close stores and shut themselves in their homes. Angry Liberals stage a demonstration in the night. Don León María disbands their march by throwing sticks of dynamite into the crowd. He manages to save the town's school without killing anyone and thus instantly becomes a hero of the Conservative Party. At the same time, he is respected by the Liberal leaders for having averted potential rioting and destruction in their quiet town. After the Conservative Party authorizes Don León María to assure that its principles and institutions are upheld, dead bodies begin appearing with increasing frequency all over the region. As people speculate about the political nature of the deaths, fear grows. In church, where Conservatives and Liberals pray side by side, the priest denounces the violence and the murder of innocent men, women, and children. The townspeople, realizing that Don León María is behind the tragedies, fear him more and more.

Don León María decides to rid the region of opposition by ordering all Liberals to leave. Finally indignant, the citizens begin to resent Don León María and rebel against him. An assassination attempt leaves León María and his wife gravely ill. Waiting for them to die, a festive crowd gathers outside their home, dancing and carousing into the night. Don León María and his wife recover. The musicians are found dead by the side of a rural road later the next day. The funeral march circles Don León María's home at least three times, indicating the town's recognition of his culpability. Finally, the Liberals are restored to power in Bogotá, undermining Don León María's legitimacy. He and his wife pack up their belongings and prepare to flee by cover of night. Don León María stops to light a candle and is gunned down as he returns to his cart. Like many of his victims, he is shot in the back. The film ends with a long take of his dead body on the dark street.

Confesión and *Condores* both demonstrate the transformation of private lives by public events. *Confesión* parlays this transformation into the opportunity to pursue personal dreams. *Condores,* on the other hand, illustrates the potential destruction of a perfectly average life and the ensuing suffering. Privately or publicly enacted, the metamorphoses enabled by 9 April and the ensuing Violencia are more available to men than to women. The women facilitate male transformations yet are not themselves permitted to break gendered social codes. In *Confesión*, Josefina and Laura remain in their homes while Santiago crosses the street, moving between the apartments and, finally, escaping down the same street. Josefina, alone in her apartment, reacts to the street riots by taking inventory of her pantry and listening to the radio. Feeling a need to control her surroundings, she telephones Laura every few minutes to advise her on emergency preparations. Eventually, Josefina rigs a pulley across the street, physically connecting the two apartments. The telephone, windows, and radio demarcate Josefina's confinement and her inability to act. The camera enhances our sense of Josefina's containment through close-ups and by frequently framing her with the window. Disembodied male voices on the radio and on loudspeakers in the streets direct her every move. In the end, Josefina's impotence abets Santiago's escape — when she runs downstairs to look at the dead body, sniper fire prevents her from crossing the threshold. Thus, an unseen man immobilizes Josefina and she can only assume that the dead man was indeed Santiago.

Laura also remains trapped in her apartment, reacting not so much to the terror of the streets, but to Santiago, a relative stranger whom she calls Don Santiago during the first part of the film. She nervously calls him Santiago only after he insists and they must hide this note of intimacy from Josefina. Laura's reactions are manifested in typical domestic actions: at Josefina's suggestion, she takes inventory of the pantry; like a proper hostess, she offers Santiago a brandy; like a good mother, she irons his pants to dry them after they get soaking wet; and, like a younger sister, she coaxes him to sing along with the tango records. More visibly nervous than Josefina, Laura continually errs in fulfilling her feminine duties. Too addled to make tea, she breaks into hysterical tears, crying that she does not want to die, especially on her birthday. Santiago comforts her, sits her down, and takes over in the kitchen.

Taking care of Laura clearly moves Santiago, whose own wife seems emotionless in comparison. In Laura's home Santiago's nurturing side emerges. And, furthermore, Laura responds positively to Santiago's dreams of being someone other than who he is. He explains that he wants people to believe he is a man who smokes since to him the act of smoking cigarettes epitomizes sophistication and confidence. Showing her how he pretends to be a smoker while he waits for the streetcar, Santiago confides in Laura that he knows he does not fool anyone. "Why not?" Laura answers, "I believe you. I believe you are a man who smokes." She encourages him to practice his stance and gives him pointers on achieving the effect he seeks.

Laura and Santiago discover a mutual love for the tango. Eventually, they turn off the radio to listen to records on the gramophone. Santiago sings along and Laura compliments him on his singing voice. As she sits and watches, Santiago dances around the living room, singing and reminiscing about his youth. A phone call from Josefina, who has been vigilantly watching them through her lace curtains, interrupts this interlude. She admonishes Laura and Santiago for being so nonchalant about such a serious situation. As the afternoon lengthens, Josefina's calm crumbles, not because she fears the riots, but because she cannot control Santiago and Laura. Increasingly jealous, she insinuates to Santiago that Laura is trying to seduce him. A few hours later a truck passes and orders everyone to snuff their candles. Josefina, now frantic because she cannot see into Laura's apartment, insists that Santiago return. He acquiesces, leaving Laura sobbing over the spaghetti dinner he had cooked for them. A shot rings out. Both Laura and Josefina, peering out their windows, see a man in a hat and overcoat lying facedown in the street and assume it is Santiago.

Socially defined gender roles guide Laura's actions and emotions until Santiago reappears at her door a few minutes later. An unmarried woman alone with a married man, she had remained modest and chaste, even embarrassed by her growing feelings for her neighbor's husband. When she sees Santiago after he has been "shot," however, she falls into his arms, governed now by emotion and fear far more powerful than social codes. Laura and Santiago make love, an adulterous act unthinkable outside of the circumstances of the violence and the curfew. When morning comes, Laura convinces Santiago to flee down a back alley. Laura masterminds Santiago's escape, sacrificing her own happiness in doing so. It never occurs to either one that she should go with him. Laura cannot leave because she is confined to her domestic space and actions. Like Josefina, Laura reacts, rather than acts, in response to the events outside her home. In the end, Laura returns to her apartment, a space where changes affected by a historic event are only fleeting.

The domestic space of the apartment fosters Santiago's personal transformation, but remaining itself unchanged by external events, this space cannot help perpetuate these internal metamorphoses. A gendered space, the apartment reflects the continuity in women's social roles; it symbolizes how women's lives evolve slowly rather than change radically in the face of historic events.[7] Santiago thus joins the public on the streets, taking his personal discoveries into the public realm, where change occurs swiftly and relentlessly. In Laura's apartment, a nurturing Santiago expresses his desire to be a different sort of man. The circumstances that throw them together initiate Santiago's self-discovery. But Laura's sympathetic nature and the hominess of her apartment provide a locus for change. Although they never discuss politics, Santiago finds a flip-book of photos of Gaitán on Laura's bookshelves and revels in finding a woman who shares his political beliefs. This little book completes Santiago's growing sense of comfort in Laura's home. Increasingly, he exudes an ease and confidence that were absent in his own home and in his conversations with Josefina. Laura and her home enable Santiago to leave his own home to follow his dreams.

At the end of *Condores*, Don León María also leaves his home. Unlike Santiago, who ventures into public alone to pursue his new life, León María runs away from angry, vengeful villagers, attempting to flee his public persona and reclaim his quiet, private life. His wife Agripina accompanies him silently. The majority of the action in *Condores* takes place in the town's public spaces— the marketplace, the town square, the streets, or in places specifically coded as masculine such as bars and back rooms. León María's metamorphosis is completed in these spaces from which he issues orders and creates hit lists. But the women rarely venture beyond the buildings whose institutions define their gender roles—the home, the church, and the school. Doña Gertrudis, a powerful Liberal matriarch, exerts her influence from her own library and in the church. She holds meetings in the library of her estate mansion where, seated in her thronelike armchair, she directs other Liberal leaders in handling León María. After one of her close advisers is killed, she interrupts the priest's Sunday sermon to condemn the senseless murders in the village. Yet, when she holds a meeting at which she intends to demonstrate to León María that the village's Liberals are still strong, Don León María does not attend. She responds by breaking the curfew he has imposed and going alone under cover of dark to his house. The servant tells her that she can find Don León María at the Happy Bar, where the only women to be found are lower-class barmaids. Socially restricted from going to the Happy Bar, Doña Gertrudis is prevented from delivering her message. The walls of her home and the church mark the boundaries of Doña Gertrudis's ability to act and transform her power into impotence after 9 April. Outside of her home, Doña Gertrudis is ineffectual against the Condor.

The "home" structures gender roles, defining expected behavior of men and women. In the urban setting of *Confesión a Laura*, the Bogotazo creates a circumstance in which the home serves as a cocoon in which Santiago metamorphoses. In *Condores*, León María's home life contrasts with his public persona. The comparison makes his transformation after Gaitán's death less radical, demonstrating that the changes affect his public self more than his private self. Before Gaitán's assassination, León María *only* wields power as maker of law in his own home. Within this situation, León María's actions are governed by social expectations for a man and his wife. A fervent Catholic, he follows a strict moral code and is fiercely loyal to the Conservative Party. He admonishes his wife for being topless in the privacy of their bedroom because "It's a question of principles." When his daughter Amapola flirts with a young man León María does not like, León María uses his newfound influence to arrange a scholarship for her at a distant boarding school. Agripina and Amapola, subject to his domestic sovereignty, obey his rules without question.

At home, Don León María controls his family's power structures, proving his moral strength. In public, however, León María appears weak. He suffers from asthma attacks, which vary in intensity according to what space he is in. The asthma disables him, leaving him gasping for air as the bookstore owner lets him go.

The owner gives him a bellows and explains that his grandfather used it to get more air when asthma inhibited his breathing. Ventilating himself with the bellows, León María explains that he is convinced an asthma attack will kill him in the street someday. Yet, the asthma rarely bothers him when he is dictating to his family. As the film progresses, the attacks increase in frequency while decreasing in severity, paralleling León María's transition from ineffectual observer to powerful actor in village life.

After the assassination, León María's public persona changes. He instigates, rather than observes, events in village life. At his orders, Liberals receive invitations to leave the village, farmers are threatened, and any opponents die. When León María yells at one of his lackeys to quiet a barking dog, the lackey shoots the offending animal. Ever a man of principle, León María placates the dog's owner by making a gift of a new puppy. Don León María, now a public figure, follows his strict moral code by day — always attending his victims' funerals and going regularly to Sunday Mass. But by night, his henchmen wreak death throughout the village and its environs. As León María gains power, murders take place on the sunny streets and in the village offices. Ultimately, Don León María dies in the street, as he himself predicted, not as victim of asthma, but of an unseen assailant.

In *Condores*, the assassination of Gaitán transforms public spaces. Before 9 April, the conflict between the Conservative and Liberal parties causes minimal upheaval in this village. The peaceful coexistence of the parties is emphasized in the third sequence of the film: the priest speaks about the horrible murders that are decimating families and condemns all who might be responsible. Doña Gertrudis leans over and whispers ironically to her neighbor, "He thinks you Conservatives are innocent and we Liberals are to blame for everything." They exchange smiles. She later arranges a new job for León María, saying to the employer, "I want Don León to have the job, even if he is a Conservative." Political differences are directly spoken and acknowledged in public spaces and conversations. This tense but peaceful coexistence typified the fifteen years before Gaitán's death, a period when Conservatives and Liberals forged coalition governments and appeared, at least, to be sincere in their efforts to govern peacefully.[8] Even as tensions build, León María is approached in the marketplace to purchase a raffle ticket in support of the Liberal Party. He refuses, tersely but politely. Only after the ticket seller leaves does León María's anger surface. Shortly before Gaitán's death, León María dares to gloat about the electoral victory of a Conservative candidate before Doña Gertrudis in the town square. In doing so, he violates the mutual respect that governs village politics. After 9 April, political differences and fierce party loyalties catalyze the village's degeneration to bloody civil war. The senseless murders that tear the town apart further erode the unspoken treaty of coexistence. No rules govern political conflicts once the *pájaros* take over. Gaitán's death instigates social chaos, which, as represented in *Condores*, "reformulate[s] patterns of conflict and restructure[s] ideological contradictions" (Burgoyne, 35).[9] Because conflict and contradiction are prohibited in the home, they assume public form, converting town squares into menacing deadly spaces.

Historical Violence and Cinema in Present-Day Colombia

Gaitán's assassination constitutes a pivotal moment in both *Confesión* and *Condores*. The specific date and historic event are not randomly chosen. Rather, it may be said that Gaitán's death and the Violencia presage political violence in Colombia in the 1980s, stemming from the drug wars, anticommunist militias, and guerrilla actions. Contemporary drug-related kidnappings and murders committed by *sicarios*—the contemporary *pájaros*—are not dissimilar to the events set in motion by Gaitán's death. In the late 1980s, the escalation of the drug wars caused the deaths of thousands of innocent Colombians. Since the mid-1980s, Colombian political scientists specializing in violence, *violentólogos*, have examined the causes and effects of a century of bloodshed and fear.[10] They are especially interested in exploring the links between the Violencia and the insurrections of the 1970s and 1980s. As historical narratives, *Confesión* and *Condores* serve multiple functions: each provides a new perspective on a historical event that changed Colombia forever and each permits the viewer to consider how one historical moment affected the country's future (their present). Further, both films allow the viewer to contemplate the effects of contemporary violence on their own lives.

Only a modest amount of cultural output examines the Violencia, the Bogotazo, and the aftermath. Gonzalo Sánchez notes the impact of the Violencia on Colombian art and literature, commenting that "in the subject matter of most of these works we find a stress on the dead, the victims. Rarely do the executors, the beneficiaries, or the rebels appear. The *Violencia* is shown almost wholly as tragedy, as an impersonal and destructive force" ("La Violencia in Colombia," 806). *Confesión* and *Condores* show, respectively, the beneficiaries and the victims of the Violencia. In portraying personal transformations catalyzed by the Violencia, both films chart a new path in depicting this moment in Colombian history. Adapting for the screen a novel about a legendary assassin, *Condores* reenvisages the public tragedy and the transformation of quiet village life into violent struggle. Almost as a complement, *Confesión* reminds its viewers of the private triumphs made possible by this event, the personal metamorphoses made possible (and in some cases necessary) by social and political changes. These films, taken with a small number of other films made in the past ten years, reflect a concern with violence that is being expressed in all forms of Colombian art. It is probably too soon to determine whether they signal the beginning of a "national cinema," but we would be remiss to ignore the exploration of Colombian reality in this group of films.

Although neither *Confesión* nor *Condores* is a pure historical narrative, both films reflect historiography and how history is known in Colombia. Both cinema and historiography present us with an absence, the represented past. Further, in each there is the implicit absence of the represented future (Rosen, 31). Both films illustrate how one historical event changes lives and each speaks to the transformative power of continued violence in Colombian life. *Confesión* depicts a private episode triggered by the public event, using fiction to create a plausible tale that fills in the gap of unknowable history. When Santiago joins the morning pedestrians, he walks into the future, unknown and ambiguous. The viewer lives in Santiago's future and thus can connect the film to her/his own reality. Similarly, the viewer does not recognize León María's death at the end of *Condores* as a turning point in the Violencia. Rather, when the camera pulls back from a close-up of León María's dead body on the street to an over-head long shot of the street with the body lying still, small, and insignificant, the viewer realizes that the violence masterminded by the Condor will continue without him.

Forty years after Gaitán's death, both *Confesión* and *Condores* serve as parables for the working out of contemporary violence by permitting their audiences to experience social violence at a historical distance, while at the same time presenting intimate, personal transformations with which a viewer may identify. The results of acts of public and political violence are not limited to public lives and spaces; they affect family relations and everyday private lives as well. *Confesión* and *Condores* narrativize these changes, parlaying the experience of a definable historical period, the Violencia, into an exploration of how a social phenomenon, violence, continually transforms the ways in which Colombians live and act.

Notes

1. In English-language scholarship, this ellipsis can be seen in John King's *Magical Reels: A History of Cinema in Latin America.* Colombia and Venezuela are considered together in a chapter subtitled "Cinema and the State." King begins with Colombian filmmaking in the 1960s without mentioning the cinematographic attempts of Colombians since the turn of the century. Thus, King's history neglects the growth of a filmgoing culture, the output of documentary films, and the creation of virtual distribution and exhibition monopolies, which began early in Colombia and continue to influence Colombian feature filmmaking. Paul Lenti's essay on Colombia, "State Role in Film Production," in *Mediating Two Worlds: Cinematic Encounters in the Americas,* is another case in point. Lenti, a freelance reporter for *Variety,* is more concerned with the institutional aspects of state involvement in production. His essay, while providing useful information, limits the discussion to a chronology of Colombia's legislative efforts to promote film production. In doing so, it ignores the films made outside of the system in the past fifteen years and avoids any discussion of artistic and ideological content of Colombia's films. Octavio Getino discusses Colombia briefly in sections subtitled "The Andean Region" in each section of *Cine Latinoamericano: Economía y Nuevas Tecnologías Audiovisuales,* making important and interesting connections between how cinema and film industries have (or have not) evolved throughout the region.

2. Rodríguez and Silva are interviewed by Julianne Burton in *Cinema and Social Change in America: Conversations with Filmmakers.*

3. This and other translations from Spanish-language sources are mine.

4. *Confesión a Laura* is distributed on video in the United States through Facets Multimedia in Chicago.

5. Isabel Sánchez has compiled six Colombian screenplays that incorporate themes of social and political violence. Three of these scripts won the Concurso Nacional de Guión, a national screenwriting contest sponsored by Colombia's Compañía de Fomento Cinematográfica (Focine, the now-defunct state-operated film office dedicated to stimulating domestic film production) from 1979 to 1992. These three are *Los días de miedo* (written by Antonio Montaña, 1979 winner), *Efraín* (Jairo Anibal Niño, 1980 winner), and *Siete colores* (Dunaz Kuzmanich with Jairo Obando and Javier Ponce, 1981 winner). Despite winning this prestigious award, none of these films has been produced because of the censorship regarding the Violencia. The other screenplays in the volume are *Condores* and *Canaguaro* (directed by Dunaz Kuzmanich, 1981) two of Colombia's best-known films and *El día de las Mercedes* (directed by Dunaz Kuzmanich and Antonio Montaña, 1985).

6. The term violentólogos refers to political scientists who since the 1980s have focused on the effects of the Violencia both in its time and in today's Colombia.

7. Jorge Eliécer Gaitán began advocating women's suffrage and full rights to citizenship in the 1930s. Colombia, however, only granted voting rights to women in 1957, becoming the second-to-last Latin American country to do so. Perhaps because of its historic ties to the Catholic church, Colombia has consistently been a country where women's rights have been won slowly and arduously.

8. For more on the period of *convivencia*, see Herbert Braun.

9. Burgoyne is writing here about a general notion of how historical narrative cinema functions.

10. The most important studies have been published by the Universidad Nacional de Colombia and by Amnesty International. For more information and a review of the scholarship in English and Spanish, see Ricardo Peñaranda.

Works Cited

Alvarez, Carlos. *Una década de cortometraje colombiano: 1970–1980*. Bogotá: Arcadia va al Cine, 1981.

Arbeláez, Ramiro. *El espacio audiovisual en Colombia: Infraestructura y marco jurídico*. Colombia: Centro Editorial Univ. del Valle, 1992.

Bernal, Agosto. Interview with Ilene S. Goldman. July 1993.

Braun, Herbert. *The Assassination of Gaitán*. Madison: Univ. of Wisconsin Press, 1985.

Burgoyne, Robert. *Bertolucci's 1900*. Detroit: Wayne State Univ. Press, 1991.

Burton, Julianne. *Cinema and Social Change in Latin America: Conversations with Filmmakers*. Austin: Univ. of Texas Press, 1986.

Bushnell, David. *The Making of Modern Colombia: A Nation in Spite of Itself*. Berkeley: Univ. of California Press, 1993.

de Certeau, Michel. *The Writing of History*. Trans. Tim Conley. New York: Columbia Univ. Press, 1988.

Duzan, María Jimena. *Death Beat*. Trans. Peter Eisner. New York: HarperCollins, 1994.

Gerdes, Dick. "Estaba la pájara pinta sentada en el verde limón: Novela testimonial/documental de 'la violencia' en Colombia." *Revista de Estudios Colombianos*, no. 2 (1987): 23–26.

Getino, Octavio. *Cine Latinoamericano: Economía y Nuevas Tecnologías Audiovisuales.* Buenos Aires: Editorial Legaso, 1988.

Johnson, Randal. "In the Belly of the Ogre: Cinema and State in Latin America." In *Mediating Two Worlds: Cinematic Encounters in the Americas.* Ed. John King, Ana M. López, and Manuel Alvarado. London: British Film Institute, 1993.

King, John. *Magical Reels: A History of Cinema in Latin America.* London: Verso, 1990.

Lenti, Paul. "Colombia: State Role in Film Production." In *Mediating Two Worlds: Cinematic Encounters in the Americas.* Ed. John King, Ana M. López, and Manuel Alvarado. London: British Film Institute, 1993.

Osquist, Paul. *Violence, Conflict and Politics in Colombia.* New York: Academic Press, 1980.

Peñaranda, Ricardo. "Surveying the Literature." In *Violence in Colombia: The Contemporary Crisis in Historical Perspective.* Ed. Charles Bergquist, Ricardo Peñaranda, and Gonzalo Sánchez. Wilmington, Del.: Scholarly Resources, 1992.

Rosen, Philip. "Securing the Historical: Historiography and the Classical Cinema." In *Cinema Practices, Cinema Histories.* Ed. Patricia Mellencamp and Philip Rosen. Los Angeles: American Film Institute, 1984.

Rowe, William, and Vivian Schelling. *Memory and Modernity: Popular Culture in Latin America.* London: Verso, 1991.

Sánchez, Gonzalo. "La Violencia in Colombia: New Research, New Questions." *Hispanic American Historical Review* 65 (1985): 789–807.

———. "The Violence: An Interpretative Synthesis." In *Violence in Colombia: The Contemporary Crisis in Historical Perspective.* Ed. Charles Bergquist, Ricardo Peñaranda, and Gonzalo Sánchez. Wilmington, Del.: Scholarly Resources, 1992.

Sánchez, Isabel. *Cine de la violencia.* Bogotá: Univ. Nacional de Colombia, 1987.

Chapter 4
When the Mountains Tremble: Images of Ethnicity in a Transcultural Text

Teresa Longo

Crucé la frontera, amor...
Rigoberta Menchú

When U.S. filmmakers document the lives of people from other countries, especially Third World countries, they risk making a film that objectifies and mythifies the cultural other.[1] The challenge, according to filmmaker and cultural theorist Trinh T. Minh-ha, is to "re-create without re-circulating domination" (15). My purpose in writing about *When the Mountains Tremble*, a documentary on civil war and ethnic survival in Guatemala, is to examine the possibilities it offers for overcoming the film industry's tendency to dominate — to mythify and objectify — its subjects. *When the Mountains Tremble* (1983 and 1993)[2] is, strictly speaking, a *U.S.* documentary: it was created by the founders of Skylight Pictures (Pamela Yates and Thomas Sigel, directors, Peter Konoy, producer), was funded by the Public Broadcasting System (PBS), and is distributed by New Yorker Films to a largely U.S. audience. Yet in spite of their U.S. interests and national origins, Yates, Sigel, and Konoy have made a concerted effort to create a documentary whose focus is more transcultural than ethnocentric and objectifying. The most important evidence of this effort may be found in the decision to involve Rigoberta Menchú as an active participant in the work's creation.[3] Indeed, Menchú is not the object, but the narrator—or speaking subject—of *When the Mountains Tremble*. As the primary storyteller, Menchú is also the creator of the text's verbal images of ethnicity. As my investigation probes the ideological significations of ethnic imagery in *When the Mountains Tremble*, I analyze Menchú's imagery not in isolation but in relation to its visual counterparts.[4] I argue that the conjoining of the visual (images selected by U.S. filmmakers) and the verbal (images composed by Menchú)[5] challenges delineations based on nationality, stretches the boundaries between the filming subject and the filmed object, and renders this text transcultural. As a result, Yates, Sigel, Konoy, and Menchú address the practice whereby documentary filmmakers reproduce exotic cultural others. Thus, the creators of *When the Mountains Tremble* begin to re-create without recirculating domination.

Earth/Corn and Mother/Father

Menchú begins her narration of *When the Mountains Tremble* by underscoring Guatemalan ethnicity as the thematic focus of her text: "Me llamo Rigoberta Menchú, indígena quiché del pueblo de Guatemala... les voy a contar mi historia que es la historia de todo el pueblo de Guatemala."[6] As the voice of the people, Menchú then begins to define her culture in terms of its ancestral ties: "We are descendants of the Maya. Most of us live in the high mountains... we cultivate corn... Before planting... we ask permission from our mother earth for the wound we're going to create..." In correspondence with Menchú's opening remarks, Yates, Sigel, and Konoy begin the text's visual narration by acknowledging the importance of an ancient tradition—the cultivation of corn—in contemporary Guatemalan culture. By beginning the documentary with images of earth and corn, the U.S. filmmakers, like Menchú, recognize the indigenous Guatemalans' respect for the earth that sustains them. According to Rigoberta's people, this respect has profound roots: Rigoberta Menchú's ancestors—the ancient Quiché Maya—conceived of the earth as a divinity and corn as the source of their humanity (Tedlock, 14, 47). The visual and oral representations of the relationship between earth and corn—used by Menchú and her U.S. colleagues to introduce Guatemalan ethnicity—are, therefore, extremely important: the opening images of *When the Mountains Tremble* portray Guatemalans as a people with age-old connections to the divine, a people with ancient and sacred rights to their land.

Dual images like earth and corn abound in *When the Mountains Tremble*. For example, while Menchú introduces herself and Guatemala, viewers see Mayan women and men in pairs approaching the camera. As in the opening scene of earth and corn, the text's dual imagery reflects the teachings of the ancients: according to the Maya Quiché's story of creation, the first people modeled from corn dough, the first Quiché leaders, were dual entities—the mother/fathers of their lineage (Tedlock, 47).[7] In *When the Mountains Tremble*, the mother/father duality, like the earth/corn duality, ultimately symbolizes the Guatemalan people's rights to the land. This is the case in the filmmakers' controversial dramatic re-creation of a conversation between María and Jacobo Arbenz and the U.S. ambassador to Guatemala.

The scene, based on declassified U.S. documents, was staged by the Skylight group in order to clarify the historical background of U.S. involvement in Guatemala beginning in 1954 (Barnouw, 302)[8]: viewers hear Jacobo Arbenz, the president of Guatemala, and his wife, María, explain to U.S. ambassador John Peurifoy why Guatemala will no longer allow the United Fruit Company to control its finest land. Yates, Sigel, and Konoy's work here has been criticized for its oversimplification of Guatemalan history.[9] I would argue, however, that this dramatic performance is not as simple as it seems: in terms of the text's symbolic meaning, what viewers hear is secondary to the highly suggestive images that they see. The visual presentation of María and Jacobo Arbenz is an image of two complementary figures. When Jacobo speaks, María listens knowingly. When she speaks, he nods in agreement. Side by side, the partners address their adversary, the U.S. ambassador, seated at the opposite side of the table. The ambassador attends dinner with his wife as well, but she never speaks and camera angles diminish her size. In contrast with the grandiose figure of the ambassador and his silenced wife, Mr. and Mrs. Arbenz emerge as two equally dignified individuals who act as one.[10] They are the mother/father leaders of their nation—dedicated to their people's right to cultivate the land. As a result of the dual imagery of this dramatic re-creation, the U.S. filmmakers demonstrate a transcultural understanding of Mayan culture. They have sacrificed the complex rhetoric of U.S.-Guatemala diplomacy, but it was a sacrifice worth making, for it reveals — on a level more subtle than the verbal — the complexity of Guatemalan ethnicity.

Beauty in the Land of the Quetzal

Included among the images that Rigoberta Menchú uses in order to subtly convey her people's ethnicity is an image of Guatemala as the "land of the quetzal." Menchú's mention of the brilliant national bird native to Central America ("...hace diez años... acababa de salir de la tierra del quetzal") evokes a Guatemala that values natural beauty and indigenous life. Like Menchú, Yates, Konoy, and Sigel also portray Guatemala as the "land of the quetzal." In contrast with the natural brilliance suggested by Menchú, however, the Skylight group (assuming a position critical of U.S. intervention in Central America) reveals a Guatemala that is neither indigenous nor natural, a Guatemala whose "beauty" is imposed — and purchased — from abroad.

The scene from the documentary that most clearly conveys this new and imposed vision of Guatemalan beauty centers on a Miss Guatemala Pageant around 1982. Just prior to the pageant scene, viewers hear an address in which President Ronald Reagan thanks U.S. business leaders for their resourcefulness in Central America and encourages them to further expand their enterprise throughout the hemisphere. Also prior to the pageant scene, viewers see a series of billboards advertising the products of U.S. companies: a shot of a Pepsi billboard, an advertisement for Viceroy, and a close-up of an ad for Wrangler — a U.S. flag inside an unzipped pair of jeans with the caption, "Wrangler, the American Way of Jeans." The montage ends as contestants of the Miss Guatemala Pageant dance across a stage in jeans while the pageant's emcee announces that "tonight there is beauty in the land of the quetzal." Viewers perceive the full ironic impact of the emcee's statement as a result of the Skylight group's careful and creative editing: even before we witness the pageant, the jeans and the flag have already informed us that beauty and culture, in the land of the quetzal, are profoundly and intimately dictated by U.S.

business interests and backed by the U.S. government.[11] As the reigning Miss Guatemala adjusts her crown and proceeds down the runway, images from the pageant itself continue to reinforce the new standards: were it not for the Spanish-speaking emcee, it would be difficult to say that the fair-skinned, blonde-haired, evening-gowned queen was not Miss North Dakota or Miss Virginia 1980-something.

Once we have taken a final look at the reigning Miss Guatemala, Yates, Sigel, and Konoy further direct our attention to the topic of Guatemalan ethnicity — and to threats of its extinction. In their filming and editing of the beauty pageant, they include disturbing images of ladina contestants modeling the native dress of Guatemalan Indians: "luzco el traje del pueblo quiché," states a young ladina woman whose short hair and "cover-girl" makeup negate her claim to an understanding of Quiché ethnicity.[12] The young contestant's obvious act of disrespect unveils a certain acceptance by ladinos of the new, U.S. standards of beauty — an acceptance that results in the mythification (falsification) of indigenous cultures: "sure, the outfit looks pretty," states Menchú, "because it brings in money, but the person who wears it is as if they were nothing" (*Me llamo Rigoberta Menchú*, 234). And, "as if they were nothing," indigenous Guatemalans are significantly absent from "this night of beauty in the land of the quetzal." Via images from the Miss Guatemala Pageant, *When the Mountains Tremble* attests to the very real threat of extinction facing Guatemala's ethnic cultures.

"We the Indians" and International Solidarity

Menchú's reference to Guatemala as the land of native or ethnic beauty and the corresponding portrayal of the suppression of ethnicity, via the beauty pageant sequence, constitute an act of solidarity and an important transnational critique of imperialism. Throughout *When the Mountains Tremble*, Yates, Sigel, Konoy — and Menchú — will continue to stress the importance of national (Guatemalan) and international solidarity in the struggle for ethnic survival in Guatemala. Early in the text, the meaning of Menchú's "we," symbolic of her solidarity with her own people the Maya Quiché ("les voy a contar mi historia... somos descendientes de los Maya"), quickly expands to include all the indigenous peoples of Guatemala: *"We the indigenous people,"* states Rigoberta, "have no childhood. From the time we're very young we have to work hard in order to earn a living" (my emphasis).[13] Complementing Menchú's narrative are visuals of Mayan children picking coffee, native women en route to their jobs as servants in the capital, indigenous men shoveling garbage on the outskirts of a town: in all cases, the images—like Menchú's "we"—demonstrate the collective nature of the Guatemalan situation wherein a common national plight subsumes individual suffering. As Menchú continues her story, the subject of her "nosotros los indígenas" becomes ever more inclusive: "the landowners' security forces arrived to kick us off our small plot of land. They violently took us from our homes... That's why my father joined with workers, unions, Christian students, and other sectors."[14] The Skylight group reinforces Menchú's focus on the solidarity between ladino workers and indigenous peasants with archival images documenting the mineworkers' strike of 1977: as workers and peasants march to the capital together, their banners proclaim the unity of the people.[15]

The emphasis on solidarity in *When the Mountains Tremble* reaches an international level when Menchú offers her insights on the Americas: "For us indigenous people, it isn't exactly a bad time... and I'm completely sure that in many countries of America the indigenous will live forever and I hope that's so; it depends on society."[16] In this statement, Menchú promotes solidarity not only with Native Americans but also ("y depende de la sociedad") with an extensive international audience, which would include nonnative communities in the United States. Clearly, she has already established solidarity with the U.S. filmmakers who demonstrate their transnational sensitivity by portraying visual images of the righteous nature of Menchú's cause.

Yet, for even the most sensitive of U.S. filmmakers, the imperialist point of view is hard to avoid. For example, immediately after the beauty pageant sequence, the filmmakers cut to the testimony of a Mayan woman who speaks out in open defiance of the mythification and objectification of Guatemala's indigenous people: "The government uses us when it's in their interest. They exhibit us in our native dress in a park as though we were in a zoo. The army and the rich consider us unskilled brutes who don't know anything." It is obvious that Yates, Sigel, and Konoy see this testimony as important for they present to their international audience the image of an intelligent, articulate, honest woman whose very presence defies domination. The U.S. filmmakers, however, fail to acknowledge the speaker's ethnic origins, to identify her native language, or to introduce her by name. To a certain extent, the oversight reveals an act of unintentional ethnocentrism on the part of the filmmakers.[17] The people's unity promoted by the Skylight group in *When the Mountains Tremble* is a real necessity in Guatemala: the success of the resistance movement clearly depends on strength in numbers, the ability to organize, and international understanding and support. Nevertheless, an overwhelming focus on solidarity without an affirmation of the individual contributes to a negation of ethnicity:[18] when viewers see the twenty-two separate ethnic groups in Guatemala "unify" or merge into one category called "Indians," Guatemalans are denied the very ethnicity Menchú and the U.S. filmmakers hope to protect. It is impossible to "re-create without re-circulating domination" when individual and ethnic identification are not acknowledged on the screen.

Ethnicity and Humanity

In *When the Mountains Tremble* Rigoberta Menchú relates the shocking story of the torture and killing of community members — including her younger brother. Her testimony reveals intense government repression of Guatemala's ethnic population. (Like Menchú, those tortured are descendants of the Mayans.) The images of Rigoberta's testimony also reveal government efforts to deny the Indians their very humanity:

> The army kidnapped my brother. His crime was to have been the secretary of a small agricultural cooperative in the village. They tortured him for fifteen days. They cut out his fingernails. They sliced his body. Then the army published a document telling people to go see the punishment that they were going to give the guerrillas in their power. We went to the Plaza de Chajul. There were twenty tortured men there. Among them was my brother.

Their swollen bodies were without fingernails, without ears. An army official spoke for three hours, threatening the people by saying that whoever participated in subversive activities would meet the same end as these men. He gathered the men together and, while they were still alive, he poured gasoline on them. They were burned in the plaza.[19]

The images that communicate dehumanization most thoroughly here refer to acts of bodily torture that render individuals unrecognizable.[20] These twenty men, cut up and swollen from abuse, were denied their ethnicity and their humanity even before they were burned alive in the Plaza de Chajul: as a result of government oppression, the prisoners were abducted — severed from their families, their communities, and their livelihood. Now, images of severed fingernails and ears disclose not only the men's physical pain but also the torturous separations inflicted on Guatemala's ethnic communities by their oppressors. According to Rigoberta Menchú and the U.S. filmmakers with whom she collaborates, Guatemalans have been systematically split up from their families, uprooted from their land, and divided from their culture. The visual imagery that most clearly communicates the severing of humanity described by Menchú appears in a scene of the film that documents the aftermath of the government's massacre of the inhabitants of a Guatemalan village. Just prior to the massacre scene, we see drawings of war done by Guatemalan children: their subjects are machine guns, blood, and the outline of a decapitated body. Similar to the children's drawings, the images of the subsequent footage of the massacre are images of havoc and destruction. We see rows of dead bodies — their bloody hands and their faces. The imagery, like that used by Rigoberta in the portrayal of her brother's death, is highly metonymic: the focus is not on whole human beings but on isolated body parts. In this way, the U.S. filmmakers record the forced fragmentation of ethnic communities in Guatemala.

In addition to the filming of hands and faces, coverage of the Skylight group's work on the massacre scene includes close-up coverage of the intense human reactions of those who survived: a woman whose passage is blocked by a barbed-wire fence covers her face in her hands; another woman cries out in agony as she caresses the cloth covering a loved one. The scene is as painful to watch as Menchú's testimony is to hear. The question, of course, is "how close is too close?" Can filmmakers document tragedy realistically without furthering victimization with their intruding cameras? Pamela Yates maintains that part of her camera style is to really look at people, to "feel people as human beings, as having lives, dimensions" (Rosenthal, 548). She "wanted to make a film which would actually draw Americans closer to Guatemala" (ibid., 545). With this purpose in mind, it seems that the Skylight group filmed the massacre scene in the only way possible. The largely U.S. audiences of *When the Mountains Tremble* experience only a fragment of the grief affecting the survivors. But — as a result of this close-up experience — we do experience something. Pamela Yates hopes that this brief moment of shared agony will promote U.S. viewers to stop their government's intervention in Central America.[21] When this happens, the camera's momentary intrusion into the grief of the victims will become not a victimizing tool, but a component in the effort to stop the fragmentation and dehumanization of Guatemala's ethnic communities.

The Armed Struggle, Little Sisters

Ultimately, Guatemalans are portrayed not as victims but as survivors in *When the Mountains Tremble*. And according to Rigoberta Menchú, survival — ethnic survival — depends on armed struggle: "For us orphans there hasn't been any other path but that of struggle," states Menchú. "My two little sisters [*hermanitas*] have chosen armed struggle." Menchú's combination of the diminutive image "little sisters" with the notion of armed conflict suggests the intriguing, multilayered dimensions of the lives of the people — especially the women — involved in the Guatemalan struggle. Menchú's subjects are not one-dimensional, or mythical objects, but individuals whose lives are complex and even contradictory. Like Menchú, Yates, Sigel, and Konoy present this complexity successfully in their filming of the daily routines of guerrillas-in-training in the Guatemalan highlands. The documentary's highly acclaimed guerrilla scenes include coverage of initiation ceremonies and armed skirmishes as well as interviews with revolutionaries.[22] In her own interview with Alan Rosenthal, Yates refers to the filming of the guerrilla scenes as an extraordinary "once-in-a-lifetime" experience: "the general oppression in Guatemala is so intense that you can't just ask someone their candid opinion, because they won't tell you. At least not above ground in the capital. But when we went with the guerrillas, it was like crossing an invisible line. All of a sudden, everyone would tell you anything you wanted to know... And to me that was a revelation" (546). To Yates's comments, I would add that, for the viewers of *When the Mountains Tremble,* the real "revelation" of the guerrilla scenes lies not only in the information we hear but also, and perhaps even more poignantly, in the images we visually perceive. As the filmmakers draw their viewers into the day-to-day workings of revolution, we catch glimpses of some of the essential and unexpected elements of the guerrillas' existence: this is a world of army fatigues, black berets, guns, and dog tags. It is also a world of intricately woven *huipiles,* delicate earrings, and sewing needles.

The complexities of revolutionary existence apparent in the juxtaposition of such incongruent images come to life when the Skylight group interviews two very young Mayan women who, like Rigoberta Menchú's little sisters, have both chosen a life of active participation in armed revolution. During the interview, one of the young women speaking leans against her gun and embroiders. Her companion, with a rifle resting at her side, brushes her hair and listens. The seemingly contradictory images of the young guerrillas' life—guns, a hairbrush, and an embroidery hoop—parallel the sharp distinction between the innocence of their years and the gravity of their message: "In the future when we win, we're going to achieve a new society very slowly," states the first young woman, "but we the guerrillas will be able to adapt to the new life that is coming. We will be able to go into the villages and nourish the old culture, the best part of our folkways." Here "to nourish," with all its feminine implications, is associated with the preservation of ethnic culture and with the success of the revolution. Women—and some very young women, indeed—have found a place in the Guatemalan revolution. As the young guerrilla interviewed by the Skylight group states, "It's good to be here: everyone is equal." In the Guatemalan revolution, young people articulate adult concerns; women feminize the masculine enterprise of war: the hairbrush and the gun may not be as incongruous as they seem.[23]

Before the Skylight group could capture on film this young woman's insights on revolution, before Yates, Sigel, and Konoy could document the complexities of her life as a revolutionary, they had to cross what Pamela Yates has called an "invisible line." It is hard to imagine that the group's line or border crossing was not in some way facilitated by the identification in gender between Yates and her subjects. In *I, Rigoberta Menchú*, Menchú maintains that women have played an incredible role in the revolution: "It is unbelievable. Mothers with their children would be putting up barricades, and then placing 'propaganda bombs,' or carrying documents. Women have had a great history. They all experienced terrible things, whether they be working-class women, peasant women, or teachers" (233). And to this list of female participants in the revolutionary struggle, it seems that Menchú has also added a U.S. filmmaker and her collaborators.

When she agreed to narrate their documentary in her own words, Menchú and her U.S. colleagues opened a border that has for so long blocked international dialogue through film. *When the Mountains Tremble* is not a flawless piece of transcultural communication. Neverthless, Menchú's "border crossing"[24] together with Yates, Sigel, and Konoy's "step over the invisible line" may constitute an important direction to be taken by U.S. documentarists — a direction that subverts ethnocentrism by recognizing the complexity of the hairbrushes alongside the guns.

Notes

When the Mountains Tremble can be purchased from New Yorker Films at 16 W. 61st St., New York, NY 10023.

1. See Christian Hansen, Catherine Needham, and Bill Nichols, "Pornography, Ethnography and the Discourse of Power," in Nichols, *Representing Reality: Issues and Concepts in Documentary.* As an alternative to discourses of domination, the authors propose documentaries based on "dialogue, heteroglossia, political reflexivity, and the subversion of ethnocentrism" (227). The "dialogue" proposed here is apparent in *When the Mountains Tremble* in the cooperative efforts of Rigoberta Menchú and the creators of Skylight Pictures.

2. *When the Mountains Tremble* was originally produced in 1983 and then rereleased with additional narrative by Menchú in 1993. On the original production, see Erik Barnouw, *Documentary: A History of the Non-Fiction Film* (300–302).

3. Rigoberta Menchú is a Maya-Quiché activist, a spokeswoman for indigenous rights, the 1992 recipient of the Nobel Peace Prize, and the narrator of the testimonial *Me llamo Rigoberta Menchú y así me nació la conciencia* (Elizabeth Burgos, ed.). She is currently recognized as an international authority on justice and ethnic survival. See Teresa Longo, "Authority and Reconquest in *Me llamo Rigoberta Menchú.*"

In an interview with Alan Rosenthal, published in Rosenthal's *New Challenges for Documentary,* Pamela Yates clarifies Menchú's participation as follows:

> We knew that our main problem in the editing of *Mountains* was that we had very few central characters, and we had no one, central character to act as the thread to weave the film together. And then, about three days after I met her, I knew that she would be the best choice. Then it was Tom's idea that we film her in isolation the way we did, to give her that storytelling quality . . . and to represent her as the voice of the Guatemalan people . . . [We filmed her] at the very beginning [of the editing process], before we really had an assemblage. She came and looked at all the footage with us, and we discussed the kinds of scenes we were going to put together. Of course, we knew her whole story. We had tried to gather every article that had been written about her, and we also had many long conversations with her. Then she sat down and wrote the script, her own personal story, over a period of three days. Afterward we went into a studio and filmed her. (546)

4. My analysis of signification relies on Roland Barthes's theory of the image. In "The Third Meaning," Barthes writes that signification or symbolic meaning is referential to history (52). On the relationship between verbal and visual imagery, see W. J. T. Mitchell, *Iconology: Image, Text, Ideology.* Mitchell's theory centers on the notion that the "dialectic of word and image seems to be a constant in the fabric of signs that a culture weaves around itself" (43); "we create much of our world out of the dialogue between verbal and pictorial representations" (46).

5. The editors also selected the portions of Menchú's oral testimony that would be included in the documentary. My focus, here, however, is not on the selection or deletion of entire narrative passages but on the imagery within those passages that Menchú uses to tell her story.

6. Menchú's opening statement also introduces a dialogue between *When the Mountains Tremble* and *Me llamo Rigoberta Menchú y así me nació la conciencia* (Elizabeth Burgos, ed.), which begins in much the same way. The first edition of Burgos's work was published in 1985, although she began recording Menchú's story in 1982 — just one year before Skylight Productions filmed the Guatemalan activist. Menchú's narration of *When the Mountains Tremble* closely resembles a "condensed version" of *Me llamo Rigoberta Menchú.* In the cinematic representation of the activist's story, the details are provided not by the narrator but by Yates, Sigel, and Konoy.

7. In the introduction to the *Popol Vuh,* Dennis Tedlock writes that even today there are individuals called mother/fathers who serve in ritual matters as symbolic androgynous parents to everyone in their respective lineages (47). In *Me llamo Rigoberta Menchú,* Rigoberta herself offers additional information on the responsibilities of mother/father. In Menchú's community, the leader is not a single

person who symbolizes a duality; the community leader is an actual mother/
father pair.

> En la comunidad de nosotros hay un elegido, un señor que goza de
> muchos prestigios. Es el representante. Tampoco es el rey pero es el
> representante que toda la comunidad lo considera como padre. Es el caso
> de mi papá y de mi mamá, que son los señores elegidos de mi
> comunidad. Entonces, esa señora elegida, es igual como si toda la
> comunidad fueran sus hijos. (27)

8. This is one of two dramatic re-creations in the documentary. The second
scene dramatizes the CIA-backed overthrow of Arbenz and the installation of
Castillo-Armas in 1954. See Barnouw, 302. Although Yates, Sigel, and Konoy have
been criticized in the United States for mixing drama and documentary, this aspect of their work is, in fact, a principal characteristic of New Latin American
Cinema. See Ana M. López, "An 'Other' History: The New Latin American Cinema" (315).

9. In response to this criticism Pamela Yates argues that the Skylight group
"made the film for an American audience, most of whom know little about Central
America . . . about the role of the United States in the war there." She adds that
because they want a more complex analysis, "political analysts and film critics of
the left have criticized [the] film . . . They've been very narrow-minded in terms
of documentary film form, arguing that the dramatic sections ruin the film" (Rosenthal, 550).

10. In *Radical Thought in Central America*, Sheldon B. Liss also acknowledges
the first lady's role as a national leader. According to Liss, "Secretary of State
John Foster Dulles believed that U.S. investment was threatened by nationaliza-
tion and the socialist thinking of Arbenz' friends and advisors and his wife, María
Cristina Villanova" (30).

11. See also Grupo Chaski's 1986 film *Miss Universe in Perú*, available through
Women Make Movies, which offers a similar critique of the corporate commodification of women.

12. Indeed, according to Rigoberta Menchú, the appearance of the young
beauty contestant would contradict, rather than support, Quiché tradition: "mi
madre me decía que una mujer indígena sólo es respetada cuando lleva su... traje
completo... 'No cortarse el pelo', decía mi mamá. 'Cuando te cortas el pelo, ya se
fijan en ti y dicen, esa mujer está rompiendo muchas cosas y ya no te respeta la
gente' " (*Me llamo Rigoberta Menchú*, 236).

13. "*Nosotros los indígenas*," states Rigoberta, "no tenemos niñez. Desde niños
tenemos que trabajar duramente para ganar la vida."

14. "las fuerzas de seguridad de los terratenientes llegaron a despojarnos de
nuestra pequeña tierra. Nos sacaron violentamente de nuestras casas... Así es
como mi padre se juntó con obreros, sindicatos, estudiantes cristianos y otros
sectores más."

15. Accompanying the archival footage of the mineworkers' strike is a speech
by a popular leader who declares that for the first time in Guatemalan history
Indians and ladinos sharing the same suffering will build a powerful movement. Also significant in this context is the Skylight group's interview with a labor
lawyer who reiterates that "it is the unity of [the] Indian population with the

non-Indians—the unity of the workers with the peasants—that allowed the mass movement to grow."

16. "Para nosotros los indígenas, no es un tiempo malo, exactamente... y yo estoy completamente segura que en muchos países de América los indígenas viviremos eternamente y ojalá que así sea y depende de la sociedad."

17. In "Colonialism, Racism and Representation," Robert Stam and Louise Spence address the ways in which the filmic medium and filmmakers produce Others.

18. According to John Beverley, "an affirmation of the individual self in a collective mode" is a principal characteristic of the testimonial genre. Menchú asserts her individuality in the declaration, "Me llamo Rigoberta Menchú": she is not, therefore, subject to "the 'facelessness' that is already [hers] in the dominant culture" (96). In *When the Mountains Tremble*, this kind of affirmation needs to be extended to other indigenous speakers as well. The filmmakers do provide the names of the lawyers, church officials, and army officials who also contribute their testimonies.

19. "El ejército secuestró a mi hermano. Su crimen era ser secretario de una pequeña cooperativa agrícola de mi aldea. Lo torturaron durante quince días. Le cortaron las uñas. Le cortaron el cuerpo. Después, el ejército publicó un documento llamando a la población a que fuera a ver los castigos que iban a darles a los guerrilleros que tenían en su poder. Fuimos en la Plaza de Chajul. Habían veinte hombres torturados. Dentro de ellos estaba mi hermanito. Estaban hinchados de los cuerpos, sin uñas, sin orejas estas personas. Un oficial del ejército echó un discurso por tres horas amenazando a la población si se metían en subversión le tocaba el mismo destino como estos hombres. Los juntaron. Vivos les echaron gasolina. Los quemaron en esta plaza."

20. In *Me llamo Rigoberta Menchú*, Rigoberta asserts that her brother's body was, indeed, beyond recognition. See chapter 23, "Tortura y muerte de su hermanito quemado vivo junto con otras personas delante de los miembros de la comunidad y familiares."

21. In his interview with Yates, Rosenthal states that "one hopes that these kinds of films will bring about change, though what documentary does is absolutely undocumented. What would you like this film to do?" and Yates responds, "Well, I'd like the film to help organize Americans to stop U.S. intervention in Central America. And also, in doing that, to aid in the organization efforts for social change in the United States" (Rosenthal, 551).

22. Erik Barnouw refers to the Skylight group's work with the guerrillas as "an unprecedented close-up look at...men, women, and children under constant government bombardment" (302).

23. Yates also addressed this issue in her interview with Alan Rosenthal. Rosenthal: "Were you conscious of the very gentle, very human way the women guerrilla recruits are shown in the film? Was there a conscious attempt to get shots that would show them in that way? The women are soldiers but still seem very tender and feminine." Yates: "Yes, I like those scenes with the young women recruits...they combine tender and childlike qualities with a very serious and sophisticated understanding of what they're doing, why they're fighting. They are wise beyond their years" (549).

24. The phrase comes from the poem by Rigoberta Menchú, "Crucé la frontera, amor," which concludes *When the Mountains Tremble*.

Works Cited

Barnouw, Erik. *Documentary: A History of the Non-Fiction Film*. New York: Oxford Univ. Press, 1993.

Barthes, Roland. "The Third Meaning." In *Image, Music, Text*. 1977. Trans. Stephen Heath, 1977. New York: Hill and Wang, 1985.

Beverley, John. "The Margin at the Center: On *Testimonio*." In Sidonie Smith and Julia Watson, *De/Colonizing the Subject: The Politics of Gender in Women's Autobiography*. Minneapolis: Univ. of Minnesota Press, 1992. 91–114.

Burton, Julianne. "Toward a History of Social Documentary in Latin America." In *The Social Documentary in Latin America*. Ed. Julianne Burton. Pittsburgh: Univ. of Pittsburgh Press, 1990. 3–30.

Hansen, Christian, Catherine Needham, and Bill Nichols. "Pornography, Ethnography and the Discourses of Power." In *Representing Reality: Issues and Concepts in Documentary*. Ed. Bill Nichols. Bloomington: Indiana Univ. Press, 1991. 201–28.

Liss, Sheldon B. *Radical Thought in Central America*. Boulder, Colo.: Westview Press, 1991.

Longo, Teresa. "Authority and Reconquest in *Me llamo Rigoberta Menchú y así me nació la conciencia*." *Revista Interamericana de Bibliografía* 43 (1993): 247–56.

López, Ana M. "An 'Other' History: The New Latin American Cinema." In *Resisting Images: Essays on Cinema and History*. Ed. Robert Sklar and Charles Musser. Philadelphia: Temple Univ. Press, 1990. 308–30.

Menchú, Rigoberta, and Elizabeth Burgos. *Me llamo Rigoberta Menchú y así me nació la conciencia*. Mexico City: Siglo Veintiuno, 1988.

Minh-ha, Trinh T. *When the Moon Waxes Red*. New York: Routledge, 1991.

Mitchell, W. J. T. *Iconology: Image, Text, Ideology*. Chicago: Univ. of Chicago Press, 1987.

Nichols, Bill. *Representing Reality: Issues and Concepts in Documentary*. Bloomington: Indiana Univ. Press, 1991.

Rosenthal, Alan. "*When the Mountains Tremble*: An Interview with Pamela Yates." *New Challenges for Documentary*. Berkeley: Univ. of California Press, 1988. 542–53.

Stam, Robert, and Louise Spence. "Colonialism, Racism and Representation." *Screen* 24 (March–April 1983): 2–20.

Tedlock, Dennis. *Popol Vuh*. New York: Simon and Schuster, 1985.

Yates, Pamela, Thomas Sigel, and Peter Konoy. *When the Mountains Tremble*. New York: Skylight Productions, 1983 and 1993.

Chapter 5

How Real Is Reel? Fernando de Fuentes's Revolutionary Trilogy

John Mraz

What can we learn about history from the films Fernando de Fuentes made on the Mexican Revolution? Movies about the past have traditionally been viewed with much skepticism by historians. Perhaps one of the more extreme instances is the premise of G. S. Metraux, editor of a volume dedicated to cinema and history, who maintained that "every film that is inspired by history provides an escape into the past" (9). The hyperbole notwithstanding, the statement reflects a typical disdain for history on the screen. For the vast majority of historical films, this scorn is as well earned as is the contempt expressed by Jorge Ayala Blanco for the "sublime exemplary anecdotes" that make up most movies about the Mexican Revolution (26).

Nonetheless, as historically fallacious as many of these films are, even they have their uses as objects for an analysis of the period in which they were made. This is the characteristic position among historians who have attempted to "rescue" cinema for their discipline, for they feel that these films tell us much more about the context in which they were produced than they do about the past they purport to represent.[1] This is a path already relatively well marked in the study of literature, and it is clear that de Fuentes's films reflect the ideological context in which they were made; in that sense, they are filmic-historical myths about the revolution.

Fernando de Fuentes's movies do indeed present different aspects of the revolution. Although I will compare here what historians tell us happened with what the films show us, I believe that the most important question we can ask about historical cinema is, What facets of history is cinema particularly—perhaps even uniquely—apt at communicating? To seriously think about cinema as a form of history is a relatively new undertaking, but recent scholarship indicates that this may well be a more interesting issue than that of situating films in their context.[2]

The Mexican Revolution is the definitive political event in the history of that country's twentieth century. In this cataclysmic civil war were established the fundamental elements of national identity. However, as Enrique Florescano has pointed out, the revolution "is not just the series of historical acts that took place between 1910 and 1917, or between 1910 and 1920, or between 1910 and 1940; it is also the collection of projections, symbols, evocations, images and myths that its participants, interpreters, and heirs forged and continue to construct around this event" (71). Perhaps the most pervasive of the myths is that propagated by *official history*, which, concerned with legitimizing the ruling party as sole heir, essentially maintains that this was a prolonged struggle of the revolutionaries—Francisco Madero, Venustiano Carranza, Álvaro Obregón, Emilio Zapata, and Pancho Villa—against the old regime of the Porfiriato and its sequel, Victoriano Huerta, which they eventually overthrew and replaced. In conflating these figures into the same camp, official history attempts to deny the fact that this struggle was defined more by the warfare among the revolutionaries than by the battle between the old and new orders (Gilly, 11).

At the level of mass culture—textbooks, statues, monuments, and so on—official history has dominated the representations of the revolution. Cinema has been one of the important staging grounds for officialist evocations, images, and myths, as more than sixty films have been made in which the Mexican Revolution serves as the context for the movie's story (*Filmoteca* 1, 120–25).

Among the best films made by Mexicans on this struggle is the "revolutionary trilogy" directed by Fernando de Fuentes, *Prisionero 13* (1933), *El compadre Mendoza* (1933), and *¡Vámonos con Pancho Villa!* (1935).[3] The trilogy does not in any way glorify the civil war, as, for example, Miguel Contreras Torres had done in the first sound film made on it, *Revolución (La sombra de Pancho Villa)*, whose "exalted and patriotic pretensions" would become typical of films about this event—and about Villa (García Riera, *Historia documental del cine mexicano*, 32). Rather, looking at the trilogy in terms of Mexico's best-known twentieth-century muralists, I find the movies more in the tone of José Clemente Orozco than of Diego Rivera or David Alfaro Siqueiros: they emphasize the pain and torment, rather than the transformations; they exude a disenchantment with the revolution's shortcomings, instead of celebrating its achievements. Two of the works, *El compadre Mendoza* and *¡Vámonos con Pancho Villa!*, do address the issue of social ideals through their protagonists, though the question is never really developed.

Considered as a whole, the trilogy is perhaps most interesting because of the fact that de Fuentes has chosen to focus on the three losing sides: Huertismo, Zapatismo, and Villismo. In the period during which de Fuentes made these works, it was still possible—perhaps even inevitable—to take account of the differences between the Zapatistas, Villistas, and Carrancistas. This may also have resulted from the fact that he made these films in a relatively tolerant period—that immediately preceding the accesion to power of Lázaro Cárdenas, and during the first years of the presidency he held from 1934 to 1940. Although two of the films suffered direct government interference, the ideological consolidation of the 1940s—a key element of the revolutionary institutionalization—had not yet produced the official history that would become characteristic in films about this conflict. In the future, movies about the revolution would almost always be set in either the unproblematic Huertista period (when the revolutionary forces were united against him) or in an abstracted, ahistorical situation, in which the exact allegiances of the protagonists remain unclear.

Prisionero 13, first shown in 1933, was quickly withdrawn from circulation because of objections by the army.[4] The movie follows the life of Colonel Julián Carrasco, an alcoholic officer in the Porfirian and Huertista armies. He mistreats his wife, who leaves the house with their infant son; we see the boy grow to manhood under his mother's care, as the film moves into the period of Victoriano Huerta's 1913–14 dictatorship. Some conspirators against Huerta's rule are rounded up and condemned to be shot. The mother and daughter of one prisoner bribe Carrasco to let him go free. As Carrasco has already turned in the list to the governor, he orders a subordinate to capture a substitute at random; he turns out to be Carrasco's son. The colonel is unaware of this, and the boy's mother attempts to alert him to the danger, but she is delayed by Carrasco's guard. When he comprehends that his son is to be shot, he hurries to the execution site in an attempt to save him. He would be too late, but—in an ending evidently tacked on in a vain effort to mollify the military's censure of the film—he awakens and discovers that it was all a dream caused by drinking.

Despite the artificial return to the Porfiriato at the end, the representational context of *Prisionero 13* is the period of Huerta's rule during 1913 and 1914; contemporary reviewers such as Luz Alba and Carlos Denegri clearly identified the film as taking place at this point in time (García Riera, *Fernando de Fuentes*, 93, 95). This is portrayed most directly in the photograph of Huerta on the wall of Carrasco's office (see figures 1 and 2).[5] The movie occurs largely within a military scenario of camps, offices, and barracks, reflecting the militarization of society under Huerta (Knight, vol. 2, 91–93). The historical referent in *Prisionero 13* is certainly Huerta, for Carrasco's alcoholism is a distinct allusion to Huerta's drinking, which was so commented on that one diplomat's wife remarked that the only two foreigners Huerta knew well were Hennessy and Martell (O'Shaughnessy, 48). In the visual narrative, the ubiquitous presence of the bottle and the bombshell on Carrasco's desk is a constant allusion to alcohol and militarism as the defining structure of his existence (see figure 3).

Carrasco's corruption and cruelty also are in accord with the role that Huerta has been assigned as the "corruptor de sociedades," the "usurper" and "murderer" (Garfias, 606; Rutherford, 177). Here, Carrasco's unlawful freeing of a conspirator in return for a bribe, and his cold-blooded execution of an innocent person

Fig. 1. In his office, Colonel Carrasco stands in front of Huerta's portrait.

Fig. 2. At the end of *Prisionero 13*, the return to the Porfiriato is visually indicated in the different uniform Carrasco wears.

Fig. 3. Seated at his desk, Carrasco is framed between a bombshell and a bottle, as he gives the order to capture an innocent man for execution.

reflect the generalized corruption and repression under Huerta, manifest in his unlawful overthrow and assassination of Madero, as well as in the disbanding of congress and the jailing of deputies in 1913 (Katz, 119).

The representation of Carrasco/Huerta as the villain of the revolution is very much in line with his portrayal in the official historiography that would develop during the 1940s. Most modern historians seem to concur that he was a typical counterrevolutionary military dictator, although some have attempted to tell a different side of the story (Sherman and Greenleaf; Meyer). Whatever the truth of Huerta's "black legend," it serves the purpose of "whitening" the reputations of other revolutionary leaders who may have been just as corrupt and little more revolutionary. However, it appears more likely that de Fuentes was following a widely accepted reputation of Huerta as the murderer of Madero, the usurper of power, and the corruptor of morals, rather than reflecting an official position, which had not yet consolidated itself to the degree that it would thereafter.

Historical detail in *Prisionero 13* is sorely lacking. Both military and civilian dress are obviously from the 1920s and 1930s, perhaps one of the reasons for which the army objected to its "denigrating" image and had the film retired from distribution. However, what is most wanting in a film dealing with the revolution is the development of warring ideologies, interests, and classes. The political goals of the "conspirators" whom Carrasco executes are at no point defined. They are almost all dressed in middle-class clothing, with the exception of a father and son, who appear to be from the urban proletariat. Further, the only "political" declaration in the film is when the prisoner who seems to be the leader, Enrique Madariaga, shouts "¡Viva la Revolución!" just before he is shot.

Prisionero 13 was apparently one of the first movies to address seriously the question of Mexican identity.[6] This was a pivotal issue of the period, as can be seen in the muralists' exploration of *mexicanidad,* as well as in the 1934 publication of Samuel Ramos's *El perfil del hombre y la cultura en México,* the initial philosophical indagation of what would become a long inquiry into "México y lo mexicano." In reviewing *Prisionero 13,* Juan Bustillo Oro, later a well-known director, argued that Mexican film had been a "servile imitation" of foreign cinema, because it had ignored "themes that are flesh of our flesh and the breath of our sweet and equally terrible land." Calling this "the first Mexican film," he felt that it constituted the primary step toward the creation of a national identity: "The first task before Mexicans is to discover themselves... Only by discovering ourselves can we create our country... The day that we have a theater and a cinema equal in moral and revelatory value to *Prisionero 13* we can say that our nationality has begun to develop, that we have been saved" (García Riera, *Fernando de Fuentes,* 95). The next year, de Fuentes's new film on the revolution, *El compadre Mendoza,* also provoked commentaries about national character, although in this case they were protestations by the critic A. F. B. against identifying Mexicans with a "vile traitor" (ibid., 103). The impact of these two movies within the context of the sensitivities surrounding the national identity issue in this period can be appreciated by the remarks of film reviewer Alfonso de Icaza, who wrote in 1934:

We've spent our entire life protesting the fact that our neighbor denigrates us, and now we make films that exhibit repugnant sores ... If we follow the path marked out by *Prisionero 13* and *El compadre Mendoza,* our films will assure that the fame of bandits that the Yankees have given us will be replaced by a worse one: that of traitors ... Is that how we have been? (Ibid., 104)

El compadre Mendoza narrates the travails of Rosalío Mendoza, an opportunistic *hacendado* during the period between 1913 and (roughly) 1919. Mendoza pretends to be a friend to all sides: when the Zapatistas come to his hacienda, he celebrates their arrival, feeds the troops, and dines with the officers under a photo of Zapata; with the Huertistas, he does the same, except beneath an image of Huerta; at the moment the Carrancistas become a force in the area, he buys and exhibits a photo of Carranza ... when the Carrancistas are present (see figures 4, 5, and 6). Mendoza marries Dolores, the young daughter of a ruined landowner. On the night of their wedding, they are surprised by the Zapatistas.

Fig. 4. In the beginning of *El compadre Mendoza,* the Zapatistas' arrival at Mendoza's hacienda leads to a change of portraits. The administrator removes Huerta's photograph.

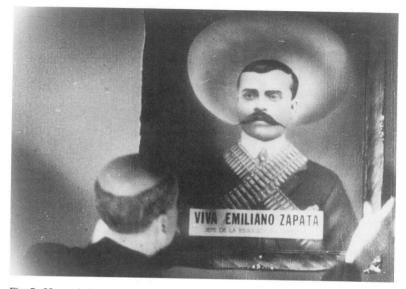

Fig. 5. Huerta's image is replaced with Zapata's portrait.

Fig. 6. After the defeat of Huerta, Carranza's portrait is interchanged with that of Zapata.

A Huertista officer is present, and Mendoza is at the point of being executed alongside him. He is saved by a Zapatista general whom he had met earlier, Felipe Nieto, with whom Rosalío and Dolores later become close friends during his frequent visits to the hacienda. Eventually, Rosalío asks Felipe to be the *compadre* of his forthcoming son, and he accepts. Felipe develops a strong attachment to Dolores, and to the boy who has been named after him. It is clear that Dolores is as attracted to Felipe as he is to her, but they deny their love because of their commitments to Rosalío. Times become increasingly difficult for both the Zapatistas and Mendoza. The *hacendado* wishes to leave for Mexico City, but this is made impossible when the train carrying his entire harvest is burned. Afraid for the safety of his family, Mendoza agrees to betray Felipe, who is killed by the Carrancistas as the *hacendado* flees with Dolores and their son.

The film's "cruel and macabre" finale was evidently much commented on, for an interviewer asked de Fuentes about that the day after the premiere in April 1934. He replied that he was searching for a Mexican aesthetic, not trying to make another copy of Hollywood's "happy endings":

> We believe that our public is sufficiently cultured to be able to stand reality's bitter cruelty. It would have been easy to make the story so that the final outcome was happy, as we're accustomed to see in American [*sic*] films; but we think that Mexican cinema ought to be a faithful reflection of our severe and tragic way of being . . . and not a poor imitation of Hollywood. (Ibid., 28)

Contemporary reviewers characterized this extraordinary work as the best Mexican film made up to that point (ibid., 104). It is still a masterpiece. De Fuentes evinces a clear sympathy for the Zapatistas. The movie opens with a tracking shot that follows what appears to be a plowed furrow; but, as the camera catches up with the "plow," we see that the "furrow" was made by a rifle's butt that an exhausted Zapatista is dragging. The opening sequence serves to create identification with the Zapatistas, the "little guys" for whom the audience naturally roots against the more powerful forces of Huerta and Carranza; it also immediately establishes the relationship between the Zapatistas and the land, a metaphor underlined by later references to the Plan de Ayala, Zapata's instrument of agrarian reform.

Zapatismo is personalized through the figure of Felipe, who is shown to be of a high moral character, capable of denying his love for Dolores and of being committed to the struggle for a common good. Within the film, identification with Felipe is effected through the fact that all the other main characters love him, and even the Carrancista who finally has him killed, Colonel Bernáldez, says that "he is not one of those who can be bought." Felipe's ideals are in contrast to the absence of any such articulated commitments on the part of either the Huertistas, embodied in Colonel Martínez, or the Carrancistas, encarnated in Bernáldez; they are depicted as being interested only in defeating the Zapatistas. Thus, the film implicitly juxtaposes the revolutionary demand of Zapatismo for an equitable distribution of land—while recognizing that there are certain Zapatistas, for example, El Gordo, who are bloodthirsty—with the lack of social programs on the part of the other groups, whose sole concern is portrayed as being to gain power. At one point, Colonel Bernáldez does use the argument of nationalism to convince Mendoza to betray Felipe, asserting that "In the end, all we want is the good of the country." By placing these words in the mouthpiece of the New Order (Carrancismo), de Fuentes acutely presaged the politics of "national unity" that would reign supreme from the 1940s on—in one form or another—as an indispensable component of the ideology of the Partido Revolucionario Institucional (PRI).

However, perhaps the sharpest difference with official history in the film is the fact that the Carrancistas take on the role of the enemy earlier occupied by the Huertistas. Embodying the Zapatista point of view, the movie's "heresy" consists of equating the two factions; to place Carrancismo and Huertismo in the same camp would be anathema in almost any form of Mexican history, filmic or written, up until very recent times. In this sense, *El compadre Mendoza* is even more critical than ¡*Vámonos con Pancho Villa!* for, in the latter, a title appears—"Año de 1914"—at the very beginning to indicate that the struggle depicted is that between the Villistas and the Huertistas. Thus, *Vámonos* implicitly subscribes to an official history that was beginning to be conceived around the time of its production, whereas *Mendoza* was an explicit challenge to the ideological concoction that would soon come to dominate Mexican culture.

Mendoza is a representative of the bourgeoisie but, although his portrayal by Alfredo del Diestro enables us to see his human side, the film precludes any identification with him by showing that his only concerns are to preserve his family and the good life he leads. The cognac he so often consumes, and which he offers to the leaders of the rival bands in their turn, functions as a metaphor for that good life and those expensive social lubricants that are used to deny the reality of class conflict. All accept the drink on the different occasions except Eufemio Zapata, who prefers mezcal, a drink "para machos" (and, by extension, "para mexicanos"). At the end of the film, when Mendoza has arranged the meeting of Felipe and Colonel Bernáldez, he serves them cognac to occupy Felipe while the soldiers who are to shoot him get into position. After he has been killed, the Carrancistas wish to hang his body from the front gate of the hacienda. This is too much for Mendoza and he cries out, but Bernáldez shrugs off his objections by offering him cognac. A Lukácsian mediocre hero caught between the warring forces, Mendoza not only arranges the meeting between them, he also brings us into human contact with both camps (Lukács, 37). He experiences no crises of either conscience or consciousness as a result of his hypocrisy, except at the end, when he is tormented by Felipe's assassination. Other than in this final agony, however, the only time that he addresses his duplicity is to convince the different forces that his friendships with the opposing bands have been useful to all concerned.

In the end, Mendoza is forced to choose between the sides, and he betrays his *compadre*. What he does not betray are his class interests. Earlier, in one of the more "politicized" sequences, Dolores asks Felipe if he could not just stop fighting. He replies that he will, some time in the future when the Plan de Ayala has triumphed, there is peace, and the campesinos own the lands they work. Felipe's voice is off-camera; Mendoza appears on screen during these statements, frowning, ostensibly at the domino game he has in front of him. However, the contradiction of a *hacendado* supporting a struggle so that campesinos could own land is made obvious; the film cuts to a close-up of Dolores toward the end of Felipe's comments, as if she shared the Zapatista's dreams.

In the film's denouement, the crisis generated by the revolution will force Mendoza to define himself; he identifies himself in terms of his class interests.

Mendoza's treachery is critiqued not only through a comparison to the solidarity—both personally and socially—of Nieto, but in the eyes of the mute servant, María, as well. She is a witness to his treason, for her capacity to read lips enables her to "hear" things that others cannot. Although women are generally peripheral characters in the trilogy, de Fuentes uses María as the witness and censor of Mendoza's crime. She is an unwelcome looking glass to him: when she first sees Bernáldez offer money to Mendoza in exchange for Felipe, she is standing in front of a mirror (see figures 7 and 8). Sent from the room, she goes outside and looks through a window to read their lips (see figure 9). The meaning of these visual references to reflective and transparent surfaces becomes clear shortly thereafter, when she watches Mendoza pace while he awaits the death of Felipe. As the film cuts between Mendoza and María, the camera moves in ever closer

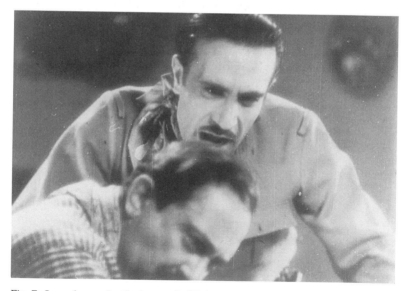

Fig. 7. In exchange for the betrayal of Felipe Nieto, Colonel Bernáldez offers Mendoza the money that will make it possible for him and his family to move to Mexico City.

Fig. 8. María "hears" Bernáldez's offer of treason.

Fig. 9. María reads the lips of Bernáldez and Mendoza through a window, while standing outside the room.

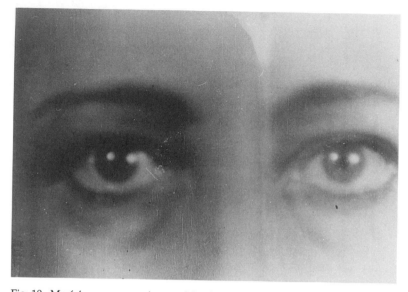

Fig. 10. María's eyes are a mirror to Mendoza's betrayal.

to her eyes, until finally they occupy the screen; we see her from
Mendoza's point of view (see figure 10). The fact that she is mute—
that she has *said* nothing—allows her to reflect back to Mendoza
his own bad conscience; he is haunted by what he reads into her
eyes, and he orders her to go away. Obviously, her muteness could
also serve as a symbol for the silent accusation of all who suffer
from the betrayal of the revolution's ideals by the opportunism
of the national bourgeoisie.

If *El compadre Mendoza* demystifies Carrancismo as a revolutionary movement, *¡Vámonos con Pancho Villa!* "demythifies" one
of the great legends of that struggle. *Vámonos* follows the fates of
six campesinos, "Los Leones de San Pablo": Tiburcio, Melitón,
Martín, Máximo, Rodrigo, and Miguel Angel. They join up with
Villa's forces after the occupation of their pueblo by the Huertistas makes life increasingly hazardous. The Leones encounter Villa
distributing corn from a train, and he accepts them into his army.
During a battle, Máximo ropes a màchine gun and dies after giving it to Villa. Martín is the next to die, again heroically while
blowing a hole in the enemy's fort. Tiburcio, Rodrigo, and Melitón

attempt to trick a Huertista officer and bring about the surrender of his forces. Their ruse is discovered and they are to be hanged in sight of their own lines; however, when they begin with fat Melitón, the rope breaks. Their *compañeros* arrive to rescue them, but, in the firefight, Rodrigo and a young Huertista lieutenant are killed by the Villistas; the latter's death provokes sympathy on Tiburcio's part. Villa incorporates the three survivors in his elite corps, the *dorados*. In a bar, the three participate in a "game" resembling Russian roulette: thirteen men sit closely around a table in a darkened room; one throws a cocked gun into the air, whose discharge is designed to eliminate one—the one with the most fear—of the unlucky number. The bullet wounds Melitón and, when the others complain that they are still thirteen, Melitón shoots himself in the head. Miguel Angel becomes ill, but accompanies the troop to Zacatecas. There, he is discovered to have smallpox, and Tiburcio is ordered to kill him and burn his body and all his belongings. Villa arrives to check out the contaminated train car and Tiburcio attempts to talk with him. Knowing that Tiburcio has been exposed to smallpox, Villa shrinks back in fear and, warning Tiburcio to keep his distance, he tells him to stay put until the danger is past. Disheartened by the death of all his friends, and disappointed by Villa's faintheartedness, Tiburcio walks away from the revolution down a train track. (In the original script, and in an existing copy of the film, Villa encounters Tiburcio some years later and urges him to rejoin the revolution. When Tiburcio declines because of his family, Villa kills his wife and daughter. Angered, Tiburcio points his rifle at Villa: in the alternative film copy, Fierro shoots Tiburcio, and Tiburcio's son rides off with Villa; in the alternative script, Tiburcio is overcome by Villa's power, he lowers his rifle, and both he and his son ride off with Villa.)[7]

The first superproduction of Mexican cinema—and still the best film on the revolution—*¡Vámonos con Pancho Villa!* cost a then-astronomical 1 million pesos, and marked the introduction of modern cinematographic equipment (synchronized sound, Mitchell cameras, and "gamma" curve developing) in national cinema.[8] If, in *Prisionero 13*, de Fuentes had been forced to dress his actors in contemporary costumes because of economic pressures, in this film he had at his disposition a train, a regiment of troops, munitions, artillery pieces, uniforms, cavalry, and military advisers.[9]

The financial support that de Fuentes received makes it clear that he enjoyed official backing for this work to a degree hitherto unknown in Mexican film. This appears to have been a result of a decision within the Cárdenas regime, prompted by various intellectuals, to promote a national cinema through government subsidies. A precedent had been set the year before, when the Secretaría de Educación Pública under Narciso Bassols had produced *Redes*, a "Mexicanist" film of penetrating social criticism.[10] Evidently, the Cárdenas government was instrumental in financing the construction of the new CLASA (Cinematográfica Latino Americana, S.A.) studios, which were equiped with state-of-the-art technology.[11] *Vámonos* was the first film produced by CLASA, and it is clear that, at the very least, the government indirectly subsidized this work, for CLASA declared bankruptcy immediately after releasing the film and received a subvention from the Cárdenas government in the amount of the movie's cost (Elizondo, 10).

The role Cárdenas may have played in relation to this film raises some most interesting questions about the cultural politics of his regime. The Cardenist period is often conceived of as one of considerable liberty, and relatively little government interference in cinema.[12] Nonetheless, the existence of an alternative ending in both script and film has led to speculation as to who was responsible for the changes. In general, scholars of Mexican cinema have tended to blame it on government censorship, which would not permit the showing of such cruelty on Villa's part (de Luna, 228; Serrano, 59; García Riera, *Fernando de Fuentes*, 38–39). Nonetheless, it is crucial to point out that, for Cárdenas, Villa was not part of the "revolutionary pantheon." In a diary entry, which Adolfo Gilly describes as the "birth certificate of the Revolution's official history," Cárdenas stated that Obregón, Madero, Zapata, and Carranza "should be venerated for their transcendent participation in the struggle for social justice" (Gilly, 10).[13] The fact that Cárdenas did not include Villa could indicate that the criticism this film renders of him (as we shall see) is in fact a result of official interests. Thus, it may well be that, after filming

the alternative ending, it was de Fuentes who decided to eliminate it because he felt it was too extreme.[14]

The allegiance of the Leones is to Pancho Villa, not to the revolution: they refer time and again in the film to the need they
feel to demonstrate their manliness to the jefe, and their actions
are motivated by this goal, rather than any other consideration,
even their own interests. In depicting the personalism of Villismo—and its lack of ideology—the film is an accurate representation of the way in which individual loyalties functioned as
the cement of that movement (Knight, vol. 2, 35; Ruíz, 193). Crucial in achieving such commitment was Villa's well-documented
charisma.[15] This may be one of the areas in which films can contribute to history, for cinema may be able to convey charisma
better than written words. The film medium allowed de Fuentes to
communicate the sensation of charisma through the actor Domingo Soler. Of course, Soler is not Villa, and the charisma he
exudes as an actor may well be entirely at odds with that of the
Centaur of the North, although he stated that he had dedicated
himself to "absorbing Villa."[16] Whether one agrees that Soler succeeds or not—and many would agree with Jorge Ayala Blanco
that Soler's personification is "exemplary"—the film at least does
give a "feel" for the intricacies of personal allegiances that might
be more difficult in writing (Ayala Blanco, 27).

Nonetheless, what de Fuentes accomplishes with the personage of Pancho Villa goes beyond immediate historical realism,
for he demystifies Villa through a complex process of identification and alienation. He does this first of all in the title: although
Villa is the personage who appears to define the work, he is not
the central figure. An early movie reviewer complained about
Villa being a peripheral character, but this is part of the film's
brilliance.[17] The title creates the expectation that Villa will be the
main protagonist, but it is the six Leones who are at the heart of
this work; Villa only appears when he is historically important—
performing public feats such as distributing corn, goading his men
in battle, and making decisions about the army's well-being, as
in having Tiburcio shoot and burn Miguel Angel.

Villa's dispensing of food to the hungry and his direct participation in battle are documented historical facts (Katz, 141; Knight,
vol. 2, 35). The incident in which Villa shows fear of smallpox,

though credible, has not been documented; disease, however, figured as one of the main causes of death during the revolution, and its inclusion is an important historical detail.[18] Nonetheless, even more crucial than its realism, this final scene represents the culmination of the long alienation process that de Fuentes has carried out in relation to Villa. In the beginning, we immediately identify with Villa because the Leones, convinced that only he can resolve the situation, join up with him. When we first see him he is engaged in a socially beneficial activity, providing corn for the hungry, and promising them land—so that no one will have to be a peon—when he wins the revolution. The people's gratitude is registered in outstretched hands and smiling faces (see figure 11). Villa's gruff but good-humored interview with the Leones assures them they have made the right decision to follow him. After the first battle, the Leones' admiration for and adherence to Villa is strengthened when he insists that Rodrigo Perea keep the revolver—his first booty—that he attempted to give Villa. Stating that he prefers his own pistol, Villa "legitimizes"

Fig. 11. A happy pueblo raises improvised containers to receive corn from the hands of Villa.

his position of caudillo by shooting the prickly pears off some cactus through a hole he has cut in the bottom of his holster. The extreme difficulty of the shot demonstrates Villa's skill, and the hole cut in the holster bottom shows Villa's intelligence and cunning; all are necessary requirements to be a leader of warriors. The fact that the Leones are greatly impressed by Villa's feat furthers their (and our) identification with him.

As the film continues, however, it insistently cuts back against that identification. In contrast to the vast majority of films about Villa, *Vámonos* is an antiepic: it contains all the elements for an epic about the revolution, but holds Villa-the-legend at bay through a constant distantiation.[19] We are confronted with Villa's legendary cruelty, as in the execution of captured band members once he has ascertained that he does not need any more bands. The film's brilliance in delineating the duality of Villa's character is demonstrated in the fact that it is Villa himself who creates sympathy for these musicians; they never appear on camera. When asked by one of his subordinates whether they should be executed, Villa responds: "No, man, how barbaric. Poor musicians, why would we shoot them? Put them in one of the brigades." Informed that all the units have their own bands, and some even have two, an irritated Villa replies: "Well, then, shoot them. Why are you bugging me with this?"

The Leones—with whom we identify unconditionally—play their part in alienating us from Villa, for his callousness is made evident in his increasing indifference as the Leones die one after another. When the first, Máximo, dies, Villa pats his body on the back; however, when the third, Rodrigo, is killed, Villa shrugs and says that it's a shame, but everybody has to die. Finally, the process of distancing the audience from Villa is completed in the last scene, when he arrives to check the contaminated train car. Tiburcio, despondent, sees Villa and his face brightens up. He moves toward and attempts to establish contact with Villa, the one real commitment of the Leones and the only thing that could make sense of all his suffering. But Villa, terrified of smallpox, makes Tiburcio keep his distance: we are as repelled by Villa's fear as we are by his insensitivity, and our rejection is corroborated by Tiburcio's disenchantment. That this distantiation is intentional can be seen clearly in the extremes of the original script where, in a shockingly powerful scene, Villa comes to Tiburcio's house some years later and kills his wife and daughter so that he will have no impediments in rejoining his forces. The fact that Villa is one of the core legends of the revolution makes it conceivable to think that the alienation de Fuentes achieves in relation to this personage could be applicable by extension to the revolutionary myths in general.

In *Vámonos*, de Fuentes makes it clear that the only commitment of any real value is to human solidarity; for that reason, he has Tiburcio look with pity into the dead face of the young Huertista lieutenant who moments before would have hanged him. Thus, the process of the Leones' deaths—the destruction of their relationships—is also demystifying, particularly when compared to the heroic demises to which we are well accustomed in films about the revolution (or war movies in general). Máximo dies a hero's death and receives Villa's commendation; Martín also dies heroically, but his body is left abandoned in the embrace of a maguey (see figure 12). The deaths of the remaining Leones could all be

Fig. 12. Killed in a heroic action against the Huertistas, Martín lies in the grasp of a maguey.

seen as metaphors for the self-destruction of the revolution: Rodrigo is a victim of "friendly fire"; Melitón participates in a suicidal game—where the fact that the revolver is tossed into the air by Tiburcio only underlines the fratricidal aspect—and then kills himself to proves his courage; Miguel Angel is shot by Tiburcio; and in the alternative filmed ending, Tiburcio is killed by Fierro, Villa's lieutenant. Through this structure, de Fuentes is referring not so much to the way in which the civil strife was a "fraternal bloodbath" as he is creating a metaphor for the murder of the revolution by the revolutionaries.

Compared to the other two movies in the trilogy—or to almost any of the other films on this struggle—*Vámonos* is rich in historical details. The form utilized by de Fuentes is crucial, for much of the film is shot in what José de la Colina described as a *"plano americano* that enabled the showing of characters in relation to their context, as well as with other characters" (García Riera, *Fernando de Fuentes,* 126).[20] Aside from the use of a visual style facilitating the incorporation of considerable contextual information, de Fuentes also employs montages of images to capture daily-life activities among the army.

The film's fertile social fabric is largely woven around the trains. When the Leones go to join Villa, the segment opens with a beautiful high-angle pan of a bustling station. Then the camera roams about through images reminiscent of the photographs from the Casasola or Brehme collections: interspersing scenes of people chatting, seated in the open doors of railroad cars—buckets of flowers and birdcages nailed to the sides—with shots of letters being written on typewriters by scribes, and film of recreational activities, such as lasso twirling in front of the customary crowd of onlookers (see figures 13 and 14). The activities of women are included in *Vámonos*: we see them selling prepared food to lines of soldiers, grinding corn, sewing clothes, and fending off the advances of unwanted suitors (see figure 15). As the trains pull out of the stations, the troops piled on top of the cars and hanging onto the front of the engine are a powerful evocation of well-known revolutionary tableaux (see figure 16). In his employment of the train, de Fuentes offers us one of the best examples of what cinema can bring to history: the capacity to present vital facets of reality that are constantly present (for example, geographic set-

Fig. 13. Villistas seated in and on top of stationary railroad cars.

Fig. 14. A literate Villista writes a letter for an illiterate *compañero*.

Fig. 15. Women soaking and grinding corn kernels to make *nixtamal*.

Fig. 16. Villistas on the front and on top of a moving train. (The lines are scratches on the 35mm print.)

tings, weather, daily-life activities, technology) without falling into aggressive symbolism or a distractingly overburdened text, as could occur by insistently mentioning them in writing.

The train, however, is not only the site for a relatively "thick" re-creation of the quotidian; it is also a permanent backdrop against which the film's dramas are played out. The train was a central protagonist of the Mexican Revolution, a struggle that was, in the words of one participant, "Made on rails."[21] In *Vámonos*, the train is at the center of the events: the film opens in a depot, where Miguel Angel is beaten by the Huertista officer; the Leones go to join up with Villa at a railroad junction, and when they first see him, he is standing in a train car; the captured Leones are marched along tracks to be hanged; the death of Miguel Angel takes place in a railroad car; and Tiburcio walks away from the revolution along the ties. As in the character of Villa, and the fate of the Leones, the train begins by promising much and ends up being the site of disillusion; it too is the revolution.

Notes

I am grateful to Eli Bartra and David La France for their comments and criti-cisms; I would also like to thank the Filmoteca of the Universidad Nacional Autónoma de México (UNAM) for providing copies of the films, as well as for making the frame enlargements that appear here. Unless otherwise indicated, all translations are mine.

1. Among others, see the works of Marc Ferro, Bryan Haworth, Paul Smith, and Pierre Sorlin. For an example of this methodology applied to historical films about Mexico, see Paul Vanderwood.

2. See the works of Robert Rosenstone.

3. It is not clear to what extent de Fuentes conceived of these three films as a trilogy. Because they deal with a common theme and were made very closely to-gether—and as de Fuentes did not return to the subject of the revolution at a later date—I have taken the liberty of denominating them a "trilogy." They are, at any rate, more of a trilogy than the three films that Carl Mora (43) attempts to identify in this way: *El compadre Mendoza*, *¡Vámonos con Pancho Villa!*, and *Allá en el Rancho Grande* (1936). With *Rancho Grande*, de Fuentes abandoned definitively any attempts to make serious cinema; henceforth, he dedicated himself to genre films such as *Rancho Grande* (the singing *charro*) and *La gallina clueca* (the self-sac-rificing mother). See Mraz, "Fernando de Fuentes."

4. Evidently, Lázaro Cárdenas, minister of war under Abelardo L. Rodríguez (1932–34), ordered the film retired from theaters because he considered it denigrat-ing to the army (de los Reyes, 158). Emma Roldán, who appears in the film as the mother of the freed son—and who was the real-life wife of Alfredo del Diestro,

who played Carrasco—stated, "The film was shown to Cárdenas, who said that the ending had to be changed" (García Riera, *Fernando de Fuentes*, 20). Apparently, neither a script nor copies exist of what must have been the "original" version.

5. García Riera states that there is a portrait of Porfirio Díaz on the wall in the film's beginning and ending sequences, which are set in the Porfiriato (*Fernando de Fuentes*, 20). In frame enlargement 2 we can see that it is impossible to determine who is in the portrait on the wall during the Porfirian sequences. (The images employed in this essay are frame enlargements, which permit the reproduction of scenes from the films, and not production stills.)

6. Aurelio de los Reyes has commented at length on nationalism in Mexican cinema.

7. On the different filmed ending, which has now been seen several times on Mexican television, and the original script, see García Riera, *Fernando de Fuentes*, 38–40. The alternative ending of the script can be found in its entirety in Serrano.

8. On the production costs and the equipment utilized, see García Riera, *Fernando de Fuentes*, 33–34, 120–21. Producer Salvador Elizondo says that the film was a commercial failure (ibid., 34).

9. The fact that he chose to dress his "Federales" in 1930s uniforms despite his funding indicates that he either still suffered from shortages or was unconcerned about such details; it could also signify that the criticism of his "denigration" of the army in *Prisionero 13* was not so far off base.

10. Given the Eisensteinian influence and the participation of foreigners such as Fred Zinneman and Paul Strand, the *mexicanidad* of *Redes* is somewhat problematic. See Mraz, "*Redes.*"

11. I say "evidently" because, although it is generally agreed among those who write on Mexican cinema that Cárdenas was responsible for the creation of CLASA, one of CLASA's founders, Salvador Elizondo, stated that it "operated entirely with private capital" (García Riera, *Fernando de Fuentes*, 33–34). García Riera believes that the Cárdenas government was deeply involved in CLASA (*Historia documental*, 90). Among those who have accepted García Riera's version are Mora (43) and Sánchez (35).

12. The director José Bohr stated: "The Cárdenas government never influenced the tendencies of productions; it never utilized censorship nor countercensorship" (Mora, 246). José de la Colina refers to the "ample liberty" of the Cardenist period (García Riera, *Fernando de Fuentes*, 119).

13. I am grateful to Eli Bartra for pointing this out to me, and for our extended discussion of this point.

14. This may well be the most convincing explanation, for one feels "beat over the head" by the excessive cruelty of the eliminated scene.

15. Villa's charisma has been commented on by many writers, among them Knight (vol. 2, 34), Katz (145), and Rutherford (155).

16. Soler stated: "Pancho Villa is the most difficult role that has ever been interpreted by anybody in our cinema . . . For that reason, I've dedicated myself to studying with great zeal, not only the part I've been given in the film, or that which is in the Muñoz novel [the source of the film script], but also the guerrilla evoked in other novels, in biographies, anecdotes, periodical articles, fantasies, and even in corridos" (Mario Galán interview with Soler, *Ilustrado* [21 November, 1935], García Riera, *Fernando de Fuentes*, 35).

17. Writing in 1937, Alfonso de Icaza expressed his disappointment at discovering the "defect" that Villa was a secondary character (García Riera, *Fernando de Fuentes*, 119).

18. Knight says that disease was the "single biggest killer" of the revolutionary struggle, and notes the importance of smallpox among the debilitating illnesses (vol. 2, 420–21). It may be worth noting that Miguel Angel's malady has often been misidentified; some authors have claimed it was cholera: García Riera, (*Fernando de Fuentes*, 119; *Historia documental*, 92), de Luna (228), and Mora (44). Jean Allard thinks it was malaria, and Gustavo García said it was plague (García Riera, *Fernando de Fuentes*, 126–27).

19. According to Gustavo García, as of 1974, there had been more than twenty films made in which Villa appeared in some form; Gustavo Montiel Pagés observed that these films were inevitably epics (Montiel Pagés, 103–4).

20. Although it seems to me that wider takes with greater depth of field would be generally preferable in historical cinema for the greater amount of detail they could include, I am also in agreement with Natalie Zemon Davis, who has argued, "There is no automatic privileging of the 'realistic' or naturalistic film as the mode for representing the past" (273).

21. So states the old railroader Guillermo Treviño in the opening interview of my videotape history of the Mexican Railroad Workers.

Works Cited

Ayala Blanco, Jorge. *La aventura del cine mexicano*. Mexico City: Era, 1979.

de los Reyes, Aurelio. *Medio siglo de cine mexicano (1896–1947)*. Mexico City: Trillas, 1987.

de Luna, Andrés. La batalla y su sombra (La revolución en el cine mexicano). Mexico City: Universidad Autónoma Metropolitana-Xochimilco, 1984.

Elizondo, Salvador. "Fernando de Fuentes." *Nuevo cine* 1:2 (June 1961): 10–12.

Ferro, Marc. *Cinema and History*. Trans. Naomi Greene. Detroit: Wayne State Univ. Press, 1988.

———. "The Fiction Film and Historical Analysis." In *The Historian and Film*. Ed. Paul Smith. Cambridge: Cambridge Univ. Press, 1976. 80–94.

Filmoteca 1, El cine y la revolución mexicana. "La Revolución mexicana: filmografía básica" (1979): 120–25.

Florescano, Enrique. "La Revolución mexicana bajo la mira del revisionismo histórico." In *El nuevo pasado mexicano*. Mexico City: Cal y arena, 1991. 71–152.

García Riera, Emilio. *Fernando de Fuentes (1894–1958)*. Mexico City: Cineteca Nacional, 1984.

———. *Historia documental del cine mexicano*. Vol. 1. Mexico City: Era, 1969.

Garfias M., Luis. "El general Huerta y el ejército federal." In *Así fue la Revolución Mexicana*. 8 vols. Mexico City: Consejo Nacional de Fomento Educativo, 1985. 605–8.

Gilly, Adolfo. "Memoria y olvido, razón y esperanza: sugerencias para el estudio de la historia de las revoluciones." *Brecha*, no. 1 (fall 1986): 7–15.

Haworth, Bryan. "Film in the Classroom." In *The Historian and Film*. Ed. Paul Smith. Cambridge: Cambridge Univ. Press, 1976. 157–68.

Katz, Friedrich. *The Secret War in Mexico: Europe, the United States, and the Mexican Revolution*. Chicago: Univ. of Chicago Press, 1981.

Knight, Alan. *The Mexican Revolution.* 2 vols. Lincoln: Univ. of Nebraska Press, 1990.

Lukács, Georg. *The Historical Novel.* Trans. Hannah and Stanley Mitchell. Harmondsworth, England: Penguin Books, 1969.

Metraux, G. S. "Editorial: When the Camera Took Up History..." *Flashback: Films and History. Cultures* 2:1 (1974): 9–10.

Meyer, Michael C. *Huerta: A Political Portrait.* Lincoln: Univ. of Nebraska Press, 1972.

Montiel Pagés, Gustavo. "Pancho Villa: el mito y el cine." *Filmoteca* 1, "El cine y la revolución mexicana" (1979): 100–109.

Mora, Carl. *Mexican Cinema: Reflections of a Society, 1896–1980.* Berkeley: Univ. of California Press, 1982.

Mraz, John. "Fernando de Fuentes." *International Dictionary of Films and Filmmakers-2: Directors.* Chicago: St. James Press, 1991. 199–200.

———. "Made on Rails: A History of the Mexican Railroad Workers," documentary videotape distributed by the Cinema Guild.

———. "Redes." *International Dictionary of Films and Filmmakers-1: Films.* Chicago: St. James Press, 1990. 747–48.

O'Shaughnessy, Edith. *A Diplomat's Wife in Mexico.* New York: Harper and Brothers, 1916.

Rosenstone, Robert, ed. *AHR Forum:* "History in Images/History in Words: Reflections on the Possibility of Really Putting History onto Film." *American Historical Review* 93:5 (December 1988): 1173–227.

———. *Revisioning History: Film and the Construction of a Past.* Princeton, N.J.: Princeton Univ. Press, 1995.

Ruíz, Ramón Eduardo. *The Great Rebellion: Mexico, 1905–1924.* New York: W. W. Norton, 1980.

Rutherford, John. *Mexican Society during the Revolution: A Literary Approach.* London: Oxford Univ. Press, 1971.

Sánchez, Francisco. *Crónica antisolemne del cine mexicano.* Veracruz: Universidad Veracruzana, 1989.

Serrano, Francisco. "¡Vámonos con Pancho Villa!" *Cine* 8 (September 1978): 60–64.

Sherman, William, and Richard Greenleaf. *Victoriano Huerta: A Reappraisal.* Mexico City: Mexico City College, 1960.

Sorlin, Pierre. *The Film in History: Restaging the Past.* Totowa, N.J.: Barnes and Noble, 1980.

Vanderwood, Paul. "The Image of Mexican Heroes in American Films." *Film-Historia* 2:3 (1992): 221–44.

Zemon Davis, Natalie. "'Any Resemblance to Persons Living or Dead': Film and the Challenge of Authenticity." *Historical Journal of Film, Radio and Television* 8:3 (1988): 269–83.

Chapter 6

Kiss of the Spider Woman, Novel, Play, and Film: Homosexuality and the Discourse of the Maternal in a Third World Prison

Patricia Santoro

The Adaptation

Reception of the cinematic adaptation of a literary work often results in a form of film bashing based on a criterion of comparison that presupposes "faithfulness" to the original. How often do moviegoers exclaim how disappointed they were that the film had not tried or could not re-create the first-person narrative of a text, that their favorite character was clearly misinterpreted by the adaptation, or that an important segment of the original had been deleted and therefore the meaning of the dramatic conclusion was altered? Given the affective relationship that the reader develops with a literary work, these complaints are justified. One might consider, however, two realities inherent in the cinematic adaptation: (1) the cinematic text intentionally alters narrational strategies and conceptual modalities; (2) novel and film are materially distinct media, and therefore narrative and representational strategies will be altered dramatically in the transcription from the verbal to the visual text. The visual medium signifies through images, movement, and sound; the verbal medium creates mental images with verbal tools. An alternative critical approach would judge the film adaptation as a success or failure on its cinematic merit,[1] just as the novel is judged on its literary merit, and would analyze the ways in which each medium creates meaning with its own set of literary tools.[2] This is not to deny the pleasure inherent in the comparison of two (or more) adaptations of an original work. Indeed, the greatest pleasure derived from this type of analysis is in the exploration of the similarities expressed by each genre. This pleasure is to be found in the analysis of Manuel Puig's *El beso de la mujer araña* (*Kiss of the Spider Woman*), novel, play, and film. The novel was published in 1976; the play, adapted by Puig himself, premiered in 1981; and the film — a North American-Brazilian coproduction, directed by the Argentine-born Hector Babenco and adapted by the American Leonard Schrader — was released in 1985.[3] All three texts share two common goals; each interweaves the political and the personal: (1) to demythologize the stereotype of both the homosexual male and the left-wing political militant, and (2) to portray the coexistence of both the material horror and the spiritual beauty that exist side by side in the Third World in general and in Latin America in particular.

Novel, play, and film structure a similar narrative framework. Two cell mates, the homosexual window dresser Molina, in prison for corruption of a minor, and the left-wing activist Valentín, a political prisoner arrested for subversive activities, pass the time in their cell mentally re-creating the old movie plots that Molina recounts to Valentín. The premise of *Kiss of the Spider Woman*, the imaginative possibilities inherent in difference, concretely that of Molina and Valentín, is the axis of narrative development. Furthermore, the narrative and structural concept of creativity born of difference relates both verbal genres and the visual genre to the same narrative family, for difference evokes the concept of montage, the basic tenet of the signification process in film. "We know, since Eisenstein, that the juxtaposition of two alien components results in a fertile clash, which then, like the montage, is capable of expressing new concepts" (Biró, 2). To this end, the texts have limited themselves to two main characters and have placed them together in the solitary confines of a prison cell. It is their interaction in a subtle montage-equals-change fashion that creates the narrative chain of discourses and action that makes up all three texts. Near the close of the narrative, the two cell mates reach a fragile state of emotional wholeness with themselves, with each other, and with the film stories. Unhappily, that illusory state, as ephemeral as the film images they have created, will be easily and inevitably shattered by the more ponderous reality of the underlying fascist ideology that has conspired to destroy both men, Molina because he is a homosexual and Valentín because he is a Marxist.

In each text, the unfolding of the narrative develops a crucial hermeneutic code regarding the behavior of Molina.[4] A little more than halfway through each text we learn that the apolitical Molina, in exchange for a parole that will reunite him with his ailing mother, has compromised himself with the authorities. He has agreed to falsely befriend the left-wing Valentín in order to gain his confidence and to relay information regarding the latter's comrades-in-arms. The revelation of the hermeneutic code causes the receptor to reconsider Molina's behavior toward Valentín. His coyness, patience, and willingness to give must be reevaluated in light of this duplicity: is he motivated by real interest or self interest? Under such scrutiny, each of Molina's actions resonates with new meaning and adds excitement to the texts. The deep emotional readings of Molina and his real motivations are at the heart of the novel and its adaptations. Narrative development resolves the hermeneutic code, and, while all three texts begin with both men at opposite ends of the political and psychological spectrum, all three narratives gradually orchestrate a rapprochement of the two characters that results in a spiritual, physical, and finally political union.

The Maternal and Psychoanalytic Film Theory

> 1. *Mother: 6. a woman looked upon as a mother, or exercising control or authority like that of a mother: to be a mother to someone. 7. the qualities characteristic of a mother, as maternal affection:* It is the mother in her showing itself. *8. something that gives rise to or exercises protecting care over something else.*
>
> Webster's Encyclopedic Unabridged Dictionary of the English Language *(1989)*

Essential to the novel and significant in the play and film is Molina's mining of Valentín's unconscious desires through his recounting of films. He tells movie stories in order to entertain Valentín, to help him sleep, and to help them both escape into the world of illusion created by the films. Molina, by his own admission, has a gift for remembering and for re-creating the visual. "And don't forget," he reminds Valentín, "I'm a window dresser, that's almost like a decorator" ("Y no te olvides que soy vidrierista, que es casi como decorador") (play, 77).[5] Carol Clark D'Lugo explains Molina's narrative and inventive powers:

> As a film enthusiast, Molina has internalized the clichés and
> stereotypes of these movies to such an extent that he is
> able to invent details when his memory fails him, something
> that happens frequently... It is significant that, early in the
> text, Molina defends his method of narration when Valentín
> accuses him of inventing half the scripts of the movie (24).
> His desire, Molina assures his cellmate, is to fill out the
> descriptions so that Valentín may see things as he does. (237)

All three texts begin in medias res with a film tale. Molina hooks both Valentín and the receptor immediately. With respect to his storytelling, Molina is conscious of his role as a maternal figure intent on tending to his charge. He tells Valentín early in the film version that the narratives are "one of Mother's many stories." At one point in the play version when Molina agrees to tell the sleepless Valentín yet another film tale, the stage directions tell the actor to speak as if "resignándose, en tono de madre de clase media" (95) (relenting, like a middle-class mother). In the novel and play, when Valentín begs off from a movie tale in order to be left alone to sort out a personal problem, Molina agrees and tells him, "Pero si se le enreda la madeja, niña Valentina, le pongo cero en labores" (novel, 43; play, 81) (But be careful you don't get it tangled, Valentina, or you'll flunk home economics). And to conclude the last movie tale in the novel, Molina ends with the set phrase used at the end of fairy tales: "Y colorín colorado,... este cuento... se ha terminado" (263) (Crimson and clover, this story is over).

Molina's positioning as mother figure and his role of storyteller of filmic tales represent integrative features of the maternal component of psychoanalytic film theory. Psychoanalytic film theory explains our unconscious fascination with the cinema based on Lacan's rereading of the Oedipus complex and subsequent theory of the mirror image. For Lacan, the small being first achieves a sense of personal identity and wholeness by seeing a more perfect image in a mirror, or in the image of the mother figure. Sandy Flitterman-Lewis describes this process:

> It mistakes this unified, coherent shape for a superior self. The child *identifies* with this image (as both reflecting the self, and as something *other*), and finds in it a kind of satisfying unity that it cannot experience in its own body. The infant internalizes this image as an "ideal ego," and this process forms the basis for all later identifications, which are imaginary in principle. (Allen, 177)

The unconscious, the locus of all desire, propels the individual through life in search of both the perfect image and the recapturing of the maternal state of oneness with the mother. Whereas for Freud, the Oedipal moment, that is, the recognition of a determined sexhood, signaled the break with the mother, for Lacan, the world of language, that is, the symbolic realm, takes the small child out of the imaginary world of perfection and maternal unity and into a world divided by symbols and the impossibility of their representation. Our unconscious, formed by those forbidden sexual longings for the parent and by the desire to be at one with the mother, is the locus of all our future desires and is what propels us through life searching to recapture and fulfill our fantasies. Flitterman-Lewis addresses the nexus of cinema and psychoanalysis, underlining its effects on the spectator: "Psychoanalytic film theory discusses film spectatorship in terms of the circulation of desire. That is, it considers both the viewing-state and the film-text alike as, in some way, mobilizing the structures of unconscious fantasy. More than any other form, the cinema is capable of actually reproducing or approximating the structure and logic of dreams and the unconscious" (Allen, 180).

The three narrative texts of *Kiss of the Spider Woman* interweave the apparently disparate threads of homosexuality, maternity, and a Third World prison cell into a mutually nurturing set of forces that reflect psychoanalytic film theory's definition of the power of the cinema to reactivate — "in ways that are pleasurable — those very deep and globally structuring processes of the human psyche" (Flitterman-Lewis, in Allen, 179). Molina, the storyteller, takes on the role of the filmmaker who creates imaginary text and who sees Valentín, the spectator, as an artificial space, a construct, whose unconscious desires will be fulfilled temporarily by Mother's stories of romance and intrigue. The film industry, a capitalist enterprise par excellence, fulfills desires in order to earn profits; the Scheherazade-like Molina will use Valentín in order to win his freedom and to rejoin his own mother. Both Valentín and Molina lose themselves in the illusion of the presymbolic in order to block out the reality of the symbolic/patriarchal system that dominates their immediate circumstances and their society at large. Their imaginations, as well as those of the receptors, become the locus of exercises in hypercreativity as they interact with the strong narrative tales spun by Molina.

The Hermeneutic Code and the Discourse of the Maternal

The hermeneutic code is interwoven into the discourse of the maternal in *Kiss of the Spider Woman*, and is born of Molina's treacherous befriending of Valentín. The unraveling of this enigma parallels the development of the complex maternal discourse that struggles for dominance over the material presence of the patriarchal order represented by the prison, the warden, and his torturers. Molina's homosexuality authorizes the feline and at the same time maternal discourse read throughout all three texts. His metadramatic role is to nurture Valentín, to tap into his unconscious desires in order to break down the rigid regimen of Marxist study and self-denial that the latter practices in the jail cell. It is clear in the film version, and implicit in both written texts, given the political regime that has sent Valentín to prison, that he has been tortured by the authorities and is therefore already in a highly vulnerable state. It is also understood that the torture has failed, and that the authorities have taken another tack. They have chosen Molina for the deception because he is a homosexual and is perceived as a "feminine" presence who is capable of creating a safe space in which Valentín will disclose the whereabouts of his comrades.[6] The hermeneutic interplay of the imaginary (Molina's mothering stance) and the symbolic (the deception orchestrated by the warden) represents a cruel irony that organizes the message in all three media. It is the symbolic world of law and authority that has motivated and at the same time co-opted the maternal discourse of fantasy and desire. This imbalance of power predicts the closure effected by all three narratives. Despite the destruction of myths and despite the spiritual beauty represented by the rapprochement of two ideologically and sexually disparate men, the political system and the brute force of its henchmen will literally dominate and destroy both Molina and Valentín.[7]

The limited spatial and temporal factor inherent in both play and film dramatizes the signs pointing to a maternal discourse. The limitations of the stage and the frame of the movie screen create a womblike setting that, for the spectator, acts as a crucible for Molina's emotional, psychological, and ultimately physical seduction of Valentín. The lights in the prison are turned out early, transforming the darkened jail cell into a darkened movie theater and subsequent dream space that makes the imaginary realm of the film stories so easily accessible. The visual paradigm of the womb as maternal and creative space is encoded in two principal ways. First, the stark background space of both stage and screen, coupled with the proximity and solitude of the two men, create a positive space in which the seeds of their friendship take root, mature, and flower. Second, both visual media frame and therefore limit the space, focusing and enabling the film viewer to hear and to observe the two characters as their sexual and political differences become blurred and their perceptions of one other become sharper. The spectator is positioned in order to analyze vocal tone, facial expression, and body language, the gradations of which mark the gradual union of the two cell mates. The film paradoxically uses warm colors such as blue and gold achieved through low contrast lighting to create the inside of what should be a harsh, Third World prison cell. In this fashion the film text itself makes a comment on a crucial narrative theme: the power of cinema to create a more perfect world. However, the seemingly safe and secure environment of the interior space of the cell is contrasted with a stark exterior space. The camera takes us outside Molina and Valentín's cell to the sadly realistic image of the exterior of other cells that are crowded with prison-ers, who, in one scene, in their only gesture of communication with the "outside" world, flail their arms through the bars like a single menacing octopus as guards walk by. In the safe womb of their own private prison cell, Molina's caring, the food, and the storytelling ultimately win the emotionally confused Valentín. The political prisoner, who at first protests the attentions of Molina, literally has no recourse but to be won by the pull of the mater-nal. He knows that torture and death await him outside that cell.

As the two men interact within the confines of their cell, signs of the homosexual Molina as the good, nurturing, albeit decep-tive, mother are highlighted in several ways. He makes certain that both he and Valentín have enough fresh water; he prepares special teas for Valentín in order to soothe his frayed nerves; he sacrifices his own provisions so that Valentín may regain strength; he inquires about his sleep and moves about silently when his cell mate is sleeping; he tries to draw Valentín into conversation, and yet respects his wishes to be left alone. At other times Molina proves to be a domineering mother who claims to know what is best for the weaker, more vulnerable Valentín. The stage direc-tions in the play indicate that the Molina character act "como una maestra de escuela... como madre sobreprotectora, dueña de la situación" (118) (like a schoolmistress...like an overprotec-tive mother, mistress of the situation) in deciding what Valentín should eat and drink. At this point in the drama he playfully chucks Valentín under the chin and asks that he be allowed to spoil him a little. Valentín reacts violently as might any grown child. This squabble, and several others throughout the narrative, only serve to bring them closer, for the driving force of novel, play, and film is the irrevocable intertwining of these two men's emotional lives.

At its most perverse, the maternal and patriarchal conspire to poison Valentín's food in order to hasten the process of entrap-ment. This narrative moment becomes a turning point in the un-locking of the hermeneutic code for the receptor. A simple clue, reminiscent of those given in standard detective fiction, hints at treachery.[8] The poisoned plate contains a significantly larger por-tion than the other, and Molina is forced to eat the larger portion by the generous but as always unsuspecting Valentín. Molina's mysterious illness and subsequent conversation with the apologetic warden reveal the conspiratorial nature of their relationship and therefore the co-optation of Molina by the system. They will try the plan again, and paradoxically, the plot moment representing Valentín's illness will render one of the most beautiful enunciations of maternal discourse in all three texts.

Valentín reacts to the poison with violent stomach pains that cause him to defecate involuntarily. The first time this happens, Molina provides Valentín with his own clothes and toilet paper so that he may clean himself as quickly and as painlessly as possible (novel, 123–24). The second time Valentín loses control of his bowels (novel, 145–46), Molina takes charge, quickly cleaning up his cell mate as a mother would her child, lifting and wiping him, and even apologizing for not having talcum powder. In the novel (145), he playfully calls him a *cagón* (one who moves his bowels a lot), a term in Spanish that a mother might use affectionately with her small child. After Valentín is cleaned up, Molina wraps him in a blanket. In the film version, at this same plot moment he wraps his cell mate in a thin blanket, like a "papoose," he says to Valentín. During this scene, the film frame briefly suggests the image of the maternal icon par excellence, the Pietà. Valentín, naked except for a towel covering his genitals, lies stretched out, helpless, and in emotional agony, in the arms of Molina. This intensely dramatic scene, punctuated by the image of the Christlike Valentín, is alive with political and social transformative messages: The homosexual "deviant," raised to the level of Madonna, cares for the martyred left-wing radical and miraculously transfigures a degrading and humiliating moment, one of many that must occur in a Third World prison, into a warm and nurturing experience that will prove to be an emotional turning point for both men and for the film viewer. The pure maternal iconography witnessed/imagined by the viewer/reader poignantly strengthens the maternal discourse and challenges the receptor, who has just learned of Molina's treachery, to sort out the blurred borders of the two embattled discourses, the maternal and the patriarchal.

Shortly after this scene, the narration of both novel and play further reinforces the image of maternal iconography. Valentín has received word that one of his comrades has died, presumably killed by the police, and tells Molina that he once changed the diapers of the baby of this same young man when they were in hiding together (novel, 146; play, 102). Valentín cries and asks Molina to hold his hand in a gesture of comfort. At that moment he recognizes the significance of Molina's earlier attentions; he sees himself as the small and vulnerable child cared for by a maternal figure. The receptor of all three texts is reminded that Molina has told Valentín early in the narrative that he is a woman in a man's body, that what he wants is a strong man to dominate his life and to form a family unit with that man. Narrative threads are drawn together in this scene as the receptor reads Molina's nurturing tenderness toward Valentín as a sign of the fulfillment of his real maternal desires and real capacity for love as woman to child and to man. His mothering of Valentín at this crucial plot moment is read as genuine in all three texts, and from this moment on in the narrative, the receptor will sense a shift in and subsequent unraveling of the hermeneutic code in the context of this unifying rather than disruptive, self-serving force.

Any disjunction will now take the form of two important plot turns: (1) Molina's manipulation of the authorities and (2) the abandonment of his mother. Molina's deceptive behavior becomes directed toward the authorities as he maneuvers adroitly between their needs, Valentín's need for his friendship, and his own emotional and spiritual need for love. Motivations shift. Instead of using food to undermine Valentín's stoicism, he is now perceived by the receptor as procuring the food for Valentín's nourishment and pleasure. Molina's resolve to contact Valentín's comrades upon his release from jail represents a radical double cross of the authorities. More important, it represents a break with his mother, for whom he agreed to inform on Valentín in the first place. He knows that contact with the subversive cell means either death or a radically new life, one in which there is no place for his mother. He explains in all three texts the motives for this decision:

> Mamá ya tuvo su vida, ella ya vivió, ya tuvo su marido, su hijo... Ya es vieja, ya su vida está casi cumplida... ¿Pero mi vida cuándo empieza?, ¿cuándo me va a tocar algo a mí, tener algo? [Novel, 258; play, 135] [Listen, my mother's had her life, she's lived, she had a husband, a son... she's old, her life is already over... But when will my life start? When is it my turn to have something?]

The tragic irony in Molina's breaking with his mother at this stage in his life is that it is too late, for he will die in the act of realizing himself as a being separate from that of his mother. He is killed at the very moment he steps into the symbolic world of opposing ideologies, specifically that of leftist guerrilla warfare and the fascist police state.

All three texts draw narrative threads together in a series of fast-paced moments that occur just before narrative closure. When Molina wins his parole at last, he risks his life for Valentín. He plays the heroine he tells us he has always dreamed of being, the beautiful Leni of the Nazi propaganda film he has recounted in both novel and film. The police, however, have anticipated his duplicity. Under police surveillance, Molina is chased as he approaches the members of the cell. Spotting the police in pursuit, Valentín's comrades shoot Molina to prevent him from revealing their identity and then speed off in their car. In the film version, in one last effort to get information out of him, the police load the dying man into their car. When he dies a few seconds later, they throw his body out of the car and onto a garbage-strewn lot in a local shantytown. Molina becomes yet another dispensable body, one of the thousands of throwaway people who live in the thousands of shantytowns all over Latin America. After Molina's "disappearance," we learn that Valentín has been tortured once again and remains near death, and in this fashion all three texts— novel, film, and play—approach closure. The brutal destruction of both protagonists and the effect on the receptor reflect the feelings expressed by Valentín at the close of the first movie tale told to him by Molina:

> Me da lástima que se terminó... Que me da lástima porque me encariñé con los personajes. Y ahora se terminó, y es como si estuvieran muertos [Novel, 47]. Es curioso como uno no puede estar sin encariñarse con algo. Es... como si la mente segregara sentimiento, sin parar... [Play, 80] [It's too bad that it ended. It's too bad because I got attached to the characters. And now it's over and it's like they are dead. It's strange how you can't help getting attached to something. It's like your brain keeps on producing feelings.]

At this early moment in the narrative Valentín has already become the ideal spectator who is caught up in the pull of the imaginary realm of film fantasy. And at this point both novel and play are laying out their own expectations for their ideal readers, hinting that they will become emotionally involved with the protagonists, and that these characters, too, will die. In this regard, the sudden death of Molina and the callous disposal of his body is especially chilling for the film viewer who has followed the Molina character through various stages of emotional development, and has formed a relationship to him.

The receptor may have become too riveted in the present both by the strong narrative pull of Molina's stories and by the strong personalities of each character to have imagined or foreseen this tragic ending for the two protagonists. However, there can be no Hollywood ending to a story that takes place in a Third World prison and whose only characters are a homosexual and a Marxist. There are, in fact, signs throughout the narrative that a tragic ending is imminent. At intervals in the three texts, and in varying degrees, Valentín cuts through the illusion created by Molina, reminding him of the sociopolitical context of the stories. His most virulent attack on the illusionist world of the film is witnessed in the cinematic version when, early on in the film in a moment of anger and frustration, Valentín abruptly interrupts Molina's dreamy telling of a Nazi propaganda film. Valentín rips off his shirt to show Molina his newly inflicted scars, a result of a brutal torture session ordered undoubtedly by the warden. Valentín attacks Molina for his extreme naïveté. "Don't you know what the Nazis did to people—Jews, Marxists, Catholics? Homosexuals?" A tearful and very frightened Molina claims to never read a political meaning into the movies he sees and relives. At an early point in the film version he has told Valentín, "Well, you see I detest politics, but I'm *mad* about the leading man." For Molina, the movie texts create beauty, love, costumes, hairstyles, and above all feelings. True to his interior perception of himself as a woman, he expresses a prototypical feminine phrase: "Look. I don't explain my movies. It just ruins the emotion." Molina's ingenuousness will prove fatal. We have seen that his desire to be the heroine ("Yo siempre con la heroina" [I'm always with the heroine], stated in all three texts) and to act on his feelings of love for Valentín will ultimately cause his death at the hands of Valentín's comrades-in-arms.

The Movie Tales

The novel recounts six film stories, six of the many films that Molina, the avid moviegoer, has seen in the cinema houses of Buenos Aires. Almost all are stories of troubled romantic love, and all vary in the degree to which they expose the societal ills of their particular culture. The first film tale is the well-known cult classic, *Cat People* (Jacques Tourneur, 1942), in which a young woman living in New York is haunted by the legend of panther women in her native Transylvania. Puig has chosen to include *Cat People* as the only film in the play version.[9] The second, a Nazi propaganda film, deals with the Nazi occupation of France. Its appearance in a Buenos Aires movie theater is a direct reference both to Argentina's alliance with the Axis powers during World War II and to the government's continuing adherence to fascist doctrine at the time of the novel's publication. This is the only film tale recreated in the film version of *Kiss of the Spider Woman.* The third film is not actually told to Valentín but is recounted mentally by Molina in order to pass the lonely hours while his cell mate studies. This film is thought to be *The Enchanted Cottage* (John Cromwell, 1945), a beauty-and-the-beast theme contrasting the purity of the soul with the ugliness of the body. There is no reference to the title of the fourth, a film that deals with the evils of colonialism in an unnamed country in South America. The fifth film, which Molina calls *La vuelta de la mujer zombie,* appears to be a variation of *I Walked with a Zombie* (Jacques Tourneur, 1943), another cult classic.[10] Molina's tale becomes an allegory, disguised as a love story and an exposition on voodoo, of the subjugation and enslavement of black slaves in the Caribbean. The sixth, an untitled film, apparently a Mexican production, is a melodrama that points to the tragedy of a woman whose life has been ruined by the ruthlessness of her business magnate lover.

Cat People, The Enchanted Cottage, and the Mexican film allegorize the overpowering forces of societal evil that control its citizens and leave them helpless. The Nazi propaganda film, and the films dealing with colonialism in the Caribbean, speak of the oppression of the suppressed minorities by strong armed "superior" races. All of these films are read both as a barometer of the societies in which they were created and as a reflection of the emotional and spiritual state of Molina, the man who has chosen to pull them from his memory. They reflect both his need for love (all the films deal with love's tragic loss) and a deep, perhaps totally unrecognized, social consciousness. They synthesize the personal and the political, the individual and the state. Valentín listens attentively, at times caught up in the comforting illusion and at other times ready to analyze the sociopolitical message whose structure underlies these fantasies. The length (287 pages) and verbal complexity of the novel allow the inclusion of the six films and enable that text and its readers to probe more deeply beneath the surface of overarching global realities in general, and into the psychological makeup of both Molina and Valentín in particular.

The limited time of both play and film results in a more concentrated social message. The play's inclusion of *Cat People* leaves the spectator immersed in the dark foreboding of the powers of the unconscious. The film's inclusion of the Nazi thriller, while hokey, bordering on camp in its presentation, foregrounds the distorted value placed on the superficial glories of fascism. Despite the beauty of illusionistic cinema, the evilness contained in the film stories, especially those with clear historical and sociological references, reflects the oppressive political situation responsible for the imprisonment of Molina and Valentín. The struggle of urban and mountain guerrillas against right-wing military governments has polarized Latin America and other Third World countries before, during, and after these countries ceased to be colonies. Fascist ideologies in Latin America are traditionally supported by a conservative Catholic clergy that condemns homosexuality. Both novel and play locate the drama principally in a Buenos Aires prison cell. Significantly, the publication of the novel and the play's premiere of 1976 and 1981, respectively, associate Valentín's arrest with those of the "disappeared" under the military junta that ruled Argentina from 1976 to 1983, and under whose rule many thousands of dissidents like Valentín were "disappeared." The film version was made in Brazil, and points to that country (which was ruled by the military until 1985) as the location of the story simply because writing visible on the prison walls is in Portuguese.

The mythology of the movies, especially the classical Hollywood-style cinema predominant since cinema's inception, considers movies a form of entertainment. They are meant to create an illusion that for an hour and a half or so mitigates the tension, the banality, or the sadness of our daily lives. The development of film criticism and film theory over the decades has exploded this myth. What is on the surface of the classic Hollywood-style film (the story, mise-en-scène, dialogue, and sound track) may engage the reader completely, and yet what lies beneath the smoothly flowing narrative reveals dominant ideological forces that are myths unto themselves. As Molina tells his movie tales, he symbolizes the more superficial reading of the film. He is the spectator who projects himself onto and identifies with the heroine (in this case not the hero, for Molina considers himself a woman). Following Lacan's metaphor of the mirror that reflects the idealized image, the heroine and the hero represent a more idealized image of the spectator whose gaze is fixed on the screen.[11] At one point in the film, Molina gazes longingly at himself in a mirror as he tells the tale of the lovely heroine. He has appropriated the lush spectacle of the Hollywood melodrama and has forgotten that he is in a Third World prison cell. He is able to transform his own reality before his own eyes and before the spectator's eyes. Yet the informed spectator reads an ideological discourse in all of these films and in all films viewed in general. The sociohistoric, economic, and psychological underpinnings of the surface text are fraught with meaning even in the most banal films.

Molina's identification with the heroine and the spectator's reading of an ideological subtext are illustrated by the first film, *Cat People*, the only film that Molina relates in the play. He reconstructs the plot, embroidering, as he says, in order to make Valentín see it as he does. He pays special attention to details, savoring elements of decor, hairstyle, and dress. Valentín, the Marxist critic, unmasks the dominant ideology, breaking the illusion, and spoiling for Molina the power of cinema to make him forget all the "garbage" of the outside world. In *Cat People* the heroine, a descendant of a line of panther women, is doomed to turn into a panther if she kisses a man. Unfortunately, she falls in love, marries, never consummates the marriage, and ultimately tries to resolve this real problem (the fact that she is a panther) by treating her condition with psychotherapy. Her fate is to turn into a panther and kill her psychotherapist and to be killed herself by a panther in a cage at the New York City Zoo. Both Molina's and Valentín's interpretation of this film (and the others) represent metacinematic comments on the role of the spectator, whose role as coproducer of cinematic text is to bring his or her own experiences to the telling of a tale, that is, to provide that information which the words and images cannot possibly supply. For his or her part, the reader/spectator of *Kiss of the Spider Woman* attributes the choice of this film and the homosexual's identification with the heroine to Molina's subconscious, for Molina recognizes that he, too, is a woman trapped in a man's body, just as the heroine is a panther trapped in a woman's body. He knows that psychotherapy will not cure him, nor will the love of a good woman. On the other hand, it is clear why the Marxist-oriented Valentín would render a Freudian reading of the film text, labeling it an allegory both of the frigid woman and the castrated man who wants a plaything for a wife. The play's choice of this film results in a more emphatic portrayal of the character of Molina. It becomes an allegory for the tragic plight of the homosexual in a society that will not accept him. As the embodiment of the maternal discourse, Molina is characterized as a good person (just as the heroine of *Cat People*, Irena, is a sweet and loving woman), yet he is too "feline," too effeminate for his society. He needs love, and finds love, yet he is doomed to die. According to the subtext of *Cat People*, unhealthy societal structures are to blame for the death of the heroine. Irena refers to the evil ways of her village, and to the dreadful events that occurred there. The zookeeper says that the panther is the worst animal. The psychiatrist speaks of corrupt passions, a canker on the mind, and the evil drive to kill. Irena says that she had to flee from her past, and yet she has no peace for "they" are inside her. In this sense, the subtext of *Cat People*, embedded in the larger text of *Kiss of the Spider Woman*, reads as a reference to the kind of society that spawned the military junta whose terror permeated Argentine society for seven years.

On the other hand, the film version's choice of the Nazi propaganda movie is an obvious sign of the military occupation of Argentina, Brazil, and of any Third World society ruled by the military. However, this movie, whose narrative and images form a significant subtext in the film version of *Kiss of the Spider Woman*, is highly problematic. Its mise-en-scène is a parody that mocks in a surprisingly lighthearted manner the inverted values of fascist ideology. The beautiful yet empty-headed Frenchwomen fall in love with German soldiers; the men of the French resistance are portrayed as foolish, depraved, and ineffectual goons; the Jews are portrayed as greedy, scheming, self-serving merchants. The film chooses not to express the true horror of Nazi ideology, and effects this by apparently portraying the film images through Molina, the omniscient narrator, who relishes its more lavish details. He leaves his role of "mother" completely behind here to become the exquisite heroine Leni, the fabulously beautiful and desirable French chanteuse whose only real love is the handsomely chiseled, blond Werner, the head of German counterintelligence. Although Molina admits he understands what the Nazis stood for, his blocking out of the horror is an ironic homage to the power of the cinema to make us forget. The image of Leni is that of the archetype Hollywood femme fatale, although here with an ingenuousness and longing for love that make her even more appealing. This political naïveté reflects Molina's own apolitical nature and his own desire to be in love with a strong man. Leni is dark, slim, with large, liquid eyes. Most important, she is the star of the film and the most famous chanteuse in all of Paris, the most glamorous city in the world. She is the mirror image that Molina desires to be because she is constructed by her film text to entrap the viewer with her beauty and charm. She symbolizes that Spider Woman quality that the Hollywood film purports to be. In Molina's rendering of the film story, this propaganda film is charged with the Hollywood aesthetic whose goal is to entertain, to make the viewer forget that there are fascistic societies that crush resistance movements. On the other hand, the mocking tone of the film with its hokey dialogue, dramatic close-ups, and exaggerated acting styles makes fun of Molina and causes the viewer to wonder if the film images are authorized by the imagination of Valentín, who clearly understands that propaganda is meant to twist reality into an ideological mold at the expense of artistic integrity. However, given that Molina's only desire is for Valentín to see the film as he does, the clichéd and melodramatic nature of the images would confirm Molina as author of the image track. The story of the Nazi film will parallel Molina's own story since

Leni is killed trying to help her lover fight the resistance. Indeed, the film text may motivate the apolitical Molina to help Valentín, his true love, fight the authorities. The Nazi propaganda film subtly evokes a crucial message in all three texts of *Kiss of the Spider Woman*: societies that support fascism as a dominant ideology glorify its strength, its patriarchal, right-wing, heterosexual values, and believe on blind faith that all differences must be erased.

Novel, drama, and film propose several major themes: the mythos and reality of the Marxist struggle against a fascist-style government; the mythos and reality of homosexuality; the power of homosexual feelings; the possibility of a loving relationship between two seemingly disparate individuals; and the power—both escapist and myth-breaking—of the cinematic apparatus. All of these themes are subtexts of a larger discourse that is never absent from the novel, the play, or the film: the horror and the beauty that coexist in the human condition, that permeate human society and affect the behavior of all its members. This message is perceived most obviously in the double dichotomies of the maternal in a Third World prison cell and the themes of the illusionistic movie tales that entangle and entrap both protagonists. The title of the triple texts also relays this message. It is Valentín who, toward the close of the novel and the play, illuminates the significance of the title, *Kiss of the Spider Woman*, when he jokingly, perhaps subconsciously, labels Molina the Spider Woman who entraps men in her web: "Vos sos la mujer araña, que atrapa a los hombres en su tela" (novel, 265; play, 137). In the film version, Molina introduces the theme briefly as another movie tale. At the end of all three texts Valentín, after another brutal torture session and sedated with morphine, dreams the story of the Spider Woman who must live forever trapped in her web, but who comforts Valentín, cries precious diamond tears for him, and provides him with nourishment. The extravagance of the dream is far from gratuitous. It is rather a direct reflection of the realism of this interactive text. In the dreamwork, Valentín's unconscious re-creates in more beautiful images the events of his conscious life. The image of the Spider Woman is the condensation of various elements: the beautiful Marta, his true love; Molina, the man who has loved and nurtured him; and the concept of entrapment, for Molina is a woman trapped in the body of a man. In the film version, Valentín and Marta row off happily into the sunset, a direct reference to the fantasy and fullness inherent in the closure of the classical Hollywood melodrama. Contextualized within the tortured mind and body of Valentín, the dream of the Spider Woman reflects the undercurrent of beauty and illusion represented by the maternal imaginary realm versus the evil represented by the symbolic, patriarchal realm that has ordered Valentín's torture.

Conclusion

Novel, play, and film present, in varying degrees, a sociopolitical critique of the Third World and an examination of the power of cinema on the human psyche. The dramatized and cinematic adaptations have compensated for their brevity by condensing the themes inherent in the original novel and by actualizing in material images the duality that is struggling to become whole in these texts. The dichotomies inherent in these texts — the maternal and the patriarchal, the domestic and the public sphere, the internal and the exterior, left- and right-wing ideologies, homosexuality and heterosexuality, fact and fiction, illusion versus reality, and the verbal versus the imagistic — are interwoven to construct a premise that concludes that these forces are ever present and are, in fact, interdependent in the consciousness of our history and our cultures. It is left to the receptor to synthesize these dichotomies, to formulate the third space that is a product of his or her own experience.

Notes

1. Yvette Biró states in the introduction to her book: "The methodology used [in the analysis of the film text] is not from the world of classical aesthetics. It has been proved countless times that neither literature's, nor the theater's, nor even the fine arts' refined methods of investigation can *automatically* be applied to the film. More than fifty years ago Béla Balázs warned that condemning the film by subjecting it to classical standards is no wiser than calling the airplane a bad automobile just because it cannot run well on the ground" (3).

2. See Dudley Andrew, *Concepts in Film Theory,* for a detailed discussion of the taxonomy and theory of the cinematic adaptation. Andrew's theorizing of the adaptation avoids the judgment of "faithful" as the only criterion upon which to base the value the film. For a variety of essays regarding theater and film as competing and complementary genres, see James Hurt.

3. For an in-depth study of Puig's adaptation of his play, see Becky Boling.

4. The hermeneutic code is defined as the "inculcation of the enigma, the question to be pursued throughout the text, in sum all the units whose function it is to articulate in various ways a question, its response, and the variety of chance events which either formulate the question or delay its answer; or even, constitute an enigma and lead to its solution. While Barthes compares the hermeneutic code to the Voice of Truth—the solution of the enigma constituting the moment of revelation—the function of the hermeneutic code is to delay revelation, to dodge the moment of truth by setting up obstacles, stoppages, deviations. The hermeneutic code regulates the pacing of the pleasure afforded by the text, engaging the reader/spectator in what Barthes calls the 'striptease,' delaying final disclosure until the ultimate moment" (Stam, Burgoyne, and Flitterman-Lewis, 192).

5. All English translations of the play version are from Holt and Woodyard. All translations of the novel are mine.

6. In *Contemporary Argentine Cinema*, David William Foster adds a new layer of meaning to the authorities' choice of Molina. Since in the film version the novel is set in Brazil, where corruption of a minor is of little interest to the authorities, his arrest may be perceived as motivated by their desire to use him expressly as an informer (124).

7. For a different perspective on the demythologizing of homosexual stereotypes, see Vito Russo, in *The Celluloid Closet*. Russo reads the Molina role as a negative stereotype of the homosexual male, since he (Molina) embodies the "destructive, masochistic identification with the cinematic downtrodden female" (284).

8. *Boquitas pintadas*, Puig's 1968 novel, also offers "clues" (although on a much larger scale) to a reader who must gather and process fragments of information in order to piece together the narrative.

9. For a discussion of the films of Val Lewton, the producer of *Cat People* and *I Walked with a Zombie*, see J. P. Telotte. For a review of Telotte's book, see *Wide Angle* 8:2.

10. According to Becky Boling (85 n. 4), *La vuelta de la mujer zombie* is a combination of *I Walked with a Zombie* and *White Zombie* (Victor Halperin, 1932).

11. For a discussion of the concept of the gaze as an integral signifying practice in film viewing, see the frequently cited articles by Laura Mulvey.

Works Cited

Allen, Robert C., ed. *Channels of Discourse*. Chapel Hill: Univ. of North Carolina Press, 1987.

Andrew, Dudley. *Concepts in Film Theory*. New York: Oxford Univ. Press, 1984.

———. "The Well-worn Muse: Adaptation in Film History and Theory." In *Narrative Strategies: Original Essays in Film and Prose Fiction*. Ed. Syndy M. Conger and Janice R. Welsch. McComb: Western Illinois Univ. Press, 1980.

Biró, Yvette. *Profane Mythologies: The Savage Mind and the Cinema*. Bloomington: Indiana Univ. Press, 1982.

Boling, Becky. "From *Beso* to *Beso*: Puig's Experiments with Genre." *Symposium* 44 (1990): 75–87.

Clark D'Lugo, Carol. "*El beso de la mujer araña*: Norm and Deviance in the Fiction/as the Fiction." *Symposium* 44 (1990): 235–51.

Foster, David William. *Contemporary Argentine Cinema*. Columbia: Univ. of Missouri Press, 1992.

Holt, Marion Peter, and George Woodyard, eds. *DramaContemporary: Latin America*. New York: PAJ Publications, 1986.

Hurt, James, ed. *Focus on Film and Theatre*. Englewood Cliffs, N.J.: Prentice-Hall, 1974.

Kiss of the Spider Woman. Directed by Hector Babenco. Island Alive, 1985.

Kiss of the Spider Woman. Screenplay by Leonard Schrader. Boston: Faber and Faber, 1987.

Masiello, Francine R. "Jail House Flicks: Projections by Manuel Puig." *Symposium* 32: 15–24.

Mulvey, Laura. "Afterthoughts on 'Visual Pleasure and Narrative Cinema' Inspired by 'Duel in the Sun' (King Vidor, 1946)." *Framework* 15–17 (1981): 12–15.

———. "Visual Pleasure and Narrative Cinema." *Screen* 16.3 (1975): 6–18.

Puig, Manuel. *Bajo un manto de estrellas, El beso de la mujer araña*. Barcelona: Seix Barral, 1983.

———. *El beso de la mujer araña* (1976). Barcelona: Seix Barral, 1982.

Russo, Vito. *The Celluloid Closet: Homosexuality in the Movies*. New York: Harper and Row, 1987.

Stam, Robert, Robert Burgoyne, and Sandy Flitterman-Lewis. *New Vocabularies in Film Semiotics: Structuralism, Post-Structuralism and Beyond*. New York: Routledge, 1992.

Telotte, J. P. *Dreams of Darkness: Fantasy and the Films of Val Lewton*. Champaign: Univ. of Illinois Press, 1985.

Chapter 7
Moving to Thought: The Inspired Reflective Cinema of Fernando Pérez

Beat Borter

"*Dying Young* will be followed by a film about Ernest Hemingway," announced the tinned voice in French, Spanish, and English on the plane that was to take me from Switzerland to Cuba in November 1991. Yet another of those documentaries enumerating episodes in the life of the famous writer, another celebration of his hunting and fishing, I thought, and dozed off. When I opened my eyes again, the screen showed a Spanish-speaking teacher explaining the passive voice to her class, using an English example that sounded vaguely familiar: "A man can be destroyed, but not defeated." Ah, yes, Hemingway. Although *The Old Man and the Sea* began to play an increasingly important part in the film, a young woman seemed to be at the center of quite a different story, one firmly rooted in Cuban reality. It turned out to be Cuban director Fernando Pérez's second feature film, *Hello Hemingway*, which had just received the prestigious *primer coral* at the International Festival of New Latin American Cinema in Havana the previous year. In this essay I explore the film's strong impact and unique appeal and trace the development of Pérez's filmmaking career.

"We Rejected Any Kind of Adaptation":
Hello Hemingway as Faithful Nonadaptation

Hello Hemingway is indeed about Hemingway in a sense, but it is not a documentary. It does not attempt to "objectively" relate Hemingway's connection to Cuba, where he lived from 1939 to 1960 and wrote *The Old Man and the Sea*. Nor does an authoritative (male) voice narrate facts and fragments from the writer's life and work. *Hello Hemingway* contains no scene created by Hemingway. Nor does it feature him on the screen—he has only a few fleeting appearances, where viewers catch a glimpse of him from afar. Yet, he is a constant presence.

Director Fernando Pérez and screenwriter Mayda Royero chose to create a story of their own, with strong and evident parallels to *The Old Man and the Sea*, while not just alluding to the novel or acknowledging their debt to it, but directly incorporating it, making its effect on the protagonist the central theme. *Hello Hemingway* is, it seems to me, one of very few successful and indeed "faithful" film adaptations of a literary work simply because it does not even attempt to be one. The film is inspired by the novel, respecting and keeping its essence: it moves beyond the problematic relationship of literature and film, addressing instead "literature and life" as it is expressed in cinematographic terms.

The action is set in the prerevolutionary Cuba of the 1950s. The story revolves around a family living next to Hemingway's grandiose *finca* La Vigía in San Francisco de Paula in the outskirts of Havana. The fifteen-year-old Larita would like to study— something unheard of for her relatives in the poor village. Yet, she is hopeful and sets her sights on getting a scholarship for the United States. Coming across the famous novel of the elusive and seemingly unapproachable neighbor, she begins to discover parallels with her own situation.

The film opens with Larita (Laura de la Uz) and her cousin Flora swimming in the pool of the *finca* where sun and rain combine with rich tropical colors. This undeclared flashback of events taking place two years earlier dissolves into Larita in front of a mirror radiantly singing, or rather imitating, a popular song expressing an engaging belief in all the happiness to come. Filled with adolescent dreams, she feels ready for what a rosy world will offer her, effortlessly switching from a sentimental Cuban song into a lip-synching of an Elvis song, which is just as much a part of her dreamworld. Although Larita herself seems hardly aware of her surroundings, the scene effectively locates her in a claustrophobic setting, introducing the grandmother's religious faith and obvious concern for Larita, the aunt's constant bickering, the uncle's disquieting background presence and his anxieties regarding his job, the superficial bond with her cousin, the lack of money and scarcity of food, and the school uniform blouse with collar turned up Elvis-style to hide the stains. Thus, while the cousin hurries on to work, Larita lingers outside the fence that encloses Hemingway's *finca* and happens to pick up a flower there.

The figure of Hemingway himself stays very much in the background. His presence remains ambiguous. His face is seen filtered through glass, a curtain, or the falling rain. His *finca* is a world apart, isolated, and towering above the neighboring shacks. Larita is ejected from this world at the very beginning and is very much aware of his presence, but has no direct access to him. She is not influenced and marked by personal encounters with him, but by his work, his creation. The film is not so much interested in his ambiguous presence or in the many popular myths surrounding him. It is not an homage to the writer, but to his work and its effect on the protagonist: Larita does not have to meet the person; she met his work, which has provoked and challenged her to become aware of her own situation, to explore her emotions, to see and understand her own life differently. "A man can be destroyed, but not defeated": this sentence on the blackboard is a rather unobtrusive introduction of the novel into the film, expressing the main theme at a time when neither the viewer nor the protagonist Larita is as yet aware of its implications.

A few scenes later Larita and her boyfriend Victor are explicitly introduced to the novel by Tomás, whose bookstore represents an inviting, sheltering world of its own. While he is looking for the book, the two exchange a first shy kiss, and while he is reading what he considers its extremely exciting opening sentences to them, their fingers tentatively touch. Thus, when Tomás comments, "see — what a beginning," their thoughts are not solely concentrated on the text. The special subtext this novel has thus acquired for them prompts Victor to present Larita with a copy. In that day's diary entry, Larita links the promise of a long journey, her beginning relationship with Victor, and the novel, which she is now starting to read.

Although her reading experience is crucial to the development of the film plot, Pérez and Royero reject a facile visualization of the novel, refusing to present and illustrate the images and associations the novel provokes in Larita. They include a number of extracts from the novel and employ various strategies, all expressing and emphasizing a great belief in Hemingway's text and in the power of the written word in the cinema. The text is foregrounded, while discreet images hint at contrasts and parallels.

The apparent disparity between the old fisherman and Larita's situation evident in the bookstore scene is nicely developed—and contradicted—in the first scene in which we see her reading the novel. The description of the old man's appearance contrasts strongly with a close-up of Larita's young face—her innocence underlined by the soft-focus effect of the mosquito net under which she is reading. But with the description of the fisherman's patched shirt, her face dissolves to an image of her threadbare school uniform blouse on the clothesline. As the blouse is too tattered to wear the following day, she is refused entry into school. She returns home and, in a conversation around the kitchen table, she reveals her plans to study literature and philosophy. Her words—and dreams—are met with incredulous and derisive laughter: for a female of the working class in Cuba in the 1950s, this ambition is highly impractical and totally unrealistic. This is cut to Larita reading, in voice-over, Santiago's dreams of Africa, of wide-open spaces, long golden and white beaches and headlands. The screen is black except for a dimly lit window through which Larita is seen sleeping with her head on the table. Then the camera pans slowly through the darkness to reveal the brightly illuminated *finca,* alluring but unattainable. The connection between the two worlds is made while the screen is completely dark, drawing particular attention to the text: "he knew it was too early in his dreams and went on dreaming." A tenuous, distantly observed link between the small house and the *finca* is established, while Larita's subjective associations and as yet vague dreams are implied, but not made explicit.

Reading the novel on the open porch in the following scene, Larita quotes the old man's thought that it is better to prepare for luck rather than just wait for it. This helps to convince her grandmother Josefa to sacrifice her precious earrings to get Larita another blouse. We see her doing this in the following sequence to Larita's voice-over: a bold mixture of sentences and phrases from the beginning of the novel, as if she were picking out passages recurring in her mind at this moment—the old man is setting out toward the open sea, full of resolution, expectation, and some hope to catch his big fish. This combination of images and words conveys a sense of movement and great elevation, of a new beginning; the impact of the words is so strong that Josefa's action, which represents a decisive development of the plot, seems quite casual and natural. The sequence also opens up the locations by contrasting street scenes of central Havana with the poor villge lanes, culminating in the image of Larita, off to school in her new homemade uniform, catching a glimpse of Hemingway leaving in his big limousine. The exposition is complete; the lonely search and struggle for the big fish has begun.

Larita goes on to quote Hemingway in her diary—"Now is the time to think of only one thing"—her single-minded purpose blocking out the serious problems at home. With school friends she visits the fishing village of Cojimar, and here she tells Victor the plot of the novel. She interprets the novel's ending in a quite hopeful way, telling Victor that at least the old man can still dream about the lions on the beach. He responds with laughter, saying that she is crazy—"tú y el viejo." Larita counters wistfully that he has no sense of imagination. Walking along the beach alone afterward, she encounters an old fisherman who seems to correspond perfectly to Hemingway's Old Man. Reality and fiction merge as Larita begins to imbue her surroundings with her literary imagination.

Her identification with the novel intensifies as things begin to go wrong. While waiting at the U.S. embassy for yet another interview, the old man's vow to say prayers and go on a pilgrimage if all goes well appears to become her own interior monologue and, like Santiago, she goes on to say Hail Marys. Similarly, in the following climactic scene, she stands alone at the Malecón looking out at the overcast sky merging with the stormy sea.

Facing probable defeat, she is reminded of and feels like Hemingway's character.

Needing a letter of recommendation from a "respectable person," she turns to Hemingway for help, but he is away in Africa, hunting. Helplessly and hopelessly, she interprets the novel more and more literally and personally, as a conversation with her sympathetic teacher shows: "He was alone, nobody helped him...I thought it happened to me...thank God, I'm not a fisherman." She feels deserted by the people around her and experiences a sense of loss similar to that of Santiago when the shark begins to devour his big fish. However, she is reminded by her teacher that the novel should not be read as a story of failure.

Thus her initial, rather dutiful reaction to authoritative influence and recommendation (if the teacher and the librarian think so, then the novel must be good, she says) changes to tentative interest and to conscious identification. She quotes "Hemingway" to her grandmother and in her diary, directly applying the text to her own situation: "every day is a new day," and "my big fish must be somewhere."

In entries to her diary she begins to reflect on her situation and these unaffected, personal conversations with herself, which we hear her read, correspond to Santiago's monologues in the novel—and reflect her development. The first entry in her diary reveals possibilities and hope (the scholarship and the friendship with Victor), the second one her changing dreams (a house, a blue car, and an elegant figure are already less important than a degree and becoming a writer like Hemingway). The many difficulties and obstacles she encounters (she feels more tolerated than accepted at her uncle's home, where there is little understanding for her ambitions; there is increasing pressure on her to leave school and start earning money; her ambitions and dreams provoke the dissolution of her friendship with Victor; and apparent irregularities in her papers due to her illegitimate birth endanger her chances for the scholarship) at first only increase her single-minded resolution (third entry), but gradually she becomes afraid of losing everything (fourth), and sees no hope (fifth). In the end she realizes that something has changed within her and, like Santiago, she accepts her defeat without feeling defeated: the dreams persist.

Although the novel is very much presented from Larita's point of view as one reader's experience, its reception is also mediated through three representatives of the world of adults. The progressive teacher Mrs. Martínez, who introduces its message, contradicts Larita's self-destructive interpretation and defends her rebellious students. The bookstore owner Tomás, who presents the novel and later sympathetically consoles her by reading her a passage about the little birds that have such a difficult time on the cruel sea, and quotes some advice that the old man gave one such bird: "Take a good rest—then go and take your chance like any man or bird or fish." The grandmother, Josefa, repeatedly comforts a distraught Larita: "Don't consider yourself defeated... Take all your might and sorrow and pride and confront things"—thus unconsciously voicing the novel's main message.

Hello Hemingway represents a near-complete shift from Hemingway's male world to a female perspective. Events are seen through the eyes of an ever-present female protagonist; female characters predominate. Male figures are secondary; their function and scope remain restricted. They are mainly characterized in relation to a particular issue or preoccupation: Victor and his struggle for a students' association, the uncle and his problems at work, the students and their differing positions regarding the association, the headmaster as the authoritarian representative of a repressive regime—even the more fully realized character of Tomás, who succeeds in passing on his admiration for Hemingway's work, while the person of Hemingway remains shadowy.

The female perspective is reinforced by the "domestic" spaces of home and school; their closed and static atmosphere predominates in the first part. Toward the end, Larita is caught up in an abortive student protest, stunned and surprised and almost unable to react and take sides: Victor and Dr. Martínez are arrested while she is dragged into the school building and the massive school gate—shown in extreme low angle—closes; she is shut in while shouting to be let out.

Yet Larita ventures outdoors into open spaces, reading on the porch, where her three crucial discussions with Josefa take place, and writing her diary in the backyard next to the pigeon loft, skirting the borders of the Hemingway hacienda—and claims, at first imaginatively, by reading the novel, then physically, a space that might be coded as "masculine," the sea. Her visit to the fishing village of Cojimar with school friends is above all an enjoyable outing to the place where the events of the novel took place. But later, standing at the Malecón and facing the sea on her own for the first time, she is shown in a long shot very much on her own — a lonely figure, slightly intimidated by this vast open stormy expanse.

There is growing awareness on Larita's part that facing the sea may be like facing life with its open possibilities — and a new readiness to do so; she eventually meets Miss Amalia, the scholarship coordinator, on equal terms, in a self-assured, slightly defiant attitude (over-the-shoulder shots underline this by making Miss Amalia appear slightly smaller). A distant confrontation with Hemingway in the last scene reminds her of the old fisherman who has lent shape to her imagined fictional hero, but she has now found an identity independent of either and will pursue her own dreams in her own way. She has intensively lived a transitional phase, moving from an initial reflection of herself in the mirror to a reflection of her situation in the novel, allowing her to go beyond the looking glass and reflect on her own situation. The story is left open for the viewer's intervention. It is the open ending of an open adaptation.

Hello Hemingway does not substitute Larita's images, or indeed those of the director, for our own. Because of the constant drawing attention to the process of adaptation and to the way in which various passages of the novel are inserted into the film, the viewer remains a potential reader. Both stories are emotionally involving and their skillful combination heightens that effect. At the same time, however, this confrontation of the two quite different plots allows some distance, an awareness that Larita is just one among so many others, thus pointing to the universal significance of both texts.

In *Hello Hemingway* careful attention is given to the use of colors to express the different narrative levels on which Larita's story develops. The everyday household scenes appear in realistic, ordinary colors, moving from a clear and luminous tonality in the first half to sharper contrasts and a more somber quality, in accordance with Larita's changing state of mind. Similarly, the extremely static camera, producing "flat" and "closed" images with little movement, is replaced by a hand-held camera, underlining the chaos and disorder when the uncle loses his job and returns home drunk and starts a fight. These scenes stand in contrast to the open spaces of Larita's dreamworld. Seen from a distance Hemingway's *finca* appears in sun-lit rich colors of tropical nature—on the two occasions when Larita actually crosses its border a curtain of rain is pouring down, creating a special intensity, setting it off from her other experiences. The protective world of the bookstore and the official world connected with the scholarship application are also characterized quite differently: warm ocher and orange colors resembling the light of a Havana sunset contrast sharply with "air-conditioned" cold blue and greyish colors, which extend to the costumes and seem to parody the harsh and cold Technicolor contrasts of numerous Hollywood films in the 1950s. These effects, which contribute greatly to the atmosphere of the story, were worked out in the planning stages and during the shooting, but remain quite unobtrusive.

Hemingway's gift was said to reside in the fact that he wrote "in the white space between the lines" (Aldous Huxley). Tomás in *Hello Hemingway* draws attention to this by echoing Hemingway's often-quoted comparison of the allusiveness of his style to an iceberg, only partly visible above the surface of the sea. His simple, direct style infers and implies meaning, suggesting rather than stating. There is no search for forced "poetic" effects or elaborate metaphors. Mayda Royero and Fernando Pérez have developed an equivalent cinematic style. The seeming simplicity of the *cine de prosa*[1] used in *Hello Hemingway* creates the conditions— or rather leaves space—for poetry to surface: the allusive poetry inherent in everyday life, in human attitudes and actions, in looks and smiles and frowns, in unexpected human warmth and *ternura*, in the grandmother pawning her earrings, in Larita's mother recalling her many sacrifices while her daughter reproaches her for not having provided her with a home and a father, in Larita's painful recognition of realities, in the very different ways she looks at her grandmother, at Miss Amalia, and at Hemingway at the end.

Fernando Pérez's primary intention as a filmmaker is to create "a cinema that provokes human and aesthetic emotions, moving the viewer to reflection."[2] *Hello Hemingway* provides a good illustration of such a "reflective cinema," one that considers the reflection of life in literature and thereby moves viewers to reflect on the ways in which the two are conjoined.

"I Stopped Reasoning and Began to Absorb": The Development of a Filmmaker

Just as Hemingway was not "merely" a writer, Fernando Pérez is more than a filmmaker. Like Hemingway, Fernando Pérez was trained in journalism. In 1976 he worked as a war correspondent in Angola (participating, among other things, in José Massip's film *Angola, victoria de la esperanza*). His experiences as a correspondent in Nicaragua shortly after the Sandinista revolution and his long conversations with experienced war correspondents there resulted in *Corresponsales de guerra*. The work of journalistic fiction, not unlike some of Hemingway's writings, earned Pérez the Casa de las Américas prize in 1981 for best testimonial writing.

Pérez, who was born in Havana in 1944, forms part of an intermediate generation of Cuban filmmakers and, like most of them, followed the usual stepping stones of starting as a production assistant, gaining experience doing newsreels, and producing documentaries, before making his first feature film in his forties. He entered ICAIC (Instituto Cubano de Arte e Industria Cinematográficos) in 1962, learning from and working with the founding generation of the postrevolution Cuban cinema, while continuing his university studies. In 1971 he was assistant director to Tomás Gutiérrez Alea for *Una pelea cubana contra los demonios*.[3]

To many Cubans Pérez is known as the creator of one of the most popular Cuban films, *Clandestinos*. The film enjoyed considerable success with the Cuban public—more than 1.5 million Cubans saw the film in the first few weeks alone—and it was met with enthusiasm on the part of critics as well. *Clandestinos*, like *Hello Hemingway*, is set in the 1950s. The films, however, present very different, almost complementary, situations of that time. *Clandestinos*, written by Jesús Díaz from an original idea by Fernando Pérez, is part heroic epic and part political thriller. The film deals with a chapter of the revolutionary history of the country that had hitherto been neglected: the struggle of urban underground guerrilla units against the Batista regime, chiefly aimed at supporting and creating publicity for the main struggle in the Sierra Madre, by hitting where it hurt (and embarrassed) the dictatorship most, in the big cities. These *clandestinos* are young and dedicated, and often sacrifice their lives for their ideals. *Hello Hemingway*, on the other hand, is about the quite unspectacular, unheroic everyday lives of ordinary people. Most people at that time were aware of the general situation, but not actively involved; they remained immersed in individual problems and preoccupied with their private dreams. It is a perfectly valid, human stance, says Pérez: "Having narrated the story of a youthful avant-garde who moved history, I also had to tell the story of the vast majority, and of myself and how I lived that time."

Yet, the division is not quite as clear-cut as this. The young "heroes" of *Clandestinos* appear very human, characters of flesh and blood with all their hopes and fears, problems and inhibitions, and basically very conventional: like everyone else they fall in love and would like to get married, if only circumstances permitted. As it is, the knowledge of impending torture and imminent death strengthens their emotions, intensifies their brief moments of happiness, and heightens the pitch of their laughter.

Fernando Pérez's first feature film is mainly concerned with the public history of the 1950s and the second fills in the more personal, autobiographical elements. It is a time to which he feels a special emotional affinity — the time of his youth — and the memory of this intensely experienced period, so important for his personal development and that of his community, seems to quicken his creative impulse. Very personal experiences and preoccupations led to Pérez's third feature film, *Madagascar,* an imaginative, fictional reflection of the author's relationship with his own children, and again, but this time very loosely, inspired by a literary text, the story "Beatles versus Duran Duran" by Mirta Yánez. Pérez creates a brief tale of the troubled relationship between a university teacher (Zaida Castellanos) and her adolescent daughter (Laura de la Uz), which also evokes the prevailing atmosphere of uncertainty in present-day Cuba. Private and public preoccupations and truths may appear less obviously connected, but have become even more meshed and certainly more complex.

Laura, the mother, is very much set in her own ways and has to come to terms with Laurita's unexpected changes and rapid developments. Laurita turns from electrified pop euphoria to extreme weltschmerz, from nature mysticism to religious fundamentalism, completely embracing each new faith and identity. At the end their roles are reversed: the daughter has returned to her studies, everything seems back to "normal," but her transformations have affected her mother, who, having taken her daughter's advice and looked at herself and her life, is beginning to change. Constantly moving from one house to another has not altered the static and stagnant realities around them, so both of them will finally set out for "Madagascar," an imaginary place summing up very disparate dreams and destinations. Laurita defines the place as "what I don't know," a departure implying a change, but also a challenge.

In a key scene Laura looks at photographs of Laurita as a child, while complaining that her daughter thinks only of herself, rejects all talk of political consciousness, and maintains that the only thing she is conscious of is that she has the right to think as she pleases. Coming across an old newspaper photo depicting a gigantic May demonstration in the 1960s, she tries to find herself in the large crowd. So what does she see looking back from the enormous distance time and changed circumstances have created? While she is scrutinizing the image, the multitude loses its contours, becomes nebulous, and disappears, revealing nothing but blurred spots: "¿Dónde estoy yo, Dios mío?" Dissatisfied with the private and public paralysis strongly evident in her present, she looks in vain for herself in the past—a time of revolutionary changes full of promise, political ideals, and euphoria.

This is a long way from the archive materials that Fernando Pérez and Jesús Díaz skillfully assembled in their first documentary, *Crónica de la Victoria* (1975), a half-hour montage of mass rallies with individual actions and reactions both presenting and representing a collective response to a general situation. It is not a chronicle of the revolution, but rather a moving testimony of the fervor and turbulence of its first few years, when self-realization seemed to lie in one's public role and function, when, as Díaz notes, "the demarcation line between social life and public life was difficult to make out, even if you had wanted to—history imposed itself with an incredible intensity" ("Das Ende der Revolution"). This is also evident in some of Pérez's other early documentaries, which testify that he did a number of newsreels for the *Noticiero Latinoamericano* and show a considerable influence of the Santiago Álvarez school in their effective juxtaposition of music, text, and picture to underline and communicate a political message. In *Camilo* (1982), for instance, extracts from letters, old newsreels and films, period music, and captions combine to an eloquent tribute to the legendary guerrilla leader Camilo Cienfuegos, who led the rebel army into Havana together with Che Guevara.

Thus there is a shift from *razonar* to *absorber*, from arguing collective causes in order to mobilize people's political consciousness to taking in, expressing, and reflecting on what is there and going on, prepared to see and express contradictions between the public and the private, encompassing both political awareness and personal preoccupations, both emotions and individual reflection. This attitude is perfectly illustrated in *Madagascar* by repeated shots of Laurita standing with her arms open on the top of high buildings, defying the vast abyss or, in one scene reminiscent of Larita in *Hello Hemingway*, the open sea. These culminate in a long shot of Havana, with the silhouettes of young people on top of every high-rise building, arms outstretched, chanting "Madagascar."

Pérez is clearly "inspired" by events taking place around him, both private experiences and public conditions, and reflects these in a personal story. Reality is his *materia prima*, and although literature is also a strong source of inspiration, as shown in *Hello Hemingway*, Pérez would share Gutiérrez Alea's view that literature interests him "like any other aspect of reality" (Chávez, 9). The story of *Hello Hemingway*, paralleling Hemingway's text, is largely based on autobiographical *vivencias*, his own and above all those of scriptwriter Mayda Royero. Royero grew up near Hemingway's *finca* in San Francisco de Paula, in a poor family, her uncle a policeman, her mother a servant—and she strove to learn and solicited a scholarship. The very format of *Madagascar* reflects realities in Cuba today: it is one of three loosely related, fifty-minute episodes that were going to be combined to create a feature-length film, the scarcity of resources being such that even for filmmakers of repute this represents the only strategy, and indeed a privileged opportunity, to be able to film at all.[4] After

Hello Hemingway, Pérez had to wait for three years until August 1993 to shoot the first takes of a film again.[5] *Madagascar* opens with close-ups of people moving slowly but steadily toward the camera, with graceful, regular, slightly swinging movements and serious, deeply concentrated, thoughtful faces. It takes a while for the viewer to realize that these are bicyclists in the streets of present-day Havana, where these pictures were shot cinema ve-rité-style. These people move slowly with considerable effort; their destination remains unknown. What may appear as a sim-ple, realistic depiction of everyday street life resonates more fully under the circumstances.

The wish to communicate with the public leads to a conscious choice of using a simple, direct cinematic language that effec-tively transmits basic (but not empty) emotions. But this simplic-ity is more apparent than real, comprising as it does a multitude of meanings, complexities, or indeed varieties of style.[6] *Clandes-tinos* is an action-packed story with strong emotions and a direct, linear development: very much a genre film, a political thriller told in the language of the action film as perfected by U.S. cin-ema. *Hello Hemingway* is more intimate, with mainly interior "ac-tion"; the story line and the character of the protagonist are more complex and developed. The structure of *Madagascar* is more com-plex still, but there is clearly an exposition, a conflict, and a solu-tion, so that viewers can create a story in their mind, and there are credible, "real" characters they can identify with. On the other hand, Laura claims to dream at night what happens to her dur-ing the day, so reality is not always easy to identify; recurring ac-tions and some locations have a distinctly dreamlike and at times nightmarish quality, but are presented in a disconcertingly matter-of-fact "realist" way: Laura and Laurita move from one house to the next; Laurita's friend and his relatives seem to be constantly chewing cabbage; the liberatingly open rooftop locations con-trast with the claustrophobic staff room at the university; Laura is officially honored for her distinguished work at a ceremony that takes place in an abandoned dilapidated factory area.

Fernando Pérez's commitment to communication is evidenced by his work as a film critic and a teacher.[7] He has taught film his-tory at the University of Havana and filmmaking at the Interna-tional School of Film and Television at San Antonio de los Baños, encouraging his students to experiment in order to develop their own individual styles. Pérez draws upon the work of a variety of directors in his teaching, including Sergei Eisenstein, Orson Welles, and Steven Spielberg, and in doing so demonstrates that "the popular" and "the intellectual" need not be contradictory. The choice of cinematic language depends on the story to be told. Traditional narrative codes need not be rejected; in fact, they can be employed in highly successful ways.

Of utmost importance to Pérez is for filmmakers to draw from their own reality. Pérez quotes Jorge Luis Sánchez, saying, "Queremos parecernos al tiempo que estamos viviendo: eso nos contagia, no ha venido por decreto," which sums up the common sentiment and impulse among a younger generation of filmmakers — and a preoccupation he shares — a rejection of ideological formulas and well-trodden routine paths to search for ways and forms to "absorb" contradictory Cuban realities.[8]

"All Styles Are Valid, What Must Be Rejected Are Formulas": A Cuban Context

When *Clandestinos* was presented in a Cuban cultural workshop in the Swiss town of Biel in 1990, quite a few spectators (including myself) found their expectations thwarted. Anticipating a "Cuban" film, we were surprised by the story of young revolutionaries in prerevolutionary Cuba presented in a cinematic language that did not seem very "Cuban." Moreover, we had organized a large selection of Cuban films to be shown in various cinemas of the town to counter the overwhelming predominance of U.S. films, and here was a Cuban director who freely admitted in a personal presentation of his film that he liked and admired good U.S. films. A year later spectators viewing *Hello Hemingway* appeared bewildered that such a sensitive study of an individual should come out of socialist country. What, then, is a "Cuban" film?

Hello Hemingway is certainly very much rooted in Cuban reality; it presents a recognizably Cuban story with human beings of flesh and blood and describes their lives with great accuracy and authenticity, with respect and tenderness. It is not merely a question of obvious surface elements of *cubanía*, such as dialogues interspersed with snatches of song, surprising poetic diction, political jokes, or abrupt changes of mood, nor of paying close attention to period detail in the sets and of shooting the film in the actual locations, though this certainly contributes to an authentic atmosphere. It is not just the streets of Havana, the beach at Cojimar, and Hemingway's *finca* that are real enough; even the interior scenes in Larita's home were filmed in a small house next to the *finca*. Impressive acting also contributes, above all the astounding performance of Laura de la Uz, a nineteen-year-old student who had never been involved in cinema and who had not passed the entrance exam for acting school. Yet, she becomes, in the words of Mayda Royero, "the soul of the film." But what stands out above all is the director's attitude of respect, affection, even tenderness toward his characters, with all their hopes and illusions and contradictions—he never ridicules their sentiments—and the sincerity with which these are presented. "In the feature films that I've made," states Pérez, "I have not started by saying I am going to make a film that tells of Cuba or of the sentiment of being Cuban ... If I have made films it is to tell personal experiences, obsessions that preoccupy me, and that I think may interest others."

Thus the Cuban elements are inherent, and are perceived as such by a Cuban audience. Pérez notes that the Cuban public has seen *Clandestinos* as "very much its own film—although it contains stylistic elements that are not new and are similar to those in other, including foreign, films." Although very much an action-genre film, *Clandestinos* contains a variety of idiosyncratic touches, especially in its lyrical scenes in which the female parts are uncharacteristically stronger than the conventions of the genre would allow. Still, a non-Cuban audience might find Pérez's reclaiming of traditional narrative codes very "un-Cuban," especially if their expectations are shaped by the few well-known classics of Cuban cinema that they may have had the chance to see: *Memorias del subdesarrollo* (1968), *De cierta manera* (*One Way or Another*, Sara Gómez, 1974), possibly *Lucía* (1968), and above all Santiago Álvarez's documentaries of the 1960s, with their philosophy of cinema as intervention, of creating new ways of seeing, expressing a new revolutionary self. These films were indeed exemplary; an insistence on their "model" character, however, does not take into account that Alea, Humberto Solás, and Álvarez went on to make a considerable number of films in varied styles.

Pérez is fond of citing E. M. Tomlinson's familiar words, "We don't see things the way they are but rather the way we are," emphasizing the importance of being aware of our own expectations and limitations, our own culturally defined attitudes.

That one can be destroyed but not defeated is not only the "super objetivo" (Pérez) of *Hello Hemingway*, but relevant for all of Pérez's feature films. Their open endings show possibilities and openings for the protagonists as individuals, whose transformations enable them to go on living and struggling, provided they retain the ability to dream. Nereida, the pregnant girl who survives at the end of *Clandestinos*, is visibly shaken and marked by the terrible experiences she has undergone, but in her last look to the camera there is an affirmation of life that transcends her expression of suffering and mourning. In *Hello Hemingway* Larita faces the old fisherman first and foremost as a grown-up individual, whose experience has made her understand the significance of that sentence she saw chalked up on the school blackboard, and not as part of a "grander design" representing nation or youth. In *Madagascar* mother and daughter are pushing their bicycles in the long tunnel that leads underneath the bay of Havana, together with numerous other people, but they are not walking toward a light at the end of the tunnel: they are simply on their way, facing new uncertainties and possibilities, apparently confident that there is a way out eventually. An additional take before the final credits shows a long train against the dilapidated factory area seen before; its steady, painfully slow movement toward an unknown destination recalls the opening shots of the cyclists in the streets of Havana. This is not facile optimism, and the director would hesitate to call it hope. In *Hello Hemingway*, and to an even greater degree in *Madagascar*, the individual's power to change is an inherent and explicit part of the plot; thus, it is not possible to instrumentalize Hemingway's survival code as an intransigent ideological appeal to "resist" in the face of overwhelming difficulties in present-day Cuba. These films hint strongly at the sheer infinity of "endings" and openings that even such a situation as that of present-day Cuba offers to the individual. As Pérez says, "In my films there will always be a nearly inexpressible sentiment that human beings—and the values that define them—will invariably have another opportunity."

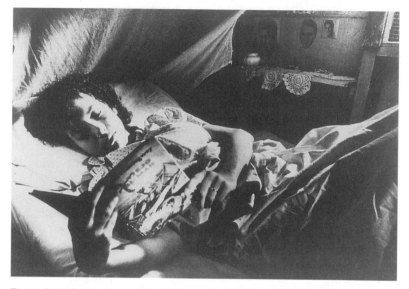

Fig. 1. In *Hello Hemingway,* Larita (Laura de la Uz) reads *The Old Man and the Sea* in her room decorated with cutouts of Elvis.

Fig. 2. Larita models her new dress for the scholarship interview.

Fig. 3. The revolutionary student organization confronts Batista supporters.

Fig. 4. Laurita in *Madagascar* facing the open sea.

Notes

I am grateful to Ann Marie Stock for her guidance in developing, organizing, and writing this essay.

1. In a very personal discussion of poetry in film and reality in "Un caracol dormido" (*Cine cubano*, 137), Pérez quotes Eric Rohmer's assertion that there is a "prosaic narrative cinema in which poetry is present, not affected, but appearing without having been looked for." Pérez sees such a *cine de prosa* exemplified in Adolfo Aristarains's *Un lugar en el mundo*, but it applies equally to *Hello Hemingway*.

2. Pérez's comments, unless otherwise noted, are from a series of conversations that have taken place over the past few years.

3. Pérez's intermediate position is underlined by the fact that in 1991 his own assistant director for *Hello Hemingway* and *Madagascar*, the talented young filmmaker Jorge Luis Sánchez, made the documentary *El cine y la memoria*, which is based on interviews with Alea and contrasts his classic *Memorias del subdesarrollo* with present-day contradictions and shows the continuing relevance of Alea's exemplary stance. Sánchez is a founding member of the Asociación Hermanos Saiz, which, since 1986, has been instrumental in supporting *cine aficionado* and young Cuban filmmakers outside the strictures of ICAIC. His documentaries have allowed people on the margins of society to express themselves: Havana *friquis*, adolescents with different views and lifestyles, in *Un pedazo de mí* (1989); people living in a slum area, which the final shot reveals to be practically in the middle of Havana, voicing their preoccupations in *El Fanguito* (1990); the little-known provincial *trovador* Raúl Torres in *Atrapando espacios* (1993–94), conveying the feeling of being young in Cuba today.

4. *Quiéreme y verás* by Daniel Díaz Torres, *Melodrama* by Rolando Díaz, and *Madagascar* all depict life in present-day Havana and were originally intended to be released together under the ambiguous title *Prognóstico del tiempo*. Production difficulties and, in the case of the outspoken farcical comedy *Melodrama*, political pressure led to different completion dates, so that at festivals the three episodes have usually been shown (and have indeed received prizes) separately. In 1995 *Madagascar* and *Quiéreme y verás* were commercially released as a double feature in some European countries.

5. Ironically, this amounted to practically "blind" filming; the allowed shooting time was four weeks and the rushes took fifteen days to return from the laboratory in Caracas.

6. For example, in the short documentary *Omara* (1983), a tribute to the popular Cuban singer Omara Portuondo using mainly personal testimony, there is a moving introduction telling the incredible love story of her parents: what sounds like a soap opera story is presented in the style of a *foto-novela*, in beautiful, slow-moving black-and-white images, allowing an emotional buildup to Omara's own story that is both efficient and effective. The short *foto-novela* sequence works and does not seem out of place because it is perfectly in tune with the actual events it relates, as well as with the songs that follow. Neither parody nor caricature, it is simply another narrative approach that combines emotionally involving and distancing effects.

7. For an early example of Pérez's work as a critic, see "Un film dialéctico y partidario," his review of *Memorias del subdesarrollo* in *Pensiamento crítico* 42 (1970). It is also included in *Alea — una retrospectiva crítica*, edited by Ambrosio Fornet (Havana: Letras Cubanas, 1987. 103–11), and in English in Tomás Gutiérrez Alea and Edmondo Desnoes, *Memories of Underdevelopment* (New Brunswick, N.J.: Rutgers Univ. Press, 1990. 227–31). In his review of Alea's film, Pérez stresses the active participation demanded from the spectator, praises the "free, open, clear" structure, characterizes the protagonist as a "being without possibilities," and prefers to speak of a "collaboration" between the author of the novel and the film director rather than of an adaptation. Even such a brief enumeration of points reveals the extent to which Fernando Pérez was marked by *Memorias*, the film he still considers to be the masterpiece of Cuban cinema.

8. Numerous film and video exercises made under Pérez's guidance testify to this. Some outstanding examples from 1993 include *Crunch* by Alvaro Silva Wuth (Chile), *Los que se quedaron* (*Those Who Stayed*) by Benito Zambrano (Spain), and *Este tiempo tiene tu nombre* (*This Time Bears Your Name*) by Edgar Pinzón (Colombia). All three videos have a clear "then-now" structure, with a communal past full of life and ideals and movement, and a present in which individuals have to redefine their place — the filmmakers registering, recording, "absorbing" that great contrast and difficult change.

Works Cited

Alea, Tomás Gutiérrez, and Edmondo Desnoes. *Memories of Underdevelopment*. New Brunswick, N.J., and London: Rutgers Univ. Press, 1990.

Chávez, Rebeca. "Tomás Gutiérrez Alea: entrevista filmada — entre fresa y chocolate." *La Gaceta de Cuba* (September–October 1993): 9.

Díaz, Jesús. "Das Ende der Revolution." *Wochenzeitung* 5 (31 January 1992).

Fornet, Ambrosio, ed. *Alea — una retrospectiva crítica*. Havana: Letras Cubanas, 1987.

Hernández, Jonathan Allen. "*Hello Hemingway*, breve instante de cine cubano." Argentina: *La Provincia* (19 March 1992).

Nodarse, Frank Padrón. "Hello Hemingway: Que los sueños, sueños son..." *Cine Cubano* 132 (1991).

Pérez, Fernando. "No creo en los premios, pero sí en mi película." *Granma* (12 December 1990).

———. "Un caracol dormido." *Cine Cubano* 137 (1993).

———. "Un film dialéctico y partidario." In *Alea — una retrospectiva crítica*. Ed. Ambrosio Fornet. Havana: Letras Cubanas, 1987. 103–11.

———. "Veo al cine cubano como soy." Typescript. 1992.

Chapter 8

Román Chalbaud: The "National Melodrama" on an Air of Bolero

Paulo Antonio Paranaguá

(translated by Tracy Devine)

In 1975, after years of petitioning, the Asociación Nacional de Autores Cinematográficos (ANAC) succeeded in obtaining protective legislation and state financing for Venezuelan filmmakers. As a stipulation for that funding, film exhibitors were required to show at least twelve Venezuelan productions per year. The first of these "funded" films was Román Chalbaud's *Sagrado y obsceno* (*Sacred and Obscene*, 1975), which was such a success that exhibitors soon needed little incentive to support the national films. The motion pictures proved to create their own audience. As one of the first artists to build such a following, Chalbaud's role in the development of the Venezuelan film industry has been decisive.

In the following essay, Paulo Antonio Paranaguá investigates the origins and evolution of one of Venezuela's best-known and most influential filmmakers. The author takes us to the 1940s movie house where a young Chalbaud admired and absorbed what would later be called the "golden age" of Mexican cinema. He then leads us through six of the director's most notable productions, giving special attention to *Caín adolescente* (*Adolescent Cain*, 1959), Chalbaud's first independent work. Paranaguá sees *Cain* as both a cornerstone and a springboard; with it we can examine the maturation of Chalbaud's work without losing sight of its theatrical origins. With *Cain* as our reference point, we are able to appreciate the development of a cinematic genre with national consciousness, a sociopolitical agenda, and widespread popular appeal. —*Trans.*

> Hay que darse cuenta
> que todo es mentira
> que nada es verdad.
> Hay que vivir el momento feliz
> hay que gozar lo que puedas gozar
> porque sacando la cuenta en total
> la vida es un sueño
> y todo se va.
> La realidad es nacer y morir
> porque llenarnos de tanta ansiedad
> todo no es más que un eterno sufrir
> el mundo está hecho sin felicidad.[1]
> Arsenio Rodríguez, "La vida es un sueño" (bolero)

In Venezuela, the year 1959 marks a turning point for two important reasons. First, at the Cannes film festival, Margot Benacerraf's *Araya* carries off two awards: the International Critic's Prize, ex aequo with *Hiroshima mon amour* (*Hiroshima, My Love*), and the Superior Technique Commission's Prize for photography, attracting first-time attention to a cinema virtually unknown to the rest of the world stage.[2] A few months later, another feature film appears on the screens of Caracas: *Caín adolescente* (*Adolescent Cain*), also by a first-time filmmaker, Román Chalbaud. At the same time, several other cinematographies begin to undergo a transformation, breaking with the past and trying, in no uncertain terms, to "discover themselves." The second and perhaps more significant major event of 1959 is that Venezuela discovers democracy; unfortunately, the new condition is not yet sufficient to ensure cultural advancement.

At first glance, Benacerraf and Chalbaud are diametrically opposed, as *Araya* and *Adolescent Cain* appear to have little in common. The only similarity is the directors' shared desire to create film in a country lacking a strong cinematic tradition. Born in Caracas in 1926, Margot Benacerraf was educated at the Institut des Hautes Études Cinématographiques (Cinematographic Institute of Higher Education, IDHEC) in Paris, after first completing university studies in philosophy and the humanities. Born in Mérida, in 1931, Chalbaud is a "country boy" who arrived in the capital when he was six years old, a "learning-disabled" yet "gifted" autodidact.

In addition to the different types of training they received, Benacerraf and Chalbaud were also influenced by different aesthetic models. In the artful tradition of Flaherty, Grierson, and Figueroa, Benacerraf's *Araya* takes on a classical lyricism, even in the text borrowed from Pierre Seghers. The film makes its mark on the future of creation documentaries, without refusing reconstruction or mise-en-scène. *Adolescent Cain*, on the other hand, integrates documentary images into a predominantly fictional drama, demonstrating indisputable debt to popular Mexican film, despite a noticeably modern inclination in regards to the film's shooting. Despite their early successes, everything seems to oppose the future of the 1959 debutantes. Margot Benacerraf, having held the rights to Gabriel García Márquez's *Eréndira* for several years, would end her directing career prematurely. She continues, however, to play a considerable role in the cultural domain of cinematography. As for Román Chalbaud, he would become the most prolific contemporary film director in Venezuela.

In some ways, *Adolescent Cain* is a "false start" for Chalbaud's career, as the time is not yet ripe for a production with such minimal continuity. During the 1960s, cinema and guerrilla seem to bandy compliments in Venezuela, both literally and figuratively. Filmmakers stick to the documentary of political denunciation, sympathizing with the revolutionaries, sharing their hopes and illusions. Yet, at the same time, producing this type of cinema supposes a kind of volunteerism and harassing tactics against the established powers, which transforms directors into true partisans. *Adolescent Cain* is a hybrid film, announcing the "new" while poking fun at the "old." As a work of transition for Venezuelan cinema and for the author himself, the film is historically and artistically significant.

At this point in his career, Román Chalbaud is already "some-one." With his friends, Isaac Chocrón and José Ignacio Cabrujas, he begins to establish a Venezuelan theater that is noteworthy for its authentically national subjects, dramaturgy, and language. Chalbaud also benefits from an important experiment working in television.[3] Chalbaud is first and foremost a playwright, but his film culture is nevertheless quite deep. Although he grew up watching Hollywood movies, like most people in the hemisphere, he was also influenced by the "golden age" of the Mexican film industry. The melodrama, at the height of its popularity, is the principal connection between Bette Davis and María Félix, Charles Boyer and Jorge Negrete, all of whom Chalbaud, a voracious spectator, admires. He demands, above all, to be moved, upset, surprised, to share the feelings of the characters on screen. Although he has ample opportunity to admire Mexican director Emilio Fernández, Chalbaud's own experience will make him a strictly urban filmmaker.

The depth of Chalbaud's relationship with Mexican cinema goes beyond the impressions of a frequent moviegoer. Loans from Argentina and Mexico funded Venezuela's tentative industrial ephemera while the Bolívar Film Studios were being established in Caracas. (Their principal success was, appropriately, *La balandra Isabel llegó esta tarde* [*The Balandra Isabel Arrived This Afternoon*, 1950].) In this context, Román Chalbaud becomes an assistant to Mexican director Víctor Urruchúa, aiding in the production of *Seis meses de vida* (*Six Months to Live*, 1951) and *Luz en el páramo* (*Light on the Plains*, 1953), and completing an informal apprenticeship on the set.

Chalbaud's first independent work, *Adolescent Cain*, includes many elements of the golden age Mexican films: melodramatic climaxes, bar and the cabaret locations, typical characters, gestures and forms, and, above all, the young girl, who is seduced, abandoned, and continuously rejected because of her loose morals.

Although it draws heavily on the Mexican cinematic tradition, *Adolescent Cain* is full of other intricacies. In an effort to "lighten up" his play, the author opens the film with documentary images (the set includes a church where amulets and other religious objects are sold) and incorporates the action of descriptive outside scenes that reveal shantytowns perched on the hills of Caracas. In the direction of these rapid shots, the angles or chosen movements, the presence of women and children, and the inclusion of "authentic" decor (an arena, an improvised baseball camp, a garage), there is a certain vitality of Italian neorealism, common in Latin America at the time. In this respect, the film corresponds to its contemporaries, announcing a renovation of and a rupture with a tradition to which it otherwise adheres.

The principal weakness of *Adolescent Cain* stems from its originality; that is, the author's personal universe is entirely present, but the cinematic adaptation leaves a lot to be desired. The previously mentioned "openings" toward outside locations offer an unedited version of a metropolis that is clearly beginning to go mad. A sequence at the Coney Island amusement park introduces moments of visual brilliance (which, unfortunately, become dated rather quickly), but more important, a nocturnal atmosphere that will progressively imbue the action itself, as well as a musical piece fully retained in the final edition. Chalbaud attempts to use images, sounds, and music as transitional mechanisms in *Adolescent Cain*, but his effort fails, at times, to produce the necessary continuity. In addition to technical problems, the film suffered from the lack of material resources and various unexpected turns of fortune. The fifty-nine-day-long shooting took more than two years to complete, a fact that is apparent to the spectator. In light of such unfavorable conditions, the final product is nonetheless a remarkable accomplishment.

Adolescent Cain reveals that "Chalbaud-adapter" does not yet know how to deceive or distance himself from "Chalbaud-author." He does not know how to eliminate or rewrite dialogues, how to edit monologues, or how to arrange the dramatic, intersecting lines of his story. As a result, the audience can easily lose the plot or arrive at an erroneous ending. The film's interpretation, entrusted in large part to the same actors who had previously created their work on stage, pushes the film too much toward its theatrical origins.

Despite these problems, *Adolescent Cain* reveals, at a very early stage, certain traits that would later be considered characteristic of Chalbaud: the frequent fusion of Christian forms and references, the extreme opposition between the lost paradise of the countryside and the hell of the city, the weight of syncretism and folk-lore (the Christmas songs, the masques from the Carnival), and, above all, the sensitive and sympathetic choice of places and pop-ular characters.[4] Another curious aspect of this transitional work is the contradiction between the author's apparent intentions and the inclination suggested by his dramaturgic options. Román Chal-baud opposes, as a matter of principle, numerous prejudices: he manifestly defends Juana's right to sexual pleasure, despite the reticence of her son Juan, who initially objects to his mother's black, fugitive lover, Encarnación.[5] The author rejects the moralism that victimizes the young, pregnant Carmen and lauds Juan's de-cision to accept responsibility for a child who is not necessarily his.[6] But, as the melodrama has motives that sometimes lack rea-son, the author hurls the naive Juana into hell, condemning her to death, to be trampled by a panicked church crowd.[7] Suggested from the beginning, the end is presented in an elliptical form. Anyway, Juana is punished because she did not wait for her first boyfriend, who was equally attached to nature and country values.

By a stroke of fate, Román Chalbaud's career and Venezuelan cinema rebound with his next feature film, *La quema de Judas* (*Burn-ing the Judas*, 1974).[8] Chalbaud's biting humor has a major role in his second film, though it was hardly evident in *Adolescent Cain*. The style is more relaxed, the language and the characters lose their artificially popular quality, and perhaps most important, the dramaturgy becomes truly cinematic and no longer appears bor-rowed from theater. Yet, as with his other major productions of the time— *Sagrado y obsceno* (*Sacred and Obscene*, 1975) and *El pez que fuma* (*The Smoking Fish*, 1976) — *Burning the Judas* is an adap-tation of one of Chalbaud's plays. Although the film version of *Adolescent Cain* respected the three acts of its theatrical predecessor ("Christmas," "Carnival," and "Easter"), Chalbaud's later adapta-tions would be less faithful to the structure of his original text. If ambivalence or ambiguity exists, it is now implicit in his outlook or internalized by his characters.

Constructed through successive flashbacks and multiple per-spectives, the protagonist of *Burning the Judas* symbolizes the evolution of Chalbaud's work. Carmona, a cop who is murdered by guerrillas and mourned as a martyr for his government, iron-ically proves to have been a con man.[9] Carmona possesses the traits of Miguel Angel Landa, Chalbaud's star actor and associ-ate producer. In many respects, the "marginal" or "delinquent" of society will become the antihero par excellence of the Venezue-lan cinema, which descended from its rustic utopia without be-ing able to share in the nouveau riche self-sufficiency and self-satisfaction of petroleum and corruption.

In coming down from the hills of Caracas toward the popu-lated districts, Chalbaud's world does not lose its roots; instead, it gains universality. This theater man obviously knows his clas-sics, especially the Hispanic tradition of the short playlet, the *cos-tumbrismo,* and the picaresque. In one comical scene, he ridicules the capital city's bourgeois belief in diverse forms of mysticism; however, he himself remains equally attached to the dramatic use of religious forms, symbols, rites, and ceremonies. Moreover, compared to titles as explicit as *Adolescent Cain* and *Burning the Judas, Sacred and Obscene* conveys an excited tension that amplifies the author's inspiration. *Burning the Judas* is not satisfied with evoking the ever-popular guerrilla drama; it also questions offi-cial manipulations and, at a deeper level, a society based on lies and hypocrisy.

Sacred and Obscene is the first feature film to benefit from state funds. Finally, the prosperity resulting from Venezuelan petrodol-lars will give film production some much-needed continuity, and for the first time Venezuela will be able to count on a large staff of technicians and filmmakers. The public is so supportive of the enhanced production that many other young directors and pro-ducers are—temporarily—able to share in the profit within a single, local market. Chalbaud's films are responsible for a large part of this success. *Sacred and Obscene* reopens the gaping wounds left by guerrilla warfare and the repression,[10] but also pursues the exploration of places preferred by the director in his descrip-tion of the little people: the boarding house, "Ecce Homo," with its bizarre combination of tenants,[11] the cantina, the barrio, the pop-ular quarter. Unlike many Venezuelan and contemporary Latin American filmmakers, Chalbaud is not very interested in the mid-dle classes or the petit bourgeois; he prefers to work with more marginalized characters.

Where *Burning the Judas* relies on a dismal wake scene, *The Smoking Fish* takes up with the funeral ceremonies for a pimp.

Buñuelian in its grotesque procession of dwarfs, blind men, thugs, and other riffraff, the scene clearly demonstrates Chalbaud's admiration for Mexican cinema. A true classic of the Venezuelan "boom" of the 1970s, *The Smoking Fish* can be viewed as a throwback to the old cabaret films popular in 1940s Mexico.[12] Though black and white has given way to color, and the fake luxury has been replaced by real kitsch, the prostitutes, the metaphoric microcosm, the boleros, and the tangos are still there. The songs are more than mere illustration or digression, and actually work as a source of dramatic energy. The use of music is a constant stroke of inspiration, an appeal to the complicity of a public well acquainted with the familiar repertoire. The direction breaks with the flatly naturalist treatment of "marginal society" dominating Venezuelan screens at the time. The Smoking Fish brothel is the site of the inevitable showdown for power, a struggle that takes place, of course, on the madam's bed.[13] La Garza, played magnificently by Hilda Vera (another of Chalbaud's star actresses), has a line deserving of an anthology of devouring women, descendants of María Félix:[14] "I haven't had men, I've had meters of men, kilometers of men, motorways of men."

Useless to continue with macroanalysis, with metaphor reflecting the entire nation, because the man behind the camera concerns himself with the country just as he expresses himself through multiple behaviors and individual mentalities. A single mention of Maracaibo is enough to remind one of the oil industry and its short-lived bonanza. Of course, the end product is a collective portrait, "marginal society," identifying itself with a nation that pretends to believe in its own respectability. Marked by sympathy and humor, the portrait is willingly subjective. Although the drama and tragedy of Venezuela are often simplified in political and sociological rhetoric, Chalbaud presents his country with intricacy and ironic distance. His vision is a "national melodrama" that will not be a dupe of its own mechanisms. The director sets up *The Smoking Fish* in excess from the very beginning with a shocking opening scene depicting the distribution of new mattresses.[15] This type of apparent realism within a sordid framework often hides a repressed expressionism. Although the unusual secondary characters have hardly any dramaturgical justification, their presence intensifies the visual delirium: the cashier spends his free time at the telescope studying flying saucers; La Garza's brother, a cripple, guards the entrance to the corridor leading to the prostitutes' calling rooms. To parallel this grotesque dimension, the relationship between the two pimps arguing over rank is full of subtleties. A cocaine trip on a beach suggests a lost nature-placenta: the mother and the whore, archetypes of Mexican cinema, are confounded and no longer discernible.[16] Once more, urban chaos is rejected.

Carmen, la que contaba 16 años (*Carmen, Who Was 16 Years Old,* 1978) is a very free adaptation of Mérimée's classic, situated in the modern-day Venezuelan port of La Guaira.[17] The film helps us to understand better Chalbaud's relationship with some cultural models. Behind Mérimée's tragedy, the filmmaker fleshes out the Hispanic heritage of the melodrama. Under Bizet's music, Chalbaud enhances the bolero, musical expression par excellence of the melodrama, again reminiscent of the golden age of the Mexican film industry. The centrality of the music in the film emphasizes emotion, perception, and memory over dialogue and words. Chalbaud adopts melodies, forms, and figures easily recognized by his public because they belong to popular culture (either profane or religious culture). It would not be fitting to label this attention to popular culture as a generational characteristic, because even younger Latin American directors share Chalbaud's musical tastes. This group includes both men[18] and a number of women who appear relatively unaffected by the incorrigible misogyny of this musical tradition. This is the case of Mexican María Novaro (*Danzón,* 1990), Chilean Valeria Sarmiento (*El hombre cuando es hombre* [*When a Man's a Man*], 1982), and Venezuelan Marilda Vera, whose film *Señora Bolero* (1990) simultaneously explores the meandering of national history and the skein of national feelings. Like any other composers from the grand epoch, Marilda Vera and Román Chalbaud would affirm that "the truth is located in the bolero." And too bad for the ideologies that claim to dispute the destiny of humanity.

La oveja negra (*The Black Sheep,* 1987), Chalbaud's most uncontested success after *The Smoking Fish,* begins with a procession of Easter penitents (in reality, a bunch of conniving thieves) and ends on a contemporary and apocalyptic variation on the Nativity, one that could be lived by the Third World poor. The thieves, in a constant struggle for rank, live together in a utopian commune directed by a strong woman and a vaguely mystical magician. Their old abandoned movie theater of a home resembles a modern version of Ali Baba's cave.

At times, Chalbaud surrenders too much to chance, giving his films a certain sense of irregularity. For this reason, the 1986 production of *Manon*—which was similar to *Carmen* in its parodic intentions—did not resemble the earlier film's ability to reveal its many levels. The director had been caught in his own trap. In *The Black Sheep*, on the other hand, Chalbaud accomplishes what is, without a doubt, his most masterful work. Remarkable in detail, interpretation, photography, and music, and equipped with an extraordinary set, the film is a poetic construction in which one rediscovers Buñuelian accents and an original vision.

Román Chalbaud commands respect for many reasons. He paved the way for cinema in his country several times. He succeeded in transposing to the screen a personal universe, a catalyst for the chemistry of *costumbrismo*, humor, religiosity, affectivity, parody, and music. In the quest for a popular cinema, one shared by so many directors throughout Latin America, he did not merely appropriate an artificial facade. Instead, Chalbaud fuels himself with tradition, cultivates it with sincerity and, at the same time, transcends it, as is becoming to a true creator. Chalbaud revived the old foundation of pop culture, in which the melodrama and the bolero slumbered. In doing so, he demonstrated that, like the filmmakers who had fascinated him as a child, he too could express emotion, win approval, and inspire awe in his audience.

Notes

1. One must realize that everything is a lie, that nothing is true. One must seize the happy moment and enjoy whatever is possible because in the end life is a dream and everything disappears. Reality is to be born and to die because we fill ourselves up with so much angst, everything is no more than eternal suffering, the world is made without happiness.

2. The only precedent, also at Cannes, was the photography award given to Carlos Hugo Christensen's 1950 film *La balandra Isabel llegó esta tarde* (*The Balandra Isabel Arrived This Afternoon*).

3. Chalbaud was a television pioneer, becoming the "artistic director" of Televisión Nacional after only five years of working at the station. He was also the first Venezuelan to initiate television programming with actors (Naranjo, 20).

4. The film tells the story of Juana and her son, Juan, who move from the country to the city, where they encounter much of the banality and wretchedness of urban life. Juan seeks out an apprenticeship with Matías, who becomes like an older brother to him, and introduces him to an already formed circle of friends. One of these friends is Carmen, the young girl who becomes Juan's obsession.

5. Encarnación is wrongly accused of murder and hides out in Juana's house for more than a month while the police conduct a search for him. Although he is eventually found guilty of the crime, he never behaves like a criminal; instead, he demonstrates great virtue through his sincere and selfless relationship with Juana and her son (Naranjo, 45).

6. The child's father turns out to be Juan's closest friend, Matías, who had treated Juan as a younger brother, "protecting" him from the turbulence of city life.

7. Juana and Matías visit the church together in an effort to reconnect with God and understand the complexity and unhappiness of their lives. When someone falsely alarms the congregation of a fire in the church, Juana becomes the victim of the terrified crowd.

8. In the interim period, there had been one "fake" feature film—that is, the three sketches of *Cuentos para mayores* (*Stories for Adults*, 1963)—and a short film, *Chévere o La victoria de Wellington* (*Fabulous or the Wellington Victory*, 1971).

9. At Carmona's wake, several people appear to bid him a final farewell. Each attendant reminisces about a different episode shared with the dead man, thereby revealing the policeman's crooked past.

10. The film tells the story of Pedro Zamora, an ex-guerrilla who returns to Caracas after a ten-year absence to avenge the deaths his wartime comrades. Zamora seeks to eliminate Diego Sánchez, who commanded the political group responsible for the assassination of the young guerrillas.

11. An ex-guerrilla, single women and their illegitimate children, a young revolutionary, a mistress, and a soda vendor. None of the tenants have anything in common; they seem to be brought together by a strange twist of fate.

12. The film centers around the dynamics of personal relationships as they occur in The Smoking Fish, a bordello located in the outskirts of Caracas. The result is a "grotesque metaphor for the social structures of power in Venezuela" (Naranjo, 106).

13. The two pimps fight for "the favours of the ageing madame, their rights to her body and to her empire. Shots are fired, she is killed by mistake, and her funeral is gloriously accompanied by the tango 'Sus ojos se cerraron'" (Her eyes closed) (King, 220).

14. Perhaps the best-known actress of 1940s Mexico, María Félix emerged as a new type of woman and broke the virgin/whore mold prevalent at the time in the cinema industry.

15. When the administrator of the bordello approves a "mattress change" for all inhabitants, a jubilant celebration ensues. In the street, neighborhood children play around the bonfire made up of the flaming old, worn-out mattresses.

16. After sharing a cocaine trip on the beach, La Garza and one of the pimps share childhood memories, comparing remembrances of their mothers. What initially appears to develop between the two characters is a mother-son relationship, which soon becomes twisted and confused when they sleep together in their inebriated state.

17. Carmen is a young woman whose relationships with men tell the story of civil war in a Latin American country. Her lovers include a revolutionary guerrilla leader, a former member of the National Guard, and an apolitical bullfighter. Jealousy leads Carmen to her death, when her jealous boyfriend discovers that she is in love with the torero. He brutally stabs Carmen to death while her true love—simultaneously engaged in a bullfight—looks on from the ring.

18. For example, Paul Leduc from Mexico and Argentine Fernando Solanas.

Filmography

Caín adolescente (*Adolescent Cain*, 1959), *Cuentos para mayores* (*Stories for Adults*, 1962), *Chévere o La victoria de Wellington* (*Fabulous or the Wellington Victory*, 1971), *La quema de Judas* (*Burning the Judas*, 1974), *Sagrado y obsceno* (*Sacred and Obscene*, 1975), *El pez que fuma* (*The Smoking Fish*, 1976), *Carmen, la que contaba 16 años* (*Carmen, Who Was 16 Years Old*, 1978), *El rebaño de los ángeles* (*The Angels' Flock*, 1978), *Bodas de papel* (*Paper Wedding*, 1979), *Cangrejo* (*Crab*, 1982), *La gata borracha* (*The Drunk Cat*, 1983), *Cangrejo II* (1984), *Ratón de ferretería* (*Hardware Store Mouse*, 1985), *Manon* (1986), *La oveja negra* (*The Black Sheep*, 1987), *Cuchillos de fuego* (*Knives of Fire*, 1990), *La historia del cine venezolano* (*History of Venezuelan Cinema*, 1991 [a three-part video series]).

Works Cited

King, John. *Magical Reels: A History of Cinema in Latin America*. London: Verso, 1990.
Naranjo, Alvaro. *Román Chalbaud: un cine de autor*. Caracas-Mérida: Cinemateca Nacional/Foncine/Instituto Municipal de Cultura, 1984.

Chapter 9

The Persistence of Vision:
Going to the Movies in Colombia

Gilberto Gómez Ocampo

In "The Poetics and Practice of Iranian Nostalgia in Exile," Hamid Naficy writes about the importance of visual images for the Iranian community in exile.[1] Mostly in Los Angeles, but also in places like Vancouver and Stockholm, Iranians cling to an idealized vision of the country they have lost. Nostalgia feeds and purifies this vision of the lost country where for various reasons many of them cannot step foot again. Naficy—himself an Iranian, an exile—analyzes how this nostalgia thrives on an idealized vision of the motherland and transforms it into a mother indeed: pure, protective, and natural. Iranian films and TV programs, as well as music videos produced in exile, therefore, seek to nurture this vision of the motherland and, in doing so, are powerful agents for maintaining the cultural identity of Iranians abroad, especially those who resist cultural assimilation in their host countries.

Here I write about experiences that took place a long time ago when I was growing up. For adults, childhood is like a remote territory once visited. I am trying to evoke these experiences just by the powers of memory, the only means adults have to retrieve their childhood. But memory brings nostalgia with it, and nostalgia that is, as Julio Cortázar tells us, "a word that stinks like a dog." The child, the adolescent, the young man who saw those movies did not know back then that one day he would be called upon to put in writing, in a language different from his own, the joy that came from the simple pleasure of watching films. What follows are musings about those experiences.

Sunday Afternoon at the Movies: The Lingering Silents

I heard from my grandmother about *películas mudas,* silent films where you had to read in order to make sense of the plot. She often used films as an example of the degree of *progreso* the nation had experienced in her lifetime: from the donkey to the jet plane, from silent movies to Technicolor. Yet she never developed an interest in the talkies, preferring the apparent simplicity of the silent era. The *películas mudas* were always with her. In her disorganized dresser I found old stills of actresses of the silent era, who were for her the prototype of female beauty: Scarlett O'Hara, Mabel Normand, Gloria Swanson, Maria Feht, and—towering over them all—Greta Garbo. There were others whose faces I have forgotten completely, but whose hairdos stick in my memory.

While growing up in the 1960s, long after the talkies had replaced silent movies, I had opportunities to view silent films from time to time. Occasionally a silent film would be projected at the *matinales*. The *matinales* were bargain-priced Sunday morning shows with audiences made up mostly of children under twelve. Noisy affairs, the *matinales* typically showed old, stale reruns that more mature people did not want to see, but that obviously were big affairs for the younger audiences. Going to the movies in Colombia was (and is) like this: You stand in line waiting to buy tickets. As time goes by, you realize that you are not getting closer to the box office; instead, you are moving away from it. The people in front of you let their friends and acquaintances in. After ten or fifteen minutes of waiting, you realize that your chances of getting in are slim.

Silent movies were shown at *matinales,* I believe, when nothing else was available. The managers of movie theaters were free to choose any combination of two films for those Sunday shows. Since their young audiences were pleased with anything at all, theater managers never bothered to choose films very carefully. I remember being scared stiff night after night after seeing *Drac-*

ula, starring Christopher Lee. In the movie, young newlyweds leave on a terrifying honeymoon and end up at Dracula's castle, where the young woman—not unpredictably—loses her blood at the fangs of Dracula. Another terrifying movie whose title I do not remember depicted the efforts of a concerned scientist to save the world from a nuclear disaster. The scientist first had to counteract a ring of spies within the U.S. forces who were secretly plotting against the White House to start a war. Essentially a good-guys-versus-bad-guys story, this movie had an intensity then that few others matched. As I watched that movie, I was totally bewildered at the gratuitousness of the bad guys, as they would have certainly died in the ensuing explosion. This movie contributed to shaping my perception of right and wrong, I think, far more effectively than the preaching of priests at school. In a way, it also shaped my perception of the United States as a land of technology where people in laboratories wearing white coats and aprons made terrible decisions that affected the rest of the world.

Hollywood Endings: And They Lived Happily...

The first movie I ever saw was a rerelease of *Gone With the Wind.* The sense of expectation is still vivid in my memory. My mother had a seamstress sew a new dress for the occasion. She reread many times an article about the movie that she had clipped out of what I later understood was a Spanish version of *Good Housekeeping* (I suppose it was the Cuban edition, perhaps one of the last issues before the magazine folded under the then-new Castro government). Why my mother took me to see this movie in particular—I was less than five years old—escapes me, but I think she wanted to make sure I would not miss what for her was *the* great movie classic. Besides, it was "in color," carrying with it all the prestige that technology inspired and holding appeal for a child. Sublime entertainment that was also wholesome (my grandmother would make sure about that) and, like Halley's comet, came through town only once in a great while. I guess that was not the first time she saw the movie. On the brink of a failed marriage, I imagine she harbored an attraction to Clark Gable, or maybe identified with Vivien Leigh. In any case, it was indeed a cold and windy night when my father drove us to the theater in his new pale green Studebaker Champion. He dropped us at the entrance, telling us he'd pick us up after the show. (We went home by taxi.) I now realize that this incident, almost totally lost in my memory, became an important precedent: there is nothing like a dark, rainy day to set the right mood for a good movie.

Another Hollywood film I saw as a very young child was *The Sound of Music*. My mother, a confirmed Germanophile, wouldn't have missed it. By then her marriage was in shambles, and this romantic, saccharin-filled, and highly improbable love story had to be the most glorious thing on earth for her. She took me to see it and then eagerly convinced other mothers in the neighborhood to take their own children. Everything about the movie seemed contrived to me: the goodness of the good ones, the badness of the Nazis. As a result of this heavy dose of make-believe, I took an early dislike to happily-ever-after Hollywood endings.

Movie Houses in the Central Andes

When I was a child in the 1960s there were high-brow and low-brow theaters, better known in Spanish as theaters for *los de arriba* and *los de abajo*. The distinction was—and is—clearly delineated in Colombia, a society so divided by class. I began to realize this during my teenage years, especially when, on Saturday evenings or Sunday afternoons, boys wearing their Sunday best would attempt to impress the girls they were taking to the movies. It always shocked me when fellows who would normally chat with me on weekdays in the school yard would so ostentatiously ignore me if I bumped into them at the entrance of one of the fancier theaters. I remember Gonzalo, who pretended to be wellborn and elegant. I would generally hang around with him, unless he got a date for a Saturday evening movie. Then he would transform himself into a totally different person, putting on airs just as much as any of the characters in the movie. One night I saw him and, as I crossed his path, he looked away, lighting a Kent cigarette with a most dexterous movement of his hand. He had a fancy golden Colibri cigarette lighter—coolest thing on earth. (It must have been borrowed from a relative, just like the fancy jacket he was wearing.) With such glamour—and arrogance—I could have sworn that he had just jumped out of one of the James Bond movies.

As a youngster wildly interested in movies, I had a chance to go to the most unusual movie houses. Take, for instance, the first movie house I actually went into on my own, in the early sixties, the Teatro Izcandé, in my hometown of Armenia in the central Andes. I was seven. We had very little money for frills like movies but by chance I discovered a dilapidated theater about half a mile from home where admission was only fifteen cents for a double feature. What a bargain! A lollipop cost another fifteen cents and a small round mirror, useful for blinding other kids at midday, when the sun was strongest, was a mere five cents. I soon found myself queuing up for movies at the Izcandé on Saturday mornings, the only time when movies were shown there. What was projected was probably worth less than the admission price, but to us children it was a thrill to watch these old black-and-white movies and take sides with the good guys in their never-ending fight against crime. Whether bank robberies or police car chases, it was all the same—all exciting, made more so by the fact that it was in black and white, which, to me, was more real. My mother, upon finding out where I was spending my money, strongly warned me against going to such a place, good only for bad kids, she said.

One such place was indeed a lesser theater; in fact, it was part of a church under construction. The screening area, located behind the nave, was surrounded by piles of bricks and sand. Occasionally, some wild kids would hurl pieces of brick at the villains, disrupting the movie and sometimes punching holes in the screen. The entrance to this makeshift theater was at back of the building, through the parish office behind the church. About an hour before the show, the construction site would be transformed into a makeshift movie house. The manager would come out of the building and using some old, crumpled movie posters and stills, he would cover any wedding or funeral announcements posted. (The posters were always the same, and were never related to the movie being shown.) Occasionally, he would attach a small hand-written scrap of paper with the current title. He then climbed a ladder to hang a "Teatro Granada" sign over the more permanent "Despacho Parroquial" sign. Finally, he sold the tickets, locked the theater to prevent others from sneaking in without paying, and ran upstairs to the projector. With all of these tasks to perform, it's no wonder that the projectionist slipped up once in a while and showed the second reel of film first, or awakened from his nap to find he had miscalculated the running time of a particular reel. Then the pieces of brick would fly in *his* direction rather than toward the screen. Nobody ate popcorn at the Granada.

Another cinema not too far from my high school became a favorite spot for us students. The place, called the Cine Colombia when most movie houses were called *teatros,* was located in the red-light district. I kept my trips there a secret—until I ran into classmates and teachers who shared the same interest in movies. There I became addicted to movies starring Humphrey Bogart, long before I knew he was a cult figure among grown-up moviegoers; I must have seen *African Queen* at least five nights in a row. I doubt that Ingmar Bergman's *The Seventh Seal* was shown in a red-light district anywhere else in the world, but it was in this theater that I saw it for the first time, amid the snoring of an indifferent public. Another great film that I saw there was *The Wages of Fear.* I recall the suspense in Clouzot's film, the wonderful camera work that gets the most out of black-and-white photography, and the director's honesty in dealing with the subject of hopelessness.

At the Cine Colombia, the audience often became quite boisterous. If the projectionist mixed up the reels or took too much time in changing them, the audience would scream insults like "¡Suelte el pollo, suelte el pollo, bobo!" "El pollo" or "the chicken" was slang for a teenager; the insinuation was that the projectionist was involved in some kind of hanky-panky with a male teenager. Indeed, the darkness of the smoke-filled place (never mind the posted warnings of "Se prohíbe fumar" from the Ministry of Public Health) was undoubtedly an enticing milieu for all kinds of encounters. The incredible thickness of the curtains that covered the walls in the theaters in my hometown seemed to invite various kinds of *pecadillos,* as well as, I am sure, *pecadotes.* For most people in the gregarious Colombian society, finding a secluded, private place was not easy. I saw all kind of secret encounters in the theaters of my city.

In the Cine Doble theater, two B-movies were shown for the price of one; the two movies ran continuously from 11:00 A.M. until midnight. I came into the theater, as always, in medias res. The movie that was being shown at that moment was an Italian spy film. My attention began to wane and my eyes started wandering. The person sitting to my left caught my attention because of his young age (maybe thirteen) and especially because of his preppy look. I wondered what such a "good boy" was doing in such a place when classes were in session. The good guys in the movie were chasing the bad guys in the streets of Rome, who were disadvantaged by the brightness of the Italian skies. They could not hide. At this moment, a big, tall man entered the theater and sat next to the boy. A sudden turn of the camera flooded the theater with a very bright take of the skies of Rome (a police helicopter was coming in to help the good guys) and just then the light shone on the face of my Spanish teacher, who had also cut classes. The good guys chased the bad guys into one of the older buildings of Rome, not far from the Coliseum. Taking advantage of the ensuing darkness, I fled the scene, leaving the clandestine couple in the theater's own darkness.

Going to the movies in Colombia was, of course, more common for people living in cities than for those in rural areas. This gave rise to a business opportunity for traveling entrepreneurs who went from place to place showing movies, their portable screens sometimes nothing more than a few sheets sewn together. The movies were often rather obscure westerns with lots of shooting and "bad" Indians, or else police movies with car chases or PelMex movies about *charros*.[2] Tickets for seats facing the screen, which permitted viewers to read the subtitles of foreign films, were more expensive than those for the other side of the screen, where the subtitles were of course reversed. Those on the wrong side of the screen managed quite well, however, pulling out their pocket mirrors to read the captions. I have always thought of this as a good example of the indirectness of contemporary art, of its untold manipulations and distortions.

Through the Decades: Changes in Distribution and Production

Until the 1950s, most movies shown in Colombia were Hollywood productions. Since that time, however, the choice of movies in the country has been, against all odds, quite diverse. A number of significant changes occurred in the 1950s. The Cine Club de

Colombia was founded in Bogotá by Hernando Salcedo Silva, the distinguished critic and journalist. From its beginning in 1950, the organization was instrumental in bringing to the country alternative works, important movies of no interest to commercial distributors.[3] The literary magazine *Mito* brought together a group of intellectuals interested in film theory and criticism. Among the serious film scholars working together at the time were Hernando Valencia Goelkel, Jorge Gaitán Durán, and a young journalist from the Caribbean region, Gabriel García Márquez. García Márquez's interest in film, particularly the work of the neorealists, led him to Rome, where he studied cinema.[4] The 1950s, then, marks a turning point in Colombian film history.

During the late 1960s, censorship in Colombia was very strict. In fact, the Junta de Censura had complete control over the movies available to the Colombian public. Members of the Junta were often *notables*, that is, individuals of good social standing. Appointed by the Ministry of Communications and OK'd by the church, the members of this committee had the final word on which films would and would not be shown; their decisions could not be appealed. Movies like Pasolini's *Teorema*, I later realized, were censored by these "guardians of public morality." I have never seen a list of movies banned by the Junta de Censura, but I suspect it might be quite long. Even as recently as the late 1980s, Martin Scorcese's *The Last Temptation of Christ* had serious problems in Colombia.

Distributors, however, found ways to bypass such controls. In 1968, for example, the German movie *Helga: The Intimate Life of a Young Woman*, a semisketch of a porno flick, was shown with great success. The distributors touted it as a "scientific" film that would "illustrate" and "teach" the importance of "healthy" sexuality to the audiences while outlining the negative consequences of misunderstanding the role of sex in life. A great deal of publicity succeeded in generating interest all over the country. What was this sensational film *Helga* about? To raise expectations even higher, viewers (only adults over 21, of course) had to *preregister* at the theater the morning of the screening they planned to attend. Projections of *Helga* were scheduled to begin at midnight in order to minimize the disruption of the city's normal life. The effect, of course, was just the opposite: people lined up patiently waiting to get into the theater and others gathered to find out who was going to see *Helga*. The would-be spectators became the spectacle: there was a show inside the theater as well as outside. My friends and I managed to watch the spectacle inside the theater, having obtained — for a price — false ID cards.

Another way to circumvent the strict censorship was to create alternative screening spaces. The 1970s saw the proliferation of *cine clubes*. These clubs became increasingly popular during this decade, not only as a form of resistance to censorship but also, I think, because people grew tired of Hollywood films and local television programming. It was at this time that society became more radicalized as the political activism of the universities spread beyond the campuses. The first *cine clubes* of this period were politically motivated, serving as they did to showcase the virtues of communism and even help recruit supporters. Some of the organizers repeated what Lunacharsky, Lenin's commissar for culture, had said about film, that it was "a very important tool for the conquest of Bolshevik power." Many movies showed the struggles of the Soviet peoples to build socialism. These films, all of them in the mainstream of socialist realism, became utterly predictable. I believe I saw three or four biographies of Lenin that depicted him as a saint, as a new Saint Francis. Fortunately, many films from Cuba and other Latin American countries made their way to the public through these *cine clubes*. Films such as Octavio Getino's *La hora de los hornos* (*The Hour of the Furnaces*), Tomás Gutiérrez Alea's *Memorias del subdesarrollo* (*Memories of Underdevelopment*), and Glauber Rocha's *Antônio das mortes* were shown exclusively in these places. Although the common language should have facilitated the dissemination of these movies, their reception was confined to university audiences.

The films shown in the *cine clubes* were — like Costa-Gavras's *Estado de sitio* (*State of Siege*) — often politically charged enough to be discomforting to most distributors. The distributors were actually U.S. companies that had bought out the local competition. In fact, the decline of movie viewing in Colombia has been attributed to the demise of local and European distributors. The U.S. companies apparently supplanted European films with less costly, and therefore more profitable, products such as the spaghetti-western Trinity series starring Charles Bronson or Terence Hill. By the mid-seventies, many of the *cine clubes* had been taken over by individuals more interested in cinema as an artistic medium than as an ideological tool. Art replaced politics. This was the golden age of the *cine club*; many movies that otherwise did not have an outlet circulated throughout the country. Film series were common, highlighting French *noir* cinema, uncirculated Hollywood movies, alternative European titles, auteur works—many shown with the cooperation of the respective embassies and consulates.

In the 1980s, moviegoing decreased. In Colombia, as elsewhere, the availability of television and video contributed to the decline. Nevertheless, you could still see long lines of people trying to get tickets for good movies. By this time, something happened with the Colombian movie market that allowed it to show movies like *Amadeus* at least four months before their official release in the United States. Still, the occasional popularity of films like this was not enough to prevent the closing of some of the most remarkable theaters, some of which had been in operation for fifty years. Landmarks like the Faenza in Bogotá became warehouses and later on, striptease joints, as the city center shifted to the north. The construction in 1973 of the first American-style shopping center with its own multiplex, Unicentro, in the north of Bogotá, signaled the beginning of the end for theaters in the downtown area. The same thing has happened in other cities throughout the country.

Although there have been attempts to create a national film industry in Colombia, locally produced movies have never been a rage. This is why in the mid-1970s a law was passed requiring the exhibition of a short Colombian film at every regular film show in order to ensure an audience for the local product. But in that least nationalist of countries, theater managers quickly found their way around the law: they would exhibit the Colombian film *after* the main foreign feature, often when only the cleaning crew and those with no place to go after the movie remained in the theater.

Nevertheless, some recent Colombian films have been reviewed favorably. Víctor Gaviria's *Rodrigo D.—No Futuro (Rodrigo D., No Future)*, which deals with the drug traffic in Medellín, was remarkable in its use of nonprofessional actors, many of whom were actually members of gangs. *Confesión a Laura* (*Confession to Laura*) has also been popular in Colombia as well as abroad, as has Sergio Cabrera's *Técnicas de duelo* (*Techniques for a Duel*). His *La estrategia del caracol* (1993) won best-movie award at the Ibero-American Movie Festival in Huelva, Spain, in 1993.

Television: Real Live Entertainment

The television industry, while certainly not devoted exclusively to broadcasting movies, has gone hand in hand with the dissemination of movies in Colombia. When it started operations in 1953, the sole TV channel operated with only a handful of inexperienced actors. Television was begun in Colombia for political rather than commercial reasons. Instigated by a faction of the powerful Conservative Party and with its support, an army general had seized power in 1953 so that the unpopular conservatives could then rule from behind the scenes. The shrewd conservatives saw television as a quick fix to divert the attention of the populace from more pressing issues.

Although democracy was restored in 1958—at least in theory—I recall that frequently there were serious clashes between the government and opposition groups. Then we stayed at home and watched the lengthy films from Otto Rank studios that were shown instead of the regular news programs. We saw the same movies when the authorities, feeling threatened, would institute the *estado de sitio*, something that happened very often in the 1960s. I became familiar with the movies of Otto Rank, then, during those long afternoons when the streets were uncertain, when tension filled the air, when on occasion soldiers shouted in the distance, army jeeps sped by, and big guys walked precipitously past our house. I would cherish the hammer striking the cymbal at the beginning of every movie. Danger, tension, cunning, weapons, plots, action, mystery both on the screen and off. But movies were always more glamorous.

Concluding Reflections

As I read Naficy's article, I could not help but think of the situation of the many Colombians abroad, myself included, and wonder to what extent films help maintain a sense of a Colombian community. There are perhaps a million Colombians in the United States, mostly in the Miami and New York areas. Chapinero, one of Bogotá's traditional commercial districts, has been replicated by Colombian immigrants in New York as Chapinerito, or Little Chapinero. I had never heard of this place until the movie *El taxista millonario* (*The Millionaire Cab Driver*) came out in the late 1970s. Essentially a farce, it depicts an obese Colombian taxi driver in New York and his path to riches through a combination of tenacity, cunning, and plain good luck. I did not think much of this film when it first came out. The protagonist, Carlos "El Gordo" Benjumea was never a good comedian, and I never liked his television show anyway. Claudia de Colombia, a then-popular singer, was also in the movie, which was set in fancy New York locales. It is now apparent to me that the effect this movie had in Colombia and *on* Colombians was perhaps the opposite of what Naficy describes for Iranians: in Colombia, that least nationalist of countries, what mattered was not the idealization of the motherland (the film was shot abroad), nor the hypothetical virtues of the land or its inhabitants. Rather, what the film depicted was the capacity of its citizens to do without their motherland, the ability to cope with the challenges of other, very foreign lands on their own, with the cargo of street smarts learned in the alleys of their distant childhood. The success of that Colombian film was based on a peculiar kind of nostalgia: a type of nostalgia that would even feed on a film that — like nostalgia itself — stinks like a dog.

Notes

1. Hamid Naficy, "The Poetics and Practice of Iranian Nostalgia in Exile," *Diaspora* 1:3 (1991): 285–302.

2. PelMex movies were produced by Películas Mexicanas, a state-controlled studio that turned out hundreds of films every year.

3. An important book is Hernando Salcedo Silva's *Crónicas del cine colombiano: 1897–1950* (Bogotá: Valencia Editores, 1981). Salcedo provides valuable information about the movie industry in Colombia and interviews with some directors.

4. García Márquez's interest in film has been documented in Raymond L. Williams, *Gabriel García Márquez* (Boston: Twayne, 1984), and Robert L. Sims, *The First García Márquez: A Study of His Journalistic Writing from 1948 to 1957* (Lanham, Md.: Univ. Press of America, 1992).

Chapter 10

Mexican Melodramas of Patriarchy: Specificity of a Transcultural Form[1]

Julianne Burton-Carvajal

Recent melodrama scholarship has emphasized the historical and cultural situatedness of the form. The study of melodrama as a highlighted theoretical-critical category developed during the 1970s in a predominantly Anglo-American context, fueled by several interrelated critical trends, including politicized auteurism, Marxist-inspired hermeneutics focused on issues of ideology, and feminist approaches to film studies heavily inflected by evolving discourses of psychoanalysis.[2] Specific manifestations of this transhistorical and transcultural form are only beginning to be explored outside a nexus of primarily Hollywood-generated examples.[3] Drawing from one of the richest national traditions, this essay postulates the subgenre of paternal melodrama and theorizes the melodrama of patriarchy as a characteristic expression in classical and, to a mitigated degree, in postclassical Mexican cinema.

Foundational Features:[4] The Overpowering Presence of the Absent Father

With its release in 1943, *Flor Silvestre* inaugurated the most distinguished collaboration in the long history of Mexican cinema — between director Emilio "El Indio" Fernández, cinematographer

Gabriel Figueroa, scriptwriter Mauricio Magdaleno, and two actors who would become an emblematic national couple, Dolores del Río and Pedro Armendáriz. That same historic year also saw the premieres of three other enduring melodramas: Fernando de Fuentes's *Doña Bárbara*, Julio Bracho's *Distinto Amanecer*, and *María Candelaria* (by the same team that produced *Flor Silvestre*). Of these four now-classics, only *Flor Silvestre* presents a narrative of the Mexican Revolution. Framed by an artificially aged Dolores del Río retelling the tragic events to her grown son, dressed as a military official, as they stand surveying the rich, rolling farmland of the Bajío, *Flor Silvestre* identifies itself from the outset as a narrative of the genesis of the Mexican nation.

In the film's most emotionally hyperbolic segment, Doña Clara (Mimi Derba), the distinguished wife of the local landowner, visits the sickbed of her son's injured bride, Esperanza (Dolores del Río). Imperiously confronting the humble peasant whom her son and heir José Luis (Pedro Armendáriz) has secretly married, she orders the unworthy girl to disappear. Esperanza, exemplar of humility and self-denial, agrees, asking only that José Luis be told that she has died. Moved by this disposition to self-sacrifice, Doña Clara dissolves in tears, having recognized the true nobility of this humble peasant girl's abject devotion. In a lightning turnaround, calling Esperanza "M'ijita" (little daughter, a term of both intimacy and endearment), she begs forgiveness for her initial blindness. Esperanza's exhausted swoon at the end of this lachrymose scene elicits Doña Clara's guilty panic and frantic attempts to revive her.

This hyperfeminine sequence has its masculine counterpart in the tavern where José Luis and Esperanza's grandfather, Don Melchor (Eduardo Arozamena), celebrate, with a double baptism of tequila and tears, their new bond, which, like the one just forged by the two women, transcends the abyss of class difference. But for this affirmation of the viability of the new Mexican family that would bridge the chasm between the privileged and the dispossessed — a possibility attributed to the revolution that has only just begun — one more person must be enlisted: José Luis's father, Don Francisco (Miguel Angel Ferriz).

A long series of landscape dissolves in long shot, featuring the protagonists on horseback accompanied by a trio of musicians who sing the title song, distends the distance between the town where Esperanza was raised and the paternal hacienda from which the heir has already been expelled. José Luis, who had been perfectly sober in the canteen, arrives at his father's house an extreme state of inebriation. His sister (Margarita Cortés) tries vainly to hide him, but an outraged Don Francisco summarily dismisses first the daughter and then Don Melchor, while furiously attacking his son for drunkenness and for reportedly supporting the incipient revolution. Finally, grabbing his sword from the wall, he lunges at the son he has already pushed to the floor. Only the sudden bodily intervention of mother and sister saves the life of José Luis.

The narrative axis of this signal melodrama seems until this point to have been the newly constituted couple as prototype of the more egalitarian nation struggling into being. But, with the murder of the patriarch by "malos revolucionarios," the narrative lurches onto another axis. José Luis confronts his father's death in an extraordinary sequence in which he slowly traverses the sacked ancestral mansion from one end to the other, accompanied only by the accusatory strains of the *corrido* "El hijo desobediente" (The disobedient son) (sung by the Trío Calaveras, who are strewn randomly across the floor like so much additional debris). Don Francisco's portrait, still intact in its place of honor on the wall, dominates the beginning of this prolonged sequence; its conclusion reveals the once lofty Doña Clara rendered a pathetic and mute bundle of mourning on the floor of the family chapel. The arrogant and inflexible patriarch, earlier justly denounced by his wife and equally justly defied by his son, manages in death to annul the autonomy of both. Each instantly abandons the persona they have constructed to this point in order, in the case of Doña Clara, to mourn in perpetual catatonia and, in the case of José Luis, to dedicate himself obsessively to vengeance.

The death of the *padre/patrón/patriarca* coincides with the birth of José Luis's own son and heir, the literal embodiment of the new Mexico that is simultaneously being born. Yet, in this story, which his widowed wife (re)tells, José Luis abandons both son and spouse in favor of his dead father. The only response that the newborn elicits from José Luis is a reference to his ugliness.

The new mother, who has not only given birth unassisted but also managed to greet her returning husband gowned, beribboned, and radiant as a bride, is rewarded only with a distracted peck on the cheek.

José Luis's campaign of vengeance, which absorbs the remainder of the film, is persistently stymied. Once located and apprehended, the murdering bandit turns out to be too ill to offer sporting resistance. To add to the sense of filial frustration, the evil Torres succumbs to his illness without any intervention on José Luis's part, frustrating his strenuously laid plans to hang the assassin from one of the lugubrious cypress trees that guard the paternal tomb. This failure to exact the desired revenge (the culprit has died of typhus) still ends up costing José Luis his own life at the hands of the murderer's brother Rogelio (played by Emilio Fernández himself). In the film's conclusion, José Luis violently spurns his wife and baby before ever so briefly relenting and then letting himself be shot by firing squad as the price of securing their liberty from the surviving Torres.

In *Flor Silvestre*, not surprisingly, the "feminine" framing and narrative voice do not add up to a female point of view. As already mentioned, "mother's work" is occluded; there's no trace of the effort required to give birth to or raise a child. Furthermore, the conjugal drama is subordinated to the drama of filial remorse. The couple is sundered, the newest generation is separated from its progenitor, while the once apparently irrevocable split between antirevolutionary patriarch and prorevolutionary heir is mended through a kind of retrospective disavowal. The antagonism between Don Francisco and José Luis, which reproduces the antagonism between a feudal-patriarchal system and a less hierarchical form of socioeconomic organization, ends up canceling itself out as it becomes retrospectively clear that both have supported the same "good revolutionaries" (Esperanza's cousin) and condemned the same "bad revolutionaries" (the Torres brothers). Like the ostensible impulse to validate change, which assimilates itself into acquiescence to traditional structures of power, this "maternal perspective" turns out to be fully compatible with a profoundly and disruptively patriarchal orientation.

More than the martyrdom of José Luis that culminates the narrative, more than the long-suffering Esperanza whose "memories" are its motor, more than the land itself that, according to Esperanza, motivates "the greatest and most terrible love," more than that great upheaval which is the revolution, primarily embodied here as banditry, and much more than the quasi-invisible son who ostensibly serves as metonym of the future nation, *Flor Silvestre* as narrative is dominated by the figure of the patriarch. It is the power of the father, even more potent and pervasive in death than in life, that explains the otherwise inexplicable detours and contradictions that riddle the narrative.[5] This unbridled and self-imposing authority, capable of derailing established narrative dynamics, is an example of what provokes this call to reconsider the typology of Mexican melodrama.

Cross-Cultural Naming: Melodrama as Mode, Genre, and Subgenre in Anglo-American and Mexican Critical Discourses

As various critics and theorists have argued, following the lead of Peter Brooks in *The Melodramatic Imagination* and Christine Gledhill in the important introduction to her anthology *Home Is Where the Heart Is: Studies in Melodrama and the Women's Film*, melodrama needs to be conceptualized in the broadest terms as a way of understanding the world. Thomas Elsaesser calls melodrama "a cultural form" and a "modality of experience." David Rodowick calls it an "aesthetic ideology," a "structure of signification capable of reproducing itself within a variety of narrative forms." Beyond a (mere) typological distinction, melodrama has been redefined as a metageneric category, a way of registering experience and of understanding both individual and collective placement in the universe, a means of encoding moral and ideological concerns within registers of the aesthetic and the emotional.

Serving primarily as signposts to those who consume texts and as retrospectively imposed, heuristic systems of classification for those who analyze them, generic typologies inevitably reveal themselves, upon closer examination, as arbitrary and shifting.[6] Most contemporary critics agree that the concept of genre as a means to a coherent taxonomy of filmic expression is hopelessly flawed: tendentious, tautological, retrospectively prescriptive, either too specific or too general to function intraculturally, much less cross-culturally. Yet for lack of a better instrument, the categories of genre and subgenre must nevertheless be qualifiedly retained as a way of addressing how film practices converse with, contest, and challenge one another. "Congenital" limitations notwithstanding, generic and subgeneric classifications are an indispensable survey tool for critics and historians in both the mapping of the terrain of a particular national cinema and the retrospective reading of what identifying features that mapping process has emphasized and what equally identifying features it may have overlooked.

In what follows, I will be referring to melodrama in a dual register: as ideological (pre)disposition and structure of signification in the broadest sense, and as a category of classification in a typology of narrative filmmaking. Yet this latter sense is also dual, since even when treated as a "genre" in film studies, melodrama insists on asserting itself as a metagenre, one that subsumes and hybridizes with other generic categories. As we shall see, this is particularly true in the Mexican case.

In the table of contents of *La aventura del cine mexicano*, a synthetic study of Mexican cinema from the silent period through the 1960s, Jorge Ayala Blanco classifies the films of the the formative periods of Mexican filmmaking (origins through the 1950s) into thematic categories and those that fit—or fail to fit—into series configurations. These thematic rubrics, however, easily lend themselves to generic and subgeneric equivalences. In fact, two of the eleven thematic categories he employs in Part I—*comedia ranchera* and *horror*—are widely accepted generic denominations, and both are easily assimilable to the broader metageneric category of melodrama. If we add the term "melodrama" to Ayala Blanco's other thematic categories, they metamorphosize into subgenres: melodramas of the revolution, melodramas of Porfirian nostalgia, provincial melodramas, urban melodramas, melodramas of prostitution, melodramas of indigenous peoples, melodramas of adolescent life. A quick look at how this latter is defined validates the assumption that, lacking an explicit statement to the contrary, melodrama as metagenre subtends all these "thematic" divisions: "Mexican cinema's films about adolescents almost never exceed the features of traditional melodrama, which rapidly assimiliates them" (177). Only a thematic category called "La violencia" fails to translate into a subcategory of melodrama because it subsumes several genres, including the gangster film, the western, and a number of the subgenres just listed.

Ayala Blanco's chapter titled "La familia" begins with a brief survey of the development of Mexican film genres beginning in the 1930s. "Ephemeral" genres like the colonial swashbuckler (*aventura de capa y espada en tiempos del virreinato*), the epic biography, and the melodrama based on the nineteenth-century serial novel (*folletones*) were "hybrid and artificial" imitations of Hollywood that would, in the 1940s, make way for the consolidation of genres more genuinely responsive to national needs and popular tastes—among the most numerous, *comedias rancheras*, comic films, and barrio epics. Other genres that "are revealing when subjected to analysis are the Porfirian nostalgia films, the folkloric films of the revolution, and, curiously, family dramas" (48–49). Although Ayala Blanco only uses the term "melodrama" once in this list, very narrowly, all the genres he names are clearly subject to inclusion under the category of melodrama. Throughout the text, Ayala Blanco "coins" generic and subgeneric terms (e.g., *comedia melodramática campirana* [set in the countryside], *melodrama del pueblo, melodrama sociofamiliar, melodrama negro, melodrama blanco, melodrama conjugal, melodrama criminal*), but his cumulative usage suggests an alternative to this almost whimsical proliferation: a geohistorical mapping featuring the predominance of the rural genres up to 1947 (the exception being the melodramas of prostitution and the *cabareteras*, which flourished from 1932 through 1952), the urban genres from 1947 onward, and the "border" genres beginning in the 1960s.

The year-by-year, film-by-film organization of Emilio García Riera's *Historia documental del cine mexicano* sidesteps the issue of generic mapping, except to the degree that the period reviewers quoted invoke them. (Reviews, interview fragments, and other contemporary commentary constitute the "documents" of the title.) In the *comentarios* that García Riera provides on each film, he often uses the label "melodrama," but without any further (subgeneric) elaboration. Although each film entry begins with a schematic informational section, film genre is not included as a category.[7] Interestingly, however, in *Los hermanos Soler*, the first book in the *Cineastas de México* series dedicated to actors rather than to directors, García Riera invokes a series of generic categories, including *comedia melodrámatica, melodrama de aventuras revolucionarias, melodrama provinciano, melodrama rural, melodrama urbano, melodrama capitalino, melodrama norteño, melodrama tropical, melodrama de época, melodrama cabaretero y populachero.*

In a 1992 overview titled "Las mitologías del cine mexicano," cultural critic Carlos Monsiváis lists the following as the genres that have formed the Mexican public: "the *comedia campirana*, the films of the Mexican Revolution, urban comedy, films of nostalgia for the dictatorship of Porfirio Díaz, *rumbera* movies, adventure films," and "the variations of melodrama," which he lists first but does not elaborate, though in fact, all of the categories he offers are subject to inclusion under the latter term (19). Written in the same year, historian Julia Tuñón's doctoral dissertation on masculine constructions of the image of the female in Mexican cinema between 1939 and 1952 briefly addresses the issue of film genres, which she defines as "the complex of language, theme, symbols, and stereotypes that a series of films have in common and that permit treating them like a unit of analysis" (166). She cites Andrew Tutor's assessment of genre as a relatively fixed cultural model defining a social and moral world as well as a particular physical and historical environment, a model whose very familiarity produces a sense of individual security because it articulates the foundations of social life and its underlying norms (167; Tutor, 195, 297). She addresses the phenomenon of melodrama more extensively, emphasizing its relationship to the family and private life: "To say melodrama is to say family" (174). The use of music for emotional emphasis, the focus on problems of personal life, the device of plot reversal, the incidence of fatalism and human powerlessness in the face of implacable destiny are all characteristic of early film melodrama, whose roots stretch back to eighteenth-century theater and to a myriad of popular entertainment forms of medieval and even ancient origin. Although family melodrama is her implicit subject, the thematic clearly prevails over the generic (and subgeneric) in the conceptualization and organization of Tuñón's dissertation, which contains chapters titled "The Filmic Family," "Maternity on the Screen," "Sexuality in Mexican Cinema," and "Woman in the Public World."

In his book on Juan Orol, Eduardo de la Vega elaborates analyses of various genres and subgenres developed by Orol: the gangster film, tropical romances, *melodramas de tropicalismo, melodramas pasionales,* and the *melodrama de exaltación maternal.* He begins his account of this director's career with the latter, which he also calls *el subgénero de los homenajes maternales,* dating its emergence between 1935 and 1938 and equating it with "una visión pequeñoburguesa de la realidad" that continued to produce exemplars until 1950 (26–34).[8]

Moisés Viñas, writing in *Dicine* of film genres in Mexico, begins with the promising assertion that "Mexican cinema is basically a genre-based cinema, [though] it has seldom been analyzed from that point of view, and then always based on a model that does not correspond to its particular reality [because Mexican cinema] is based on *other genres*" (32; emphasis in the original). Viñas purports to establish a basic grid "supple" enough to accommodate the kind of national variation that Mexico represents, though he confuses his argument by designating documentary, fiction, and animation as genres, and then proceeding to apply the same name to varieties of documentary as well. His core distinction, however, is between "dramatic" and "narrative" genres—the former deriving from a theatrical and performance tradition, the latter from epic poetry and the novel. His categories of drama, comedy, and adventure correspond to the more commonly identified triad of melodrama, comedy, and epic, the latter being an acknowledged hybrid characterized by its episodic nature. He concludes his article by offering the following list of specifically national genres, without further elaboration: the *comedia ranchera,* the rural melodrama, the *rumbera* melodrama and the cabaret melodrama, the social melodrama, the political melodrama, the religious melodrama, the gangster melodrama, the thriller ("quite different from those of other countries"), and the comedies, melodramas, and adventure films of the revolution (35). The preponderance on this list of melodrama, with its patently mixed heritage deriving from both dramatic and narrative traditions, leaves the reader bewildered: despite the promise of its initial assertions, this exercise in genre clarification in the end only clarifies the pitfalls of genre analysis.

Among the (sub)generic designations invoked on the northern side of the border, the maternal melodrama (Mora; López, "Tears and Desire"), the melodrama of the revolution (Mistron; Dever), the *cabaretera* and *fichera* subgenres and the closely related melodrama of prostitution (Mora; López, "Tears and Desire"; de la Mora) figure prominently. Still, what is to date the most critically ambitious study in English of Mexican cinema—Charles Ramírez Berg's *Cinema of Solitude*—opts for a combined image-based and thematic conceptualization: two chapters titled "Women's Images," two chapters on the male image, two chapters on "communities" ("Family and Neighborhood Groups," "Political and Rural Groups"), and one chapter titled "The Indian Question." In his important opening chapter "*Mexicanidad* and the Classical Mexican Cinema," Berg opts to outline the transformation from the "classical" era to the postclassical period (1967–83), which is to be the focus of his study, through close textual analysis of *Cuando los hijos se van* (*When the Children Leave Home*), an exemplar of what he identifies as the family melodrama, in two incarnations, 1941 and 1969.

Of these various subgeneric designations, only the first and the last, the maternal melodrama and the family melodrama, are broadly transcultural; the other four—the melodrama of the revolution, the *cabaretera* and *fichera* films, and the melodrama of prostitution—are more specific to the Mexican instance. In her discussion of female representation in Mexican cinema, Ana M. López postulates a simple division: "Two basic melodramatic tendencies developed between 1930 and 1960: family melodramas focused on the problems of love, sexuality, and parenting, and epic melodramas that reworked national history, especially the events of the Mexican revolution" ("Tears and Desire," 150). Where do the *cabaretera*, *fichera*, and prostitution melodramas fit within this dichotomy? Are they family melodramas set outside the shelter of the domestic hearth, or are they, like the gangster subgenre, more "epic" in their engagement of the dystopian effects of urbanization and modernization?

However incomplete, this survey illustrates how (sub)genre as a putatively systematic category of analysis defies the very aspiration to systematicity that sets the process of categorization in motion in the first place. Generic denominations are at best a temporary working hypothesis in the service of a critical viewpoint that has opted to privilege a certain kind of phenomenon, a certain kind of agency, in pursuit of a certain end. The phenomenon of melodrama's successful "colonization" of generic territory can be detected on both sides of the border: for Mexican critics, melodrama is an implicit category so pervasive that it often goes without saying. As discussed earlier, the revival of interest in melodrama as a film genre has produced a wealth of Anglo-American scholarship arguing that the reach of the form is much more encompassing, that the category of genre can no longer contain it. If the melodramatic imagination so permeates Mexican cinema that it either obviates or multiplies the critical propensity to classify by generic category, producing on the one hand a preference for topical and thematic modes of classification, and on the other a disorderly and redundant proliferation of subgenres (e.g., García Riera's rural melodrama, provincial melodrama, *norteño* melodrama), what can be the point of postulating yet another subgenre, in this particular case, paternal melodrama, and yet another (trans)generic category, the melodrama of patriarchy?

Perhaps these are categories that are more likely to be postulated cross-culturally, or rather, extraculturally, and arguably this very fact makes the enterprise worthwhile. What categories are perceivable within the culture, but not outside it? Conversely, what possible categories are more likely to be hypothesized outside of the culture than within it, and why?

The most obvious variant of family melodrama Mexican-style has seemed to be the maternal melodrama, incarnated over numerous decades and dozens of films by the prototype of national maternity, actress Sara García (who reputedly had all her teeth extracted at the early age of forty the better to embody sexless, self-effacing, sacrificial motherhood). In his previously cited essay on feminine images in Mexican cinema, Carl Mora fails to note the profoundly patriarchal bias that subtends the melodramas that center on this emblematic "Mother of Mexico." In welcome contrast, Ana M. López suggestively, if too briefly, observes in her influential essay on female representations in Mexican melodrama:

> However, despite their self-acknowledged narrative focus on mothers and their positioning of the mother as the central ideological tool for social and moral cohesion, these and other films ostensibly glorifying mothers as repositories of conservative family values were clearly

maternal melodramas rather than women's films. This distinction is significant for the Mexican case, because it helps to distinguish between those films that focus on male Oedipal dramas and films that more self-consciously address female spectators and concerns. Indeed, one could argue that, despite their focus on mothers, these family melodramas are patriarchal rather than maternal because they attempt to preserve patriarchal values ... [T]he moral crisis created in these films revolves around the fathers' identity and not the mothers ... ("Tears and Desire," 154)[9]

Certain influential Anglo-American essays on film melodrama also reveal an awareness of what we might call the subtending patriarchal. The patriarch figures in all four variants identified by Thomas Schatz in his study of postwar Hollywood family melodrama—whose focus he identifies as "the nuclear middle-class family, the clearest representation of the patriarchal and bourgeois social order" then undergoing a process of transformation (152).[10] Sylvia Harvey's relatively early observation that the family serves as "a legitimizing metaphor for a hierarchical and authoritarian society" is implicitly or explicitly shared by numerous analysts of the family melodrama (24). David Rodowick, in a more sustained and complex argument, defines "the figuration of patriarchal authority" as "the center of a complex network of social relations whose symbolization is undertaken by the domestic melodrama" (240).

Understanding melodrama as the product of three sets of determinations—formal, social, and psychological—Rodowick argues apropos of social determinations that "the structure of institutional authority, and its function in the represented social formation, is only understood to the degree that it receives and reproduces the structure of familial politics" (239). He goes on to observe:

The domestic melodrama is attentive only to problems which concern the family's internal security and economy, and therefore considers its authority to be restricted to issues of private power and patriarchal right. The power it reserves for itself is limited to rights of inheritance and the legitimation of the social and sexual identities in which it reproduces its own network of authority. (239)

Apropos of psychic determinations, "the problematic of identity," Rodowick maintains that "individual identity is defined as a problem to the extent that it is out of sync with the relations of authority which are required to legitimate it" (239–40). He goes on to state:

In the intersection of the social and the psychic, the figuration of paternal authority plays a central role. As the linch-pin on which the structure of conflict will turn, it is a system of power against which the logic and the order of the representations of social relations are measured. Thus, the figuration of patriarchal authority in a given text will formulate the terms of conflict through the perpetuation of a series of symbolic divisions and oppositions which organize the narrative around the problem of individual identity, both social and sexual. (240)

It is this figuration of patriarchal authority that I would like to postulate as an inadequately acknowledged structuring agency within Mexican melodrama, one that subtends and often disrupts the apparent subgeneric orientation of a particular film, independent of whether or not the film explicitly addresses the dynamics of the paternal per se.

Fundamental to this enterprise is the need to delineate the cultural specificity of the concept of patriarchal authority, which, like the concept of melodrama itself, is subject to historically and culturally generated nuances and therefore risks losing rather than accruing explanatory power when transferred, without particularization, across cultural systems. Jackie Byars makes a distinction between the "historical genre of 'melodrama' " and the "theoretical genre of 'melodrama,' " arguing that the former was a functional category "long understood and accepted (though generally denigrated) by the industry and by audiences" and that the latter was a highly selective and politically motivated critical construct produced at a given historical period (14). Barbara Klinger would argue that the very denigrated status of the "historical" genre of melodrama, like the intellectually "elevated" status of the "theoretical" genre, was the product of the ultimately self-aggrandizing process of differentiation and subordination that is the very essence of "tastemaking" for reviewers and critics alike. Her chapter contrasting 1950s and 1970s reception of the films of Douglas Sirk, melodramatic auteur par excellence, concludes: "The process of tastemaking in both historical periods operated, then, to create hierarchical differences between the aesthete and the masses through the construction of canons and aesthetic positions antithetical to the perceived unrestrained and tasteless pleasures of the crowd" (96).

Notwithstanding the validity of Klinger's conclusion, the distinction that Byars attempts to draw—which might be more simply rendered as a distinction between applied and dedicated usages—seems helpful to the degree that it highlights the arbitrary selectiveness with which the concept of melodrama was ushered into the forefront of film studies. Byars observes that "constructing 'melodrama' in terms of this small group of films [Hollywood family melodramas produced by a few talented directors obsessed with stylistic manipulation] obscured the existence of other melodramatic genres, the melodramatic aspects of genres like the western, the historical variation within individual melodramatic genres, and the relationships between kinds of melodramatic genres" (14).[11] (Not to mention transcultural variations in melodramatic subgenres and modes of expression.)

In a 1993 essay, Steve Neale gives another revisionist turn of the screw by taking issue with the consensual understanding of the term "melodrama" as it has evolved over twenty years of feminist-inspired film scholarship. Based on his empirical research into the trade press, he contradicts the five standard critical assumptions about the conceptualization and usage of the term in the Hollywood industry between 1938 and 1960,[12] and concludes, "The mark of these films is not pathos, romance, and domesticity but action, adventure, and thrills; not 'feminine' genres . . . but war films, adventure films, horror films and thrillers, genres traditionally thought of as, if anything, male" (69).

Patriarchy in Colonial and Republican Mexico

Clearly, the figuration of the patriarchal, so pervasive in Mexican cinema, is related to the traditional preeminence of the patriarchal family as a social, political, and economic unit. This preeminence in turn is related to the historical importance of the father as supreme regent of the family and, by extension, as the link between the family unit and two other equally hierarchical and patriarchal sociopolitical entities, the church and the state. This "Mexican trinity," in which the father (*padre*) rules the domestic sphere, the priest (*Padre*) the ecclesiastic sphere, and the *patrón* (be he landowner, political boss, general, or president) the civic sphere, both naturalizes and totalizes patriarchal authority from cradle to grave—and beyond, to the realm of *Dios Padre,* God the Father, where mother and son are relegated to mediating and self-sacrificial roles.

In her synthetic history of women in Mexico from pre-Conquest times to the present, Julia Tuñón stresses that in colonial Mexico the organization of gender was "defined by its patriarchal character" and that, rather than an imported overlay, this patriarchal orientation "conserved a system of male privilege inherited from dual sources":

> The pre-Colombian concept [of male superiority and female subordination] seems to have adapted itself without greater discussion to the Christian one. Both centered women's role on matrimony and maternity, condemning abortion and homosexuality; both valorized submission, weakness, and surrender as qualities synonymous with the [female] gender and regarded virginity as an ideal state; both demonized the woman who strayed from the prescribed path, considering her in violation of both social morality and her ("eternal") feminine nature. (*Mujeres en México,* 47)

The work of two North American historians of colonial and early republican Mexico helps identify the particularly Mexican inflections of the institution of patriarchy. In *The Women of Mexico City, 1790–1857,* Sylvia Arrom describes the Mexican social system as a kind of patriarchal corporatism, a hierarchical form of organization, which she defines, by quoting from an 1806 opinion of the Council of the Indies, as "a graduated system of dependence and subordination [that] sustains and insures the obedience and respect of the last vassal to the authority of the sovereign." This "ideal Hispanic society" was made up of a hierarchy of *corporaciones* (the nobility, the clergy, the military, the guilds, the Indians, etc.), each with its particular functions, privileges (*fueros*), and limitations, and each ruled by a masculine authority. Arrom explains that "the nuclear family played a crucial role in preserving the system, for it was the basic social unit on which the entire structure rested," and that "the subordination of women was held to be essential to the functioning of the corporate system of social control": "Because conflict within the vertically segmented groups was unacceptable to this order, effective control from the top down required the inequality of husbands and wives" (76–77).

Arrom traces the basis of paternal authority to the venerable tradition of *patria potestas*, originating in Roman law and interpreted on the basis of the medieval code, *Las Siete Partidas de Alfonso el Sabio*, as the power of the master over his slave, the sovereign over his subject, the bishop over his priests, and the father over his children. The power of the husband over his wife is, as Arrom observes, a significant omission. Recent definitions of the concept of patriarchy have so emphasized this particular form of authority — that of the patriarch over his wife and other women — as to risk obscuring the degree to which patriarchal power also consists of the authority wielded over other men, not least among them the patriarch's own offspring. Since Roman times, the powers conferred by *patria potestas* extend to administering the punishment of death — to the unfaithful wife, the dishonored daughter, the disobedient son. The historical trajectory of patriarchal power in Mexico tended to reinforce this last category of *patria potestas*, life-and-death power over wife and offspring, while attenuating the others.

Contrary to what we might assume, the father's power over wife and children increased in the early years of the republic when compared to paternal power during the colonial period. In her fascinating study of the surviving legal records of prenuptial disputes in the reign of New Spain, Patricia Seed categorizes the beginning of the eighteenth century as the period of the establishment of "normative patriarchy." Through meticulous analysis of the documents themselves, as well as of the linguistic transformation of the related terminology of relationships, she concludes that, in the early colonial period, the need to protect the woman from any public revelation of lost or compromised honor won out over paternal ambitions to secure the most "convenient" match (*To Love, Honor, and Obey*, 72).

The historical trajectory she traces, 1574–1821, begins in a period in which the church exerts all its power and influence to protect the young couple's right to marry, and ends in a period in which the increase in political power wielded by the new republican state has displaced ecclesiastical authority and has begun ever more aggressively to reinforce paternal preference over the wishes of the young couple. The church's initial practice of conserving female honor through whatever means necessary — secret marriage ceremonies, seclusion of one or both of the *novios*, police intervention — indirectly worked to break down the corporatist hierarchy with its marked social stratification because so many families were compelled, by the church's intervention on behalf of the young couple, to accept unions that they regarded as socially and economically disadvantageous. In the eighteenth century, as a direct consequence of a growing mercantilization, Seed observes an inversion of authority in prenuptial disputes in which the concept of honor now becomes more directly linked to paternal socioeconomic position, while at the same time paternal rights are being redefined to the exclusion of maternal ones. The growing involvement of new groups of merchants, miners, and bureaucrats with global markets reinforced patriarchal authority "in a new and original way," "creating ... an essential basis for the affirmation of normative patriarchy in matrimonial selection." Mercantilism legitimated the belief "that marriage decisions were strategic rather than personal," and "the newer argument that economic power should translate into political authority within the family" reinforced the father's exclusive claim to authority over the choice of the next generation's marriage partners (122–34). Sylvia Arrom's work also associates incipient mercantilism with an augmentation in patriarchal power, arguing that even the few laws designed to protect female property had as their underlying motive the protection of male property given how the woman herself, along with all her possessions, was construed as belonging in the last instance to a man.

In *Theorizing Patriarchy*, Sylvia Walby stresses the need to distinguish between transformations in the *degree* of patriarchy and in its *forms*, the latter divisible into two coexisting types, *private* and *public*. Private patriarchy is based on the home as a unit of production and reproduction; public patriarchy is centered in the civic spheres of state and labor market. The private form of patriarchy tends to be individualistic and exclusivist; the public form is a collective appropriation that subordinates and separates women (23–24). Both forms exhibit "a strong patriarchal alliance across class differences which supports the exclusion and/or subordination of women." Like Arrom and Seed, Walby (whose analytical context is England) attributes the transformations in the location of patriarchal power to the development of capitalism, which "opened up new sites of power, and these were colonized by men because they were strategically placed to do so" (184–85).

This simple yet profound distinction between the private and public exercise of patriarchal power illuminates the distinct periods of Mexican patriarchy addressed by Arrom and Seed, as well as those that would follow. In the early colonial era analyzed by Seed, the patriarchal power of the church (both public and private) was greater than the (public) power of the state and the (private) power of the father. Both historians agree that in the eighteenth century the patriarchal power of the state worked to reinforce family-based patriarchal power in order to diminish the authority of the church, while the penetration and extension of mercantilism lent a new basis to paternal authority as an economic link to the public sector.

Arrom interprets the late colonial laws decreed in defense of paternal authority over the marriage choices of offspring as a sign of the *erosion* of paternal power, suggesting a double movement in which the effort to enforce and reinforce acknowledges a prior or potential diminution of power. She emphasizes that any subsequent tendencies to limit paternal authority over children were not accompanied by a parallel inclination to limit power over the wife. By the mid-nineteenth century, when Arrom's study concludes, the integrity of the corporatist state had been undermined by a series of decisions in favor of granting increased autonomy to various subordinate groups: the abolition of slavery, the granting of limited rights to indigenous peoples, the exempting of adult children from the exercise of *patria potestas*. These social transformations "made the wife's subjection to her husband's authority all the more anomalous"; she was "the stark exception among adults" (94).

This account of the shifting outlines of public and private forms of patriarchy in pre-Conquest, colonial, and early republican Mexico stops one hundred and fifty years short of the present. If the first several decades of the republic were characterized by tremendous political instability and the lack of a lasting leader, the three decades that preceded the revolution of 1910 found in Porfirio Díaz the supreme embodiment of the patriarchal president. The revolution that eventually swept him from power made possible, if only temporarily, the trampling of all social hierarchies, even that most recalcitrant hierarchy of gender, though a significant proportion of the possibilities unleashed during the decades of revolution and counterrevolution were curbed, if not reversed, by a series of governments ever more closely tied to the conservative interests of an increasingly transnational bourgeoisie, and by a devious politics of co-optation by dominant political interests. Imported ideologies of developmentalism and modernization, along with the series of political convulsions and economic boom and bust cycles that has characterized the last half-century, producing massive internal and external migrations and enlisting unprecedented female participation in the public labor sector, would produce many cracks in the once firmly cemented structures of patriarchal power. Private and public forms of patriarchy were challenged as women, having finally won the right of suffrage in 1953, were increasingly admitted into the public sphere. Transformations of the public sphere stimulated and reflected not always complementary transformations in the private realm of personal and family life.

Jorge Ayala Blanco finds that the late 1930s and early 1940s saw the simultaneous consolidation of the Mexican film industry and of a new kind of urban middle class.

> The Mexican middle class is made up of the old landowners [hacendados], whose privileges had been reduced by the armed revolution of 1910; the revolutionaries themselves, who had managed to prosper thanks to the institutionality and bureaucratization of social movements; the petty provincial landlords and speculators; the would-be professionals [profesionistas] barely out of university or technical school; governmental and office workers in general; businessmen and managers of nascent industries; and merchants of all types, origins, and sectors. Besides being heterogeneous, it is a class without ideology, ferociously individualistic, afflicted by a

vociferous nationalism, champion of the penetration of foreign capital, comfortably installed, thanks to its weapons of cunning and dissembling, in the realm of competence and getting ahead [*arribismo*]. (49)

Julia Tuñón's essay on images of the Mexican family in 1940s films scrutinizes the existing structures of the family in the cities, where one-third of the population was now concentrated, the vast majority new arrivals. She finds the imposition of the model of the upper-middle-class nuclear family anomalous in such a socially diverse population in which other models such as the extended family, multiple and fragmentary family groupings, and matrifocal households were equally or more prevalent; she calls the imposed model, poetically, "the silhouette of a void." Emphasizing the urban origins of film production, the middle-class origins of the producers, and the improvised, commercializing nature of production, she finds within these family melodramas "one social group's way of thinking and feeling" but argues that the inevitable infiltration of elements diverging from the moralistic vision of "the way things are supposed to be" provides a space within which the (largely working-class) audience can perceive double messages and multiple meanings ("La silueta de un vacío," 138).

> The filmic family appears as a closed, patriarchal group, a universe in itself, an isolated and secure environment. [The separation sought between home and world is absolute.] Time as depicted on the screen is eternal: the family precedes the incident that is related [either the departure of one of its members or the entry of an external problem] and will outlive it. The fundamental thing . . . is that [the family] confers protection in the face of an always hostile world. Remember that we are in a country where social security is scarce, which has just suffered through a long string of political conflicts, and that those who make the films were children or adolescents during the revolution. (140–41)

> Loyalty becomes fundamental to maintaining family unity: this type of family thus opposes individual development . . . We're dealing with a pyramid where the father occupies the cusp . . . I find in these films an image containing much earlier elements, elements that were in force throughout the

viceroyalty and the nineteenth century, such as the father's authoritarian role, his characteristic ownership of the family and of his children, the permissiveness regarding male, but not female, adultery. (142)

The female figure occupies the superior place in the melodrama, but authority is paternal. The female role centers on her nurturing function, the power behind the throne. The mother, in relation to her son, constitutes the basic nucleus, but for this nucleus to be a family, to constitute itself as a "home," the figure of the father is required. It is his presence that lends legitimacy to the offspring . . . Still, . . . when the head of the family disappears, the harmony between mother and children increases. It seems as if the paternal figure is conceived as either absent or excessively present, suggesting the idea of a leader unworthy of his power, a usurper of rights . . . The struggle between the father and the mother for control of the offspring reflects, then, another, more powerful struggle between nature [instinctive maternal love] and culture [the institution of the family, which is socially necessary to confirm the children as the father's property]. (143–44)

Tuñón concludes her book on Mexican women's history by observing:

Capitalist development complicated things still further by provoking a situation that was not only unjust but contradictory: a system that required an ideological platform of equality of individual opportunity . . . but without resolving gender oppression. Woman works outside the home, but must do so without violating her supposed nature, which stands in contradiction to ambition, competitiveness, and the capacity to earn money. She has civil and political rights but must avoid violating patriarchal norms . . . determined by a system of male privilege that has also been inculcated into her . . . Change requires other strategies, because female oppression also dwells in the terrain of ideology underlain by a mixture of ancient and modern elements. (*Mujeres en México*, 165)

From the early years of postrevolutionary national consolidation, one of the primary struggles within the Mexican film industry seems to have been between cementing over these increasingly apparent fissures and prying them open even wider.[13]

The Mexican Movie Industry's Preoccupation with the Paternal

Mexican cinema is currently in its seventh decade of sound production. The denomination of melodramas of patriarchy is applicable to films across this span—from the runaway hit of the 1930s, *Allá en el Rancho Grande* (Fernando de Fuentes, 1936) to the runaway hit of the 1990s, *Como agua para chocolate* (Alfonso Arau, 1993). A list of the many films that explicitly focus on the figure of the father as locus of narrative conflict (see Appendix), particularly in the classical period broadly defined as extending from the 1930s through the 1950s, confirms that the construct of paternal melodrama is as viable and necessary as that of maternal melodrama in the Mexican case. The melodrama of patriarchy is most useful when understood as not synonymous with paternal melodrama, but rather as a subtending disposition capable of functioning independently of and often, upon closer examination, indeed redirecting the ostensible thematics of the narrative. For the purposes of this essay, I have chosen to offer brief readings of five films, in addition to the already examined *Flor Silvestre*, in order to begin to explore how the the figuration of patriarchal authority functions across different directors, subgenres, and historical periods.

Allá en el Rancho Grande

That Fernando de Fuentes would film two versions of his megahit *Allá en el Rancho Grande* should come as no surprise since by 1937, a year after the original film's release, some twenty imitations had already been released by other directors. To my taste, the 1936 effort, starring Tito Guizar and Esther Fernández, is superior to the 1948 color remake featuring the legendary Jorge Negrete opposite an impossibly wooden Lilia del Valle, but the former, combined with some significant modifications to the remake, prompt me to base the following comments on the later version.

The double setting of the opening sequence (developed for the remake) establishes paradigms of fatherhood and motherhood — the former privileged, decisive, celebrated; the latter disempowered, vulnerable, lamented. On the one hand, potency and power; on the other, passivity and pathos. In the opening sequence, shot on the patio of the eponymous Rancho Grande, a birthday celebration situates the *padre/patrón/patriarca* Don Rosendo (Salvador Quiroz) among his myriad subordinates as the object of general adulation. Don Rosendo offers generous assistance ("All of you can count on my help as if you were my own children") while sharing his wisdom with his preadolescent son and heir: "Look and learn from this, Felipe, how a ranch owner has to be father, doctor, judge, and even at times undertaker for his poor peons." The jubilant plenitude of this patriarchal setting has just been temporarily interrupted by Angelina's (Lupe Inclán) request for money for a *comadre* in Rancho Chico who is on her deathbed (hence Don Rosendo's undertaker reference). This second setting could not be more different: a spare room, sobbing children, an image of the Virgin of Guadalupe overlooking the scene while, with her dying breath, the woman commends her two biological offspring, José Francisco and Eulalia, and her adopted daughter Cruz, to the care of Angelina. This brief exposition emphasizes popular stereotypes of a judicious, benign, and hence legitimate masculine authority and a contrasting female state characterized by destitution, vulnerability, and impotence. The paternal is cause for celebration and tribute; the maternal is best revered as loss. Female abnegation (*la madre sufrida*) achieves its apotheosis in the arbitrary pathos of negation (*la madre sufrida muerta y llorada*).

As the next sequence opens, a year later, Angelina is getting the two biological children, whom she clearly favors, ready for their first visit to the hacienda. Playing the evil stepmother, she commands Cruz, Cinderella-like, to stay behind doing domestic chores. Between the orphan from Rancho Chico and the heir of Rancho Grande a friendship is born under the benevolently watchful eye of Don Rosendo, who looks down from the portrait that hangs over his desk as the boys play-act their future roles. A dissolve reveals them in full adulthood (Jorge Negrete and Eduardo Noriega), still below the painted gaze of the now-departed Don Rosendo ("May he rest in peace," intones his son Felipe).

As in the first section of *Flor Silvestre*, the animating conflict here is ostensibly class difference, yet in fact the relationship between the two men is so free of tension that the constantly interjected folkloric spectacles and musical interludes threaten to turn the film into a kind of scrapbook of rural folklife. In a cockfight, José Francisco takes a bullet destined for his *patrón* Felipe and is in turn saved by a transfusion of Felipe's blood, but these plot developments get shorter shrift than the folkloric elements and comic set pieces, which recall the conventions of the *teatro frívolo* sketches from which the film takes much of its inspiration. In another fizzled plot situation, the dramatic tension of José Francisco's race on Felipe's horse is diffused when the competition is uncharacteristically excluded from the film's anthology of rural folkways. In narrative terms, these incidents are curiously truncated or downplayed. In the film's idiosyncratic system of signification, however, it is their symbolic significance, not their narrative weight, that matters. The substitution of José Francisco's body for Felipe's, and the saving of the former through an injection of the latter's blood, make the two "blood brothers." José Francisco's skill on Felipe's horse signals another symbolic, this time phallic, substitution.

Another potential engine of dramatic tension, equally slow to ignite, is the semisecret love between José Francisco and his oppressed adopted sister Cruz, the unwilling object of the attention of various local males. The cash prize he brings home from the race enables José Francisco to publicly declare his intention to marry Cruz. This declaration, directed at Cruz and at their unreceptive godmother Angelina, is interrupted by the masculine obligation to go to the tavern, where José Francisco repeats his declaration, only to learn, in a memorable "dueling ballads" sequence, that Cruz's honor has been sullied. The suitor thus discovers what the viewer already knows: that while José Francisco was competing at the horse race, his godmother Angelina offered Cruz to Felipe in exchange for enough money to enable her to secure a good match for her favorite, Eulalia. Only her chronic, histrionic tendency to faint when approached by a man (she suffers from asthma) saves the innocent Cruz from this heartless scheme. When Felipe overhears her murmuring José Francisco's name, he decides to restrain himself and respect the secret courtship. As he gallantly takes the flustered girl home, two voyeurs lose no time in spreading the word of Cruz's dishonor.

In the semifinal sequence, master and employee, surrounded by the local population, face off in front of Angelina's house. Without so much as asking for her side of the story, José Francisco publicly repudiates Cruz and challenges his master: "After what happened last night, there is one too many of us." Although Felipe's eloquent defense convinces José of Cruz's innocence, the dramatic issue of Felipe's own clear *lack* of innocence is passed over completely; he simply declares that his own actions were a natural response: "I am a man of flesh and blood."

The assignation of evil thus falls fully on the scheming shrew Angelina. She receives her punishment at the hands of the least manly of men, her *compañero*, the drunkard Florentino (Armando Soto La Marín, called "Chicote"), who is now publicly authorized to yell at and beat her as she has him so many times before, asserting, "From now on, I am the one who wears the pants in this house." The film ends with the conventional trope of the marriage ceremony unconventionally multiplied. In the last, long sequence shot, not one but four couples emerge from the doors of the church: the *patrón* and his bride, José Francisco and Cruz, Eulalia and her rich catch, and finally, looking absurdly gawky in her bridal gown, Angelina, engaged in heated dispute with her incongruous lord and master Florentino.

The nostalgia and humor that suffuse this prototypical *comedia ranchera*, prototype of the first Mexican subgenre to garner an international following (for reasons nicely articulated in Ana M. López's "A Cinema for the Continent"), are more ideological than innocent. Differences between rich and poor, the powerful and the dispossessed, are here represented as merely of scale rather than degree, as if the contrast between Rancho Grande and Rancho Chico resided only in their relative size. Furthermore, these differences get displaced in favor of another issue of proprietorship: who will exert ownership of the desired female body? The axis of narrative conflict is eventually revealed to be a version of *jus primae noctis* or *derecho de pernada*. This perception is shared by Emilio García Riera, who traces this plot device back to the silent film antecedents of the *comedia rachera* genre (*Historia documental*, vol. 1, 236). The master's self-control is attributable to his recognition of the quasi-filial tie between himself and his subordinate José Francisco: "We have been like brothers. Do you think that I am capable of betraying you?" The objectification of the young woman and the vilification of the mature one (Angelina as not-mother, not-wife) are consequences of this fraternal alliance.

Angelina's moral otherness, her eventual identification as the site of evil which the Manichaean moral universe of melodrama often requires, can be retrospectively anchored in an early sequence when Don Rosendo counsels her to marry Florentino. In the only reference she makes to the fact that she, too, is a mother, she says of her natural daughter, "She was only sixteen when Our Lord took her away." The "humor" resides in her amplification: it was not "Our Lord in heaven" who carried off the unfortunate girl, but "our lord of the neighboring hacienda." This impiety regarding issues of honor, this unnatural maternity, places Angelina outside and apart. Even though he was not above "buying" Cruz, Felipe is above moral criticism because he acted as nature dictates that a man should act; Angelina can become the (semicomic) personification of evil because, both as mother and godmother, her attitudes are unnatural. Self-sufficient and resourceful within the parameters of the male-dominated world she inhabits, Angelina is represented as callous and scheming and morally other.

Allá en el Rancho Grande was made two years into the regime of Lázaro Cárdenas, a president who implemented land reform, encouraged labor militancy and mass organizing in support of women's rights, nationalized the railroads and the oil industry, and organized a political party "of the revolution" that has managed to perpetuate itself in power during all the successive decades. Although Fernando de Fuentes, widely regarded as Mexico's most important director of the initial sound period, made two of the most clear-eyed and powerful films ever produced on the theme of the revolution (*El Compadre Mendoza*, 1933 and *¡Vámonos con Pancho Villa!*, 1935), *Allá en el Rancho Grande* clearly constitutes a reaction against the promises of the revolution as implemented under Cárdenas. It is a reactionary fantasy of a return to a patriarchal Eden of prerevolutionary simplicity, order, and innocence, far from the threats of urbanization and other incursions of modernity. One way of retroactively reimagining an ever more manifestly heterogeneous nation was through this nostalgic recreation of the *patria chica* of the rural hacienda as a kind of prototypical patriarchal family that contained and controlled all difference and competition.

Even more than the epic melodrama of the revolution (*Flor Silvestre* et al.), the *comedia ranchera* genre emblematized Mexican cinema at home and abroad. Integral to it is the singing *charro*. Although many actors were to play that role over the decades, none embodied it more completely than Jorge Negrete, cast as the romantic lead in de Fuentes's 1948 remake of his 1936 hit. Aspects of the *charro* also accrue to Pedro Infante in—among other films—the two paternal melodramas he made with Fernando Soler under Ismael Rodríguez's direction (see the discussion of *No desearás a la mujer de tu hijo* later in this chapter) through his singing and his (parodic?) "dancing" horse. In all these generational melodramas, the viewer is left with the sensation that the new generation never quite succeeds in supplanting the old one. Although he has an heir, the patriarch does not seem to have a true successor, because he continues to wield his power even after death through the perpetuation of values previously imposed, and those who come after, if they survive the loss of the father, fail to achieve the same stature. This seems to be a structural feature of melodramas of patriarchy, however critical of paternalistic authoritarianism. It seems expressive of a fundamental ambivalence that the specifically cinematic evolution of the charro arguably also expresses.

In symbolic terms, the *charro* is the more or less rebellious pretender to the patriarchal throne; as such, he must necessarily define himself in opposition to this dominant figure. The evolution of the cinematic *charro* often emphasizes unbridled irresponsibility (bar scenes and equestrian and other kinds of competitions) in contrast to the disciplined constancy of the patriarch, along with sentimentalized expressivity (serenade and courting sequences) in contrast to the cold, closed comportment of the *padre/patrón*. These schizophrenic behaviors denote the perpetual immaturity of the "next" masculine generation: balding screen idols play opposite fathers who look more like grandfathers yet still treat their offspring like adolescents. These latter remain caught in the role of alternately lovestruck serenaders and debauched marauders—

seldom husbands, and never fathers, because then they would have already become what they exist to oppose in a struggle necessarily frozen in time.[14]

Una familia de tantas

If actress Sara García is widely recognized as the cinematically consecrated "Mother of Mexico," Fernando Soler deserves analogous recognition as the national paterfamilias. From Fernando de Fuentes's *La casa del ogro* (1938) through Arturo Ripstein's *El lugar sin límites* (1977), he played the prototype of the authoritarian father for leading directors, including Luis Buñuel in *El gran calavera* (*The Great Madcap*, 1949), *Susana* (1950), *La hija del engaño* (*The Daughter of Deceit*, 1951); Ismael Rodríguez in *La oveja negra* and *No desearás a la mujer de tu hijo* (discussed in the next section); Alberto Gout in *Sensualidad* (*Sensuality*, 1950); Emilio Fernández in *Pueblito* (*Little Town*, 1961); and Alejandro Galindo in *Una familia de tantas* (*One Family among Many*, 1948), which many critics regard as his best role.

Fernando Soler was the eldest of eight children born to a pair of Spanish actors who arrived in Mexico in 1898. Four of the Soler sons—Fernando, Andrés, Domingo, and Julián—participated so actively in the Mexican film industry, primarily as actors and secondarily as directors that, according to Emilio García Riera's calculations, they figured in 25 percent of Mexican film production as of 1944, and the percentage remained at 20 percent as late as 1960. Interestingly, the most prominent role of the three elder brothers was that of paterfamilias. Andrés was cast in this role 66 times, Domingo 50 times, and Fernando 48 times—"más de 160 paternidades en total... y unos 300 hijos," according to García Riera's calculations (*Los hermanos Soler*, 17–25).[15] Without Fernando, Andrés, and Domingo,

> it is impossible to imagine the first forty years of Mexican sound production... Without them, Mexican cinema would not only be orphaned, since it would lose the figure of the father, but also unconfessed, since it would be at a loss for priests, and unlettered, because it would lack for convincing doctors and lawyers. Nor would it have competent figures of authority in municipal governments,

courthouses, and police stations . . . In short, traditional
Mexican cinema, so conservative and apprehensive,
would, without the Soler brothers, be left without a key
character when it comes to the maintenance of order, peace
within the family, and circumspection: the criollo. (17)

In Spanish, the term *criollo* was used from colonial times to indicate a person of European lineage born in the New World. Creole ideology divided the population into *gente decente* and the
rest, monopolizing the former category. The Soler brothers were
enlisted into a kind of filmmaking that exalted "decent" Mexico
via the representation of citizens "with neckties and good man-
ners" (*Los hermanos Soler*, 18). At the beginning of the industrial
era, it is not surprising that Mexican filmmakers would choose
to stress a Europeanized or European-like middle class in marked
counterpoint to the greaser and bandit images propagated by Hollywood since the silent era. From the 1940s, the *indigenista* strain
of many of the Emilio "El Indio" Fernández films would be perceived, accurately or not, as posing the first direct challenge to
this *criollista* paternalism. This *criollista* strain carries with it a debt
to Spanish theater with its preference for dialogue over action
and for an arguably theatricalized style of acting. García Riera
concludes, "Racist or not (and I believe that it was racist), Mexican cinema needed the Soler brothers to the degree that it needed
to give life and flesh to the social and professional classes that it
attributed to the creole sector" (ibid., 21). Among the brothers,
Fernando enjoyed the most prestige.

This concept of Fernando Soler as creole paterfamilias is important. Sara García is also a representative of the creole population, yet she is seldom if ever discussed in those terms. The case
of the symbolic father is different, less assimilable to an ideology of
homogenized Mexicanness. In his ancestry, in his casting, in his
acting style, and in the persona he projected, Fernando Soler carried (subliminal) associations with the drama of conquest. These
layered associations invest his paternal melodramas with additional layers of meaning.

Galindo's paternal melodrama *Una familia de tantas*, considered by many to be Soler's greatest performance, situates Maru
(Martha Roth), the middle daughter of a large, prosperous urban
family, between two competing masculinities, one traditional and

the other modern. Her father, Don Rodrigo (Fernando Soler), rules over wife and daughters with unrelenting severity while granting disproportionate license to his eldest son and virtually ignoring the youngest boy, barely five years old, who still remains in the women's charge. This double standard is clear from the opening "rise and shine" sequence in which the three daughters are scolded and inconvenienced by their father as a result of their elder brother's dallying in the bathroom.

At her coming-of-age party, Don Ramiro presents Maru to the match he has selected for her, her unglamorous, bespectacled paternal cousin. Maru, however, has other ideas, having been dazzled in an early sequence by a slick vacuum cleaner salesman, Roberto del Hierro (David Silva) who, despite the absence of both parents, managed to fast-talk his way into the house to demonstrate his dazzling Bright-O-Home Model M-10. Maru's eventual decision to *platicar* with Roberto outside the confines of the paternal household intensifies the confrontation between competing masculine discourses: the stifling discourse of traditional paternal authority, which stifles personal needs, and a modernized discourse of mutual support and understanding, which allows space for individual independence through horizontal relationships of friendship. Maru witnesses her father's differential treatment of her older brother and sister. Hector's (Felipe del Alba) girlfriend and the baby she has produced out of wedlock are unceremoniously incorporated into the household, but Estela (Isabel del Puerto) is battered by her father for having been caught kissing her fiancé. This double standard, combined with the complicitous intervention of the sassy servant, Guadalupe (Enriqueta Reza), provokes Maru's eventual decision to leave the household and marry Roberto without paternal blessing, in defiance of the ancient *patria potestas*. Her departure in full bridal regalia, after receiving her mother's surreptitious blessing, prompts the latter to confront her husband at last, a confrontation that takes place, significantly, on the threshold of the home rather than inside it.

One daughter has run away, the second has just left her own family for another, and first son Hector has fallen apart with the incorporation of his girlfriend into the paternal household as a surrogate servant ("Leave that and come serve me my dinner," Don Rodrigo orders her at one point). Maru's departure situates the remaining family members outdoors for the first time. When Don Rodrigo commands his two youngest children to cease their play and return to the house, remonstrating his wife that they had been forbidden to go outside, the film's crowning exchange begins. For the first time, his wife Gracia (Eugenia Galindo) dares to challenge his authority: "From today forward, nothing will be forbidden to these children."

When he responds, "This strikes me as a way of fomenting disorder," she replies, "No, Rodrigo, it is giving them the satisfaction we've never conceded, letting them be themselves. Why insist that everything submit to your ideas? I think one must yield instead to reason."

"I believe they're my children," her husband asserts. "Yes, Rodrigo, but their life does not belong to you. Their life belongs to them, and they're the ones who have to live it. I see everything clearly now. We have been only the blind instruments of God; we have given them life, but we don't have the right to shackle them. I have faith that God will continue to enlighten me so that I can guide my children solely by the rule of reason."

"Children do not understand reason," Rodrigo insists. His wife counters, "No, Rodrigo. We are the ones who don't understand the reasoning of children. The respect and obedience you have always demanded is not something that children are obligated to give; it's something that parents must earn." The film concludes with her urging him to prevent the little ones from eventually leaving home bearing the same bitter memories as their elder siblings. "Think about it, Rodrigo! Think about it!" The film ends with the beleaguered exponent of the patriarchal family literally standing on the threshold of a house that will no longer be his personal fiefdom.

The use of the inside-outside dichotomy is significant here, since threats to paternal authority are perceived as coming from outside the home. The eldest daughter is admonished to come directly home from work; the kiss that prompts her beating and subsequent flight occurs on the street in front of the house. The vacuum cleaner salesman breached the security of the family enclave while the mother was away on her only authorized excursion, her midday walk to the market. Maru uses the pretext of buying bread for the family supper to initiate her regular meetings with Roberto. Yet the film's studio-based production under-cuts this dichotomy since, with the exception of the opening and closing lateral pans of the urban landscape, all the exteriors are also, quite obviously, interiors. The eliding trope, a dissolve of bedsheets hung out to dry that "sutures" the opening and clos-ing location pans to the studio footage, seems deliberately high-lighted. Equally artificial are the frequent cutaways, in the latter half of the film, to the (painted) clock on the (painted) church tower "opposite" the house, as if ironically underlining the point that time only passes outside the paternal domain.

The majority of the film's sequences take place within the de-fined and confined spaces of the family home, a structure that is imposing without being grand, suggesting the decline of this Porfirian-style family. The camera pans in through a bedroom window to begin the film; the bedroom belongs to the household's three daughters, who rise one by one to get ready for the day. The second setting is, rather unconventionally, the bathroom, first (again, ironic) site of the imposition of arbitrary and biased pa-ternal authority. The kitchen is the third and the dining room is the fourth sequential setting, followed by the hallway and finally the living room. This "democratic" set distribution is notable be-cause, as Julia Tuñón has observed, in Mexican family melodra-mas the dining room is the setting of choice: "In the dining room, the public and private converge, her [nutritive, reproductive] work and his role as provider, thus representing the family system by combining the consumption of maternal sustenance in the space represented [and presided over] by the father" ("La silueta de un vacío," 141). Significantly, once he has gained admission to the paternal stronghold, fast-talking Roberto del Hierro heads straight for the dining room to demonstrate his wares.

The portrait of a bemedaled Porfirio Díaz, national patriarch par excellence, is prominently displayed and often included in the framing of the family living room where many of the key events transpire, the same living room that ends up temporarily accommodating first the sleek black upright vacuum and later a massive white refrigerator, imported commodities that symbol-ize impending transformations in relations within the home. The living room is also the site where del Hierro, the consummate salesman, seduces the father not once but twice, making his initial sale despite indignant resistance, and being rewarded for a second subterfuge—smuggling in the refrigerator—with a double sale: both Don Ramiro and his nephew sign on the dotted line. The living room is also the site of Maru's *quinceañera* (coming-of-age party) and of the accident that prompts her to have Roberto summoned to her aid, initiating their courtship.

What are being opposed through these contrasts are not simply discourses but ways of life. Don Rodrigo is an accountant; his son Hector exercises the same profession but with less satisfaction. For the shortsighted father, any sign of distress in his son can only be caused by a temporary problem in balancing the books. Roberto is not occupied with someone else's numbers; he generates his own as the number one salesman of multiply-coded Yankee products. The entry of the marketplace into the home, the incipient conversion of the home into a market of its own with women as the eventual consumers of devices that promise to alter the conditions of their domestic labor—like Roberto's upward career move to sales of more costly and durable imported household goods—figures the transformation of both economic and personal relations, both domestic and national economies. In *Una familia de tantas*, the nation is symbolically refigured as a child-woman poised between two imperial traditions: Porfirio Díaz and Uncle Sam. Remembering Díaz's unprecedented opening up of Mexico to foreign investment, the difference that this particular difference is meant to symbolize becomes harder to distinguish.

Emilio García Riera perceives a doubling of the positive inscription of the American model in Galindo's film—at the level of narrative (Roberto del Hierro is the most engaging character), and at the level of a narrative style heavily influenced by Hollywood: "long, airy takes and sequences free of theatrical claustrophobia despite being shot almost exclusively in a limited set of interiors" (*Historia documental,* vol. 4, 268). We could add a third level, that of acting style: David Silva's performance is above that of all the other actors except his patriarchal adversary; his much more spontaneous performance style lacks the theatricality associated with Fernando Soler's.

As the middle child and the middle daughter, Maru is the pivotal figure in the film. Just turning fifteen (the actress seems patently older), she stands on the border between girlhood and womanhood. She is still kept at home to help with the housework, though she looks forward to the dual privileges of her coming of age: having a boyfriend and being able to go to work. Yet the film's development concedes her only one hard-won prerogative: choosing which man she prefers to belong to. Obviously, this kind of choice is very different from the option to make life choices independent of male-dominated social and familial paradigms. In addition, as a character, Maru is less than congenial: she is nervous, stressed out, and severely lacking in self-confidence, presumably as a result of the strains of paternal despotism, which also broadcast their toll in the characterizations of her elder siblings. These factors undercut what is seen by leading Mexican critics as an exemplar of socially aware melodrama engaged with actual social phenomena in a meaningful way. Emilio García Riera credits Galindo's film as having "saved Mexican cinema from absolute social blindness, since it aludes in quite appropriate terms to the imminent replacement of an old and diminished Porfirian middle class by a new and much larger one" (*Historia documental*, vol. 4, 268). He also praises the way that characters who in other melodramas never break out of their stereotype "take on in Galindo's film the breath of life through real social conflict" (ibid.). Is it too carping to suggest that, in the heroine's case, she seems constrained to opt for hyperventilation over asphyxiation?

No desearás a la mujer de tu hijo

As this sequel to *La oveja negra* begins, Don Cruz Tenorio Martínez de la Garza (Fernando Soler, again) has barricaded himself in the conjugal bedroom to expiate his inconsiderate treatment of his now-departed "saintly wife" and await his own demise.[16] Expressionistic elements dominate the shooting style and mise-en-scène: dramatic lighting, aural and visual effects of rain, extreme angles, unbalanced framing, an unconventional range of camera movements. These elements will reappear in the concluding sequence, when Don Cruz finally breathes his last, and at other key points.

In the opening scenes, his son Silvano (Pedro Infante) and others try to lure him out of his self-imposed seclusion and back to the world of the living. They seem to succeed only too well: the fickle patriarch leaves his mourning behind to return to the world of drink, gambling, whoring, and partying that, by his own admission, drove his wife to the next life.

The chasm that exists between father and son, the product of the arbitrariness, abusiveness, and arrogance of the former, is bridged when the two of them, at Cruz's insistence, stand in front of the portrait of the deceased and, equally drunk, vow to replace their long-standing antagonism with a bond of friendship and swear that neither will ever bring another woman into the house. "When we're old we will remember together our great love," Cruz tells his son. This transgenerational friendship is postulated on the loss of the beloved (Cruz has been widowed and Silvano's sweetheart has married another) and mutually imposed domestic celibacy. The vow is no sooner repeated in the sober light of the following morning than a young woman with whom both father and son will fall in love crosses the threshold.

The focus of this delightful comedy is not this sexual rivalry per se, but the somewhat inverted Oedipal struggle between a father who demands the most exaggerated deference (Silvano swallows his cigarettes rather than offending his father by being caught smoking in his presence), while behaving in the most dishonorable and self-indulgent fashion (Cruz gambles away his son's inheritance, and causes the death of Silvano's prized horse), and a son who fails to protest the injustice of his subordination.

A pivotal tavern sequence invokes the ideology of *patria potestas*, the belief that the father "owns" the life of his offspring. In order to liquidate his father's unpaid gambling debts, Silvano accepts a challenge to Russian roulette, and explains his intention to his father: "To win back what you lost, which was not yours to lose, or to lose the only thing that you have given me, which really is yours, my life." This deliberate flirtation with mortality impresses Cruz, who concedes, "Now you *are* a man." Yet seconds later, this mutual understanding dissolves into intensified animosity in the face of their mutual desire to marry Josefita (Carmen Molina). At the conclusion of a long, intricately choreographed sequence that weaves its way though the streets of the town, Silvano succumbs to the pressure to humiliate himself (once again) before his father and beg his pardon, but the ever-imperious Cruz refuses his son's petition: "Before permitting you to marry her, I'll kill you, or you'll kill me, or we will kill each other."

In a subsequent confrontation, which takes place in the parental bedroom, with the same rain falling outside and the same expressionist treatment, the son boldly demands that his father recognize his advancing age. Despite the visual proof offered by his image in the mirror, Cruz insists on his youthful vigor and, with a belly laugh, heads out to demonstrate it by repeating his earlier feat of fence-jumping on horseback. This time, however, his luck deserts him: his fall requires the death of Silvano's horse and, a few hours later, causes his own, though not before he has, in characteristically arrogant and arbitrary fashion, "repaid the debt" of the dead horse by shooting his own beloved dog, adding with chilling gallantry: "If there's something more I owe you, you can hold Josefita accountable for it. I leave her to you." With characteristic hypocrisy, he proceeds to expel his son from the house on the grounds that "A vow is a vow." Silvano responds once more by kneeling down and kissing the paternal hand. Cruz then suffers an attack as a result of his fall, prompting a deathbed sequence that mirrors the ending of *La oveja negra*. He confronts death "like a man," willingly, as "another fence that has to be jumped," and his accumulated obnoxiousness does not deprive him of the solace of being surrounded by all his loved ones at the moment of his passing.

A shot of Cruz and his deceased wife reunited "on the other side of the fence," a vision anchored as much in the son's subjectivity as in the father's, concludes this satire of *patria potestas in extremis* in a way that neutralizes some of the film's most critical elements. The father's boundless egotism, arbitrariness, and hypocrisy dissolve in the pathos of his final moments and the romanticism of an afterlife where his rejuvenated and welcoming wife awaits him. With that recuperative gesture so characteristic of melodrama, a form that nourishes itself on the unmasking of vital contradictions that it does not pretend to resolve, this antipatriarchal paternal comedy ends by pardoning the patriarch.

For García Riera, this hyper-Manichaean scheme turns out to be a draw. He argues that in *La oveja negra*, director Ismael Rodríguez "is ready for anything but taking sides." In addition to the box-office boon of casting two equally crowd-pleasing actors as the opposing parties, he asserts,

> father and son represent the two sides of the highly admired macho, two interchangeable sides. Doesn't the father, whose old wet nurse still lives with him, seem to be an irresponsible, disobedient son? And doesn't his son seem to be a mature and responsible father watching over the false steps of his son-father? One and the other are, after all, one and the same, though they may seem to be opposites, as is completely confirmed when both weep disconsolately over the body of the one who might be the mother of her husband or the wife of her son. (*Historia documental*, vol. 4, 103)

García Riera does not reiterate this equation in his commentary on the sequel, but instead stresses the ironic dimension suggested by the way both films "display within themselves their initial spectators" through the device of incorporating the townspeople as constant observers of the battles between father and son (*Historia documental*, vol. 5, 105). It is hardly a stretch from these observations to a reading of this pair of films as a self-aware and highly accomplished parody of paternal melodrama. The hyperbolic performances, as well as many of the dialogues of the iconic Soler and Infante, reinforce this reading, as do the Oedipal characterization and positioning of the mother and the sweetheart, each "la mujer del hijo y la mujer del padre."

El Bruto

Consistent with its director's penchant for subverting genres from within, Luis Buñuel's *El Bruto* offers an inverted version of paternal melodrama. The domain of this particular *patrón*, Don Andrés (Julián Soler), is urban instead of rural. His lack of benevolence toward his dependents is apparent from the opening sequence in which, accompanied by a lawyer and a policeman, two extensions of the law of the father that he also incarnates, he announces a general eviction; the property will be of more value to him when put to other uses, though he piously claims he must build "a house for his father." The subsequent sequence reveals

an ill-matched couple and an inverted nuclear family. Don Andrés's wife Paloma (Katy Jurado) appears to be at least three
decades younger than he.[17] Her activities suggest her practical
status to be more that of a servant than mistress of the house, yet
this does not seem to restrain the rudeness, disdain, and sexual
disinterest she displays toward her husband. The place of this
odd couple's offspring is comically inhabited by Don Andrés's
father (Paco Martínez), an ornery and infantilized old Spaniard
with a persistent sweet tooth. When Don Andrés's hit man,
whose name is Pedro but whom everyone calls El Bruto (Pedro
Armendáriz), moves into the storeroom below the family apartment at his boss's request, the sexual alliance Paloma offers him
is doubly transgressive. This adultery is tinged with incest from
the outset by the suggestion that Don Andrés is El Bruto's father.

In Buñuel's (in)version of paternal melodrama, the (bastard)
son finally kills the *padre/patrón*. The act is in self-defense (Don
Andrés has threatened him with a gun) and provoked by Don
Andrés's threat against his girlfriend Meche (Rosita Arenas), the
only pure soul in El Bruto's sordid world. Paradoxically but tell-
ingly, the patricide takes place both on-screen and off-camera,
since the camera angle locates the viewer literally "under the
table" (like some spying child) when El Bruto repeatedly and fa-
tally bangs Don Andrés's head against it. The inserted reactions
of wife and father further undercut the criminality of this patricide: the willful Paloma, whose jealousy toward Meche and false
accusation of rape set into motion the father-son confrontation,
listens from her bed, her body mimicking the motions she hears.
The old *gachupín* crosses the adjoining room, oblivious to his son's
corpse, muttering his characteristic complaint, "In this household they abandon you like a dog," and then gleefully helps himself to the candies hidden in the sideboard.

El Bruto flees to the site of the eviction in search of Meche.
Paloma tracks him down and exposes his hiding place. El Bruto
dies at the hands of the police, the law of the now-defunct father
enduring through this official administration of "justice." The cold
stare exchanged between Paloma and a rooster perched on a wall
in the film's final shot underlines her complicity in having eradi-
cated the two masculinities on which she depended: Don An-

drés's economic and political power, and the clumsy, easily manipulable virility and brute strength of his illegitimate son ("El del gasto y el del gusto," in García Riera's wryly synthetic phrase).

In Buñuel's sardonic vision, the conflict between fathers and sons destroys both. Two patricides frame the narrative. El Bruto's "unintended" murder, in an early sequence, of Don Carmelo (Roberto Meyer), the father of the girl with whom he will eventually fall in love, dooms this love before it is born, since El Bruto's culpability for Meche's orphanhood eventually becomes the weapon used by a jealous Paloma to separate the sweethearts. At the film's conclusion, after the climactic deaths of Andrés and El Bruto, the virtuous daughter and the adulterous wife are left to fend for themselves in a world without fathers or husbands.

This film can also be read as another kind of melodrama, a melodrama of class alienation. El Bruto initially attacks the group to which he himself belongs, serving Don Andrés as the instrument through which he intimidates and displaces his working-class tenants. By eventually killing Don Andrés, El Bruto frees those who have lived under his yoke, but in keeping with Buñuel's characteristic refusal of sentimental solutions, the tenants are already dispersed, their lodgings already demolished, and, except for Meche, the few that remain on the disputed site collaborate in the final destruction of the one who has, however belatedly, saved them.

Como agua para chocolate

Like Water for Chocolate offers an oblique, revisionist version of the Mexican Revolution. Its geographical setting is on the border rather than centralized, while within the depicted domestic space the kitchen takes unaccustomed priority. The film liberally laces its realism with elements of the fantastic while elevating its female characters and stereotyping their male counterparts. That we are dealing here with a form of hypermelodrama is clear from the opening sequence in which the great-grandniece of the as yet unseen protagonist speaks in direct, wet-eyed televisual address of onions, tears, and Great Aunt Tita's cooking. The subsequent sequence, located in the historical time and place of this period film, depicts Tita's birth in a country kitchen spontaneously flooded with her intrauterine tears.

Linda Williams has grouped three commonly devalued film genres, each of which proposes to duplicate in the spectator the physical reactions depicted on the screen—terror in the thriller, sexual excitation in pornography, and tears in the melodrama—under the rubric of body genres. She theorizes that this mirroring corporeality is the source of these genres' obsessive attraction *and* of their dismissal as "low" forms. This mimetism of physiological response is jubilantly, hyperbolically exploited in *Como agua para chocolate* (both film and novel) through the narrative premise that Tita (Lumi Cavazos) has the special ability to project her emotional state onto anyone who tastes her cooking. Not just tears, but nausea and rampant sexual desire, take hold of diners at family banquets.

Such emotive fertility has its antagonistic counterpart in the emotional repressiveness of Mamá Elena (Regina Torne), a repression that is not only imposed on the daughters and female servants who live under her thumb but is also self-directed. Mamá Elena suppresses the memory and the evidence of her great transgressive love and negates the existence of her runaway daughter Gertrudis. Like Bernarda Alba in the culminating play of García Lorca's Spanish trilogy, she incarnates the domestic tyrant whose refusal of the attributes of the maternal denaturalizes and, in a grotesque way, masculinizes her. In her conviction that *her* will should be the only determining factor in her daughters' marital disposition, Mamá Elena incarnates a kind of *matria potestas*. Her exercise of this (patriarchal) power is perverse because she refuses to recognize the love between Pedro (Marco Leonardi) and Tita, arbitrarily decreeing the substitution of daughter Rosaura (Araceli Yarismendi) as Pedro's bride, and because she situates herself as the only possible recipient of Tita's devotion, proposing a life of filial service as the impediment to any matrimonial alliance.

In deference to the maternal law, Tita never marries, but in defiance of the maternal law, Tita and Pedro perpetuate their forbidden, transgressive passion for one another despite all obstacles and prohibitions. The perennial struggle between parental authority and filial autonomy, which Patricia Seed examines from the sixteenth century, resurfaces here as the conflictive nucleus of this postmodern hypermelodrama without finding resolution. Tita defies and denounces her mother, but her only escape from maternal domination turns out to be first madness (her own), and then rape (her mother's—a narratively unanchored reassertion of the supreme power of rampant masculinity). Mamá Elena's moral authority, however, endures beyond the grave; only Tita's impious declaration of hatred when confronted yet again with her mother's malicious, incriminating ghost succeeds in expelling that apparition once and for all.

The socially sanctioned union of the lead couple is displaced, through a twenty-year flash-forward, onto the marriage of Pedro's daughter/Tita's niece to the son of Tita's only legitimate suitor, the noble gringo Dr. Brown. The intergenerational conflict of authority versus autonomy is resolved in the bicultural couple, each reared by widowed fathers and maiden aunts, who immediately head off to the *real* north (Harvard Medical School—to pursue *his* career in his father's footsteps). The spectacular immolation of Tita and Pedro, the "disobedient daughter" and her illicit mate, has the blessing of an alternative, indigenous genealogy incorporated into the montage of this culminating sequence: Tita's wet nurse Nacha, from whom she learned to cook, and Dr. Brown's herbalist grandmother, who taught him the science of the empirical.

Beneath this film's captivating charm clings a misogynistic, sometimes racially inflected residue. The imputation of his wife's infidelity causes the paterfamilias, in his only appearance, to expire; sister Gertrudis finds her liberation in a brothel; both she and her daughter have a sense of rhythm not shared by other members of the family, supposed testimony to her mother's rumored alliance with a gentleman of African descent; Chencha, the servant girl, is the victim of the same marauding rapists responsible for Mamá Elena's death, yet she is reenlisted into the narrative without any acknowledgment of her ordeal or its effects; Dr. Brown's young son claims Pedro and Rosaura's daughter as his bride-to-be from the moment she is born; Tita cannot free herself from her mother's oppressive yoke except through madness and the impious declaration that the love she should feel for her mother has been supplanted by hatred; the price of Tita's long suspension between submission and rebellion is the (anti)climactic implosion of her and Pedro's relationship under the intensity of its long-deferred autonomy. Remnants of the "patriarchal imagination" cling even to counterpatriarchal (re)imaginings.

Conclusion

A hierarchized, corporativist model of social organization at whose apex stands the forbidding father as arbiter-avenger is so fundamental to Mexican culture and history that replications and contestations alike are invested with the power to illuminate cultural systems and processes of transformation. The argument developed here arises out of the conviction that, unless properly nuanced in accord with historical and cultural particularities, a term like "the family melodrama," when used in this particular cross-cultural context, is more apt to cover over than to highlight cultural specificities. At the same time, I hope to have suggested how attentiveness to the social and symbolic organization of gender reinvigorates the (always heuristic) analytical utility of the concept of genre. In the Mexican instance, paternal melodramas seem to be at least as prevalent as maternal melodramas, if not more so, and both these forms, along with a number of other subgeneric categories, are subtended by a "patriarchal disposition," which — like the "melodramatic imagination" that Peter Brooks identified as an instance of the "moral occult" that follows the demise of the sacred — pervades Mexican culture in ways that warrant further analysis in and beyond the field of film studies. The pervasiveness of the conjoined melodramatic and patriarchal imaginations in Mexican culture — in theater and the novel; in popular painting and song; in religious ritual; in national history, pageantry, and mythology, as well as in national cinematography — needs to be analyzed in regard to the particulars of the colonial experience, the process of Mexican nation/state formation, and the rise and demise of populism and the institutionalized paternal state as political paradigms. Because the Mexican movie industry rose to prominence parallel to the evolution of a new state formation, this massive cultural industry (film ranked third as a generator of gross national product during the 1940s) was integral to the process of constructing and consolidating the Mexican nation, particularly because widespread illiteracy meant that the film medium offered the most ubiquitous slate onto which inscriptions of and conscriptions into the national could be written.

The 1940s and 1950s were key decades in the critical reexamination of the patriarchal paradigm, as illustrated by the earnest critique of *Una familia de tantas*, the exaggerated parody of *No desearás*, the Oedipal layering of *El Bruto*. Yet the "work" of reinforcing and disassembling the paradigm, sometimes simultaneously, continued into subsequent decades. The pop-Freudianism gone berserk of *Pedro Páramo* in the 1960s was followed, in the subsequent decade, by Arturo Ripstein's sober rendering of a contemporary news story about one father's permanent confinement of his wife and children within *El castillo de la pureza*. In the late 1970s, Anthony Quinn returned to his Mexican roots to play an overbearing proletarian paterfamilias locked in perpetual struggle to impose his will on all his vast consanguinity, especially his protofeminist daughter Consuelo. By the era of *Like Water for Chocolate* and *Principio y fin*, revisioned gender orderings have shifted the center of household gravity to the maternal realm, but the customary powers and self-assigned prerogatives of the patriarch survive their projection onto the mother surprisingly intact. No matter which parent attempts to wield it, *patria potestas*, the semi-submerged locus of narrative conflict in *Flor silvestre*, remains at issue half a century later.

Alternatives to rigidified gender hierarchies and sociosexual identities, richly explored in recent Mexican literature and filmmaking, are being painfully played out not only in the private realm of family and personal life but also on the stage of national political life as long-cemented and more recently forged power alliances fight internecine battles, and a threatening vacuum of authority looms. The deep-seated Mexican/Iberian/Nahua disposition to patriarchal authority as the locus of order in the world has never been more subject to challenge. Feminist scholarship of various stripes has defined its task as placing women at the center of investigation. In light of that prolific and influential scholarly project, forms and expressions of masculinity can and must be read in a more adequate light. As I hope to have demonstrated here, turning critical attention to the masculinocentrism of (some) national expressions of the melodramatic imagination opens the way to deeper understandings of culturally specific and profoundly interrelated constructions of masculinity and femininity, homosexuality and heterosexuality, personal and national identifications, as well as confronting critics and theoristics with the historical and cultural determinants of their/our analytical tools.

Notes

1. An earlier version of this essay appeared as "La ley del más padre: melodrama paternal, melodrama patriarcal, y la especifidad del ejemplo mexicano," in *Archivos de la Filmoteca* 16 (1994), after preliminary presentations to members of the Program in Film and Video Studies at the University of Michigan (1993) and the Chicano/Latino Research Center at the University of California, Santa Cruz (1994). The essay evolved out of a working conference, "Movies and Melodrama in Mexico," which I organized at UC Santa Cruz in 1992 with the sponsorship of UC MEXUS, the University of California Consortium on Mexico and the United States. I would like to thank Julia Tuñón, Gastón Lillo, Norma Klahn, and Sergio de la Mora for commenting on earlier versions of this essay, with special thanks to Sergio for bibliographic assistance. Thanks to Elena Feder and Matthew Poage for careful proofreading and reformatting. All translations are my own.

2. For suggestive revisionist readings of melodrama as an object of critical attention, both written within a cultural studies paradigm, see Byars and Klinger.

3. For a significant confirmation of the global reach of film melodrama and its critical interrogation, see Dissanayake.

4. I use this term to suggest the adaptability of Doris Sommer's concept "foundational fictions" to this film in particular, as well as to numerous others that, in their attempt to narrativize the nation, and more specifically the story of the couple as analogue to the process of nation formation, function in similar ways to the nineteenth-century nationalistic novels that Sommer analyzes in *Foundational Fictions*.

5. In *Historia documental*, vol. 3 (1943–45), García Riera is at a loss to explain the narrative force of the "disobedient son" sequence. Because his analysis does not engage the film's patriarchal discourse, he is compelled to dismiss the sequence as an example of "generic contamination," arguing that the inclusion of the *corrido* "El hijo desobediente," a song he finds "inadequate to its plot moment," is simply an incongruous and unnecessary borrowing from the *comedia ranchera*, like the presence of the two comic peons who follow José Luis with feudal fidelity (18).

In "Disjointed Frames," Laura Podalsky observes: "By mapping the struggle of the nation onto that of an individual family, *Flor Silvestre* seems to glorify the revolutionary past while arguing for the need to restore the national family along traditional patriarchal lines. Rather than permanently assuaging the anxieties expressed in the film, the improbable narrative closure of *Flor Silvestre* demanded that the spectator return to similar texts to be reconvinced" (61–63).

6. Daniel Selden makes this point quite forcefully in his essay "Genre of Genre": There is a close connection in [Plato's] thought between generic prescription and political hierarchy, in this case the institutional authority of fathers, magistrates, and gods... Long after the different genres ceased to be occasional and to fulfill specific social functions, they continued to bear the marks of status, class, ethnicity, and gender, and for writers to uphold the propriety of these distinctions was felt implicitly to validate a social order" (27). Selden goes on to cite Tzvetan Todorov, Fredric Jameson, and Michael McKeon on the contingent nature of generic categories.

7. Initiated in 1969 by Ediciones Era, this compilation history of Mexican sound film has been corrected, updated, and reissued in eighteen volumes by the University of Guadalajara, 1992–95.

8. See de la Vega, 33–34 for a list of examples of this subgenre.

9. The distinction López invokes between maternal melodramas and women's films, frequently made by Anglo-American feminist scholars, has to do with the way the latter more self-consciously address the concerns of female spectators. López credits this distinction to Kaplan (123–129).

10. The variants are the male intruder-redeemer in a world of women, the widow-lover variation, the family aristocratic variation, and the male weepie.

11. The intersecting contours of this historically determined process of critical appropriation are delineated in detail in Klinger, 1–35.

12. For Steve Neale, the five "standard" critical assumptions are that the term was used pejoratively, that it was counterposed to "realism," *that its "most consistent associations were with pathos, romance, domesticity, the familial, and the 'feminine' and... its most persistent generic locations... the 'family melodrama' and the woman's film"* (my emphasis), that the woman's film was a devalued form, and that the cultural antecedent of the "lowly" woman's film was the equally "lowly" stage melodrama. In addition to illustrating once more that the impulse to redefine the term "melodrama" is a tenacious (and voracious) one, Neale's article suggests the possibility that the corrective woman-centeredness of much feminist and contemporary criticism may have overlooked aspects of generic masculinocentrism to the detriment of the fullest and most accurate understanding of the phenomena under study.

13. The disintegration of the Mexican film industry and the rise of independent production are addressed in Part III of Ayala Blanco's 1968 *La aventura del cine mexicano* and the three subsequent volumes: *La búsqueda del cine mexicano, La condición del cine mexicano* (both Mexico City: Posada, 1986), and *La disolvencia del cine mexicano* (Mexico City: Grijalbo, 1991), as well as in Berg. Analyses of the work of women directors such as Adela Sequeyro, and particularly Matilde Landeta, reveal both a refusal of and a challenge to patriarchal discourses. See Eduardo de la Vega and Patricia Torres San Martín, *Adela Sequeyro: Pionera del cine sonoro en México, 1901–1992* (Jalisco: Univ. of Guadalajara, 1996); Patricia Martínez Velasco, *Directoras de cine: Proyección de un mundo oscuro* (Mexico City: IMCINE/CONEICC, 1991), originally *La lucha de la mujer para llegar a ser directora de cine*, Tesis para título de licenciado en Comunicaciones, Univ. Iberoamericana, 1989; and Dever.

14. Ethnographer Olga Nájera Ramírez has traced the fascinating and contradictory history of the Mexican *charro* from its Spanish peasant roots, through its associations with rural banditry in nineteenth-century Mexico, and its subsequent

enlistment into the social microcosm of the hacienda as a concealer of class strat-ifications, to its twentieth-century manifestations in urban male associations (*char-reada* competitions) and officialist national(izing) folklore (the obligatory mari-achi band in *charro* garb). Although her primary scholarly focus is the *charreada*, she stresses that the cultural space that gave the *charro* broadest cultural reign was the cinema, where the figure embodied bifurcated masculinity (the aggressive action sequences and sentimentalized lyric-romantic interludes already mentioned). According to Américo Paredes in "Estados Unidos, México y el machismo," these negative qualities so exaggerated by cinematic representations of the *charro* came to be known as "machismo," a term that gained massive circulation in the 1940s, coinciding with the apogee of the *comedia ranchera* (65–84). Nájera Ramírez con-cludes: "The cinematic charro came to represent the unleashing of a conservative attitude in Mexico which recurred to an earlier social structure, idealized and ro-manticized, in which everyone knew their place and certain privileged men ruled. Their brusque and abusive comportment seemed acceptable and even nec-essary to control and guide the 'ignorant' masses. In their appeal to an idealized past, these films legitimated an iron-handed, tyrannical rule" (11).

15. Fernando Soler acted in 105 films and directed 22; Andrés acted in 192, Domingo in 152; and Julián acted in 57 and directed 82.

16. In *La oveja negra*, father and son compete in two arenas, the private and the public: the son's rejected ex-lover tries to win him back by taking up with his all-too-willing father, and father and son run against each other for election as police commissioner. See García Riera, *Historia documental*, vol. 5 (103), for a full plot summary.

17. García Riera refers to Paloma as Andrés's lover in *Historia documental*, vol. 6 (182).

Appendix

Significant titles corresponding to the sometimes overlapping categories of pa-ternal melodrama and melodrama of patriarchy include:

from the 1930s: La mujer del puerto/The Woman of the Port (Arcady Boytler, 1933); *Allá en el Rancho Grande/Over There on the Big Ranch* (Fernando de Fuentes, 1936); *La casa del ogro/The Ogre's House* (Fernando de Fuentes), *Los enredos de Papá/Papa's Complications* (Miguel Zacarías), *Dos cadetes/Two Cadets* (Jorge López Portillo and René Cardona) (all 1938); *En Tiempos de don Porfirio/In the Era of Don Porfirio* (Juan Bustillo Oro), *Papacito lindo* (Fernando de Fuentes), and *Los hijos mandan/The Chil-dren Rule* (Gabriel Soria) (all 1939)

from the 1940s: Cuando los hijos se van/When the Children Leave Home (Juan Bustillo Oro, 1941); *Flor Silvestre* (Emilio Fernández), *Doña Bárbara* (Fernando de Fuentes), *Tentación/Temptation* (Fernando Soler) (all 1943); *Bugambilia* (Emilio Fernández, 1944); *Una familia de tantas/One Family among Many* (Alejandro Galindo), *Cuando los padres se quedan solos/When Parents Are Left Alone* (Juan Bustillo Oro), *El dolor de los hijos/The Grief of the Children* (Miguel Zacarías) (all 1948); *La Malquerida* (Emilio Fernández) and the Oedipal comedies *La oveja negra/The Black Sheep* and its even more successful sequel *No desearás a la mujer de tu hijo/Thou Shalt Not Desire Thy Son's Wife* (Ismael Rodríguez) (all 1949) *from the 1950s: Azahares para tu boda/Orange Blossoms for Your Wedding* (Julián Soler), *Sensualidad/Sensuality* (Alberto Gout), *Rosauro Castro* (Roberto Gavaldón) (all 1950); *Susana, carne y demonio/Susana, Devil and Flesh* (Luis Buñuel), *El grito de la carne/The Cry of the Flesh* (Fernando Soler), *El bruto/The Brute* (Luis Buñuel) (all 1952); *Educando a Papá/Educating Papa* (Julián Soler), *Padre contra hijo/Father against Son* (Juan Bustillo Oro) (both 1954); *Cada hijo una cruz/Every Child a Cross to Bear* (Juan Bustillo Oro, 1957)

from the 1960s: La sombra del caudillo/The Leader's Shadow (Julio Bracho, 1960); *Pueblito* (Emilio Fernández), *Sol en llamas/Sun in Flames* (Alfredo B. Crevenna) (both 1961); *Cuando los hijos se pierden/When the Children Go Astray* (Mauricio de la Serna), *Los derechos de los hijos/The Rights of the Children* (Miguel Morayta) (both 1962); *Así amaron nuestros padres/That's How Our Parents Loved* (Juan Bustillo Oro, 1964), *¿Qué haremos con papá?/What Shall We Do with Papa?* (Rafael Baledón, 1965); *Pedro Páramo* (Carlos Velo), *El derecho de nacer/The Right to Be Born* (Tito Davidson), *Tiempo de morir* (Arturo Ripstein) (all 1966); and the remake of *Cuando los hijos se van* (Julián Soler, 1969)

from the 1970s: Lo que más queremos/What We Most Desire (Miguel Zacarías, 1970); *Cuando los hijos crecen/When the Children Grow Up* (Cima Films, 1971); *El castillo de la pureza/The Castle of Purity* (Arturo Ripstein, 1972); *El lugar sin límites/Hell Has No Limits* (Arturo Ripstein, 1977); the international coproduction *Los hijos de Sánchez/ The Children of Sánchez* (Bartlett, 1978)

from the 1980s and 1990s: Tiempo de lobos/Wolf Season (Alberto Isaac, 1984); *Principio y fin/The Beginning and the End* (Arturo Ripstein, 1993); *Como agua para chocolate/Like Water for Chocolate* (Alfonso Arau, 1993)

Works Cited

Arrom, Sylvia. *The Women of Mexico City, 1790–1857.* Stanford, Calif.: Stanford Univ. Press, 1985.

Ayala Blanco, Jorge. *La aventura del cine mexicano.* Mexico City: Ediciones Era, 1968.

Berg, Charles Ramírez. *Cinema of Solitude: A Critical Study of Mexican Film, 1967– 1983.* Austin: Univ. of Texas Press, 1992.

Brooks, Peter. *The Melodramatic Imagination: Balzac, Henry James, Melodrama, and the Mode of Excess.* New York: Columbia Univ. Press, 1985.

Byars, Jackie. *All That Hollywood Allows: Re-reading Gender in 1950s Melodrama.* Chapel Hill: Univ. of North Carolina Press, 1991.

de la Mora, Sergio. "Fascinating Machismo: Toward an Unmasking of Heterosexual Masculinity in Arturo Ripstein's *El lugar sin límites.*" *Journal of Film and Video* 44: 3–4 (1993): 83–104.

de la Vega, Eduardo. *Juan Orol.* Colección Cineastas de México: Univ. de Guadalajara, 1987.

Dever, Susan. "Las de abajo: La Revolución Mexicana de Matilde Landeta." *Archivos de la Filmoteca* 16 (1994): 36–49.

Dissanayake, Wimal, ed. *Melodrama and Asian Cinema.* Cambridge: Cambridge Univ. Press, 1993.

Elsaesser, Thomas. "Tales of Sound and Fury: Observations on the Family Melodrama." In Gledhill, 43–69, and Landy, 68–91.

García Riera, Emilio. *Historia documental del cine mexicano.* 18 vols. Univ. de Guadalajara, 1992–95.

———. *Los hermanos Soler.* Univ. de Guadalajara e Instituto Mexicano de Cinematografía, 1990.

Gledhill, Christine, ed. *Home Is Where the Heart Is: Studies in Melodrama and the Women's Film.* London: British Film Institute, 1987.

Harvey, Sylvia. "Women's Place: The Absent Family of Film Noir." In *Women in Film Noir.* Ed. E. Ann Kaplan. London: British Film Institute, 1978. 22–34.

Kaplan, E. Ann. "Mothering, Feminism, and Representation: The Maternal in Melodrama and the Women's Film." In *Home Is Where the Heart Is: Studies in Melodrama and the Women's Film.* Ed. Christine Gledhill. London: British Film Institute, 1987. 123–29.

Klinger, Barbara. *Melodrama and Meaning: History, Culture, and the Films of Douglas Sirk.* Bloomington: Indiana Univ. Press, 1994.

Landy, Marcia, ed. *Imitations of Life: A Reader on Film and Television Melodrama.* Detroit: Wayne State Univ. Press, 1991.

López, Ana M. "A Cinema for the Continent." The Mexican Cinema Project. Ed. Chon Noriega and Steven Ricci. Los Angeles: UCLA Film and Television Archive, 1994. 7–12.

———. "Tears and Desire: Women and Melodrama in the 'Old' Mexican Cinema." In *Mediating Two Worlds: Cinematic Encounters in the Americas.* Ed. John King, Ana M. López, and Manuel Alvarado. London: British Film Institute, 1993. 147–63. Originally published as "Celluloid Tears: Melodrama in the 'Old' Latin American Cinema." *Iris: Review of Theory on Image and Sound* 13 (summer 1991): 29–51.

Mistron, Deborah E. "A Hybrid Subgenre: The Revolutionary Melodrama in the Mexican Cinema." *Studies in Latin American Popular Culture* 3 (1984): 47–56.

Monsiváis, Carlos. "Las mitologías del cine mexicano." *Intermedios* 2 (June–July 1992): 12–23.

Mora, Carl. "Feminine Images in Mexican Cinema: The Family Melodrama; Sara García, 'The Mother of Mexico'; and the Prostitute." *Studies in Latin American Popular Culture* 4 (1985): 215–35.

Nájera Ramírez, Olga. "Engendering Nationalism: Identity, Discourse and the Mexican Charro." *Anthropology Quarterly* 67:1 (1994): 1–14.

Neale, Steve. "Melo Talk: On the Meaning and Use of the Term 'Melodrama' in the American Trade Press." *Velvet Light Trap* 32 (1993): 66–81.

Paredes, Américo. "Estados Unidos, México y el machismo." *Journal of Inter-American Studies* 9:1 (1967): 65–84.

Podalsky, Laura. "Disjointed Frames: Melodrama, Nationalism, and Representation in 1940s Mexico." *Studies in Latin American Popular Culture* 12 (1993): 61–63.

Rodowick, David. "Madness, Authority, and Ideology in the Domestic Melodrama of the 1950s." In *Imitations of Life: A Reader on Film and Television Melodrama.* Ed. Marcia Landy. Detroit: Wayne State Univ. Press, 1991. 237–47.

Schatz, Thomas. "The Family Melodrama." In *Hollywood Genres: Formulas, Filmmaking, and the Studio System.* New York: Random House, 1981.

Seed, Patricia. *To Love, Honor, and Obey in Colonial Mexico: Conflicts over Marriage Choice, 1574–1821.* Stanford, Calif.: Stanford Univ. Press, 1988.

Selden, Daniel. "Genre of Genre." In *The Search for the Ancient Novel.* Ed. J. Tatum. Baltimore: Johns Hopkins Univ. Press, 1994. 39–64.

Sommer, Doris. *Foundational Fictions: The National Romances of Latin America.* Berkeley: Univ. of California Press, 1991.

Tatum, J., ed. *The Search for the Ancient Novel.* Baltimore: Johns Hopkins Univ. Press, 1994.

Tuñón Pablos, Julia. "La silueta de un vacío: Imágenes fílmicas de la familia mexicana en los años cuarenta." *Film-Historia* 4:2, Univ. de Barcelona (1994): 137–47.

———. *Mujeres de luz y sombra en el cine mexicano: La construcción masculina de una imagen (1939–1952).* Mexico City: Colegio de Historia, Facultad de Filosofía y Letras, Univ. Nacional Autónoma de México, 1992.

———. *Mujeres en México: Una historia olvidada.* Mexico City: Planeta, 1987.

Tutor, Andrew. *Cine y comunicación.* Barcelona: Gustavo Gilli, 1974.

Viñas, Moisés. "Les Genres au Mexique." *Les Cinémas de l'Amérique Latine* 1 (1993): n.p. Originally appeared in *Dicine* 46 (July 1992).

Walby, Sylvia. *Theorizing Patriarchy.* Oxford: Basil Blackwell, 1990.

Williams, Linda. "Film Bodies: Gender, Genre, and Excess." *Film Quarterly* 44:4 (1991): 2–13.

Chapter 11
Queering the Patriarchy in Hermosillo's
Doña Herlinda y su hijo

David William Foster

Haz patria: ten hijos.
official government slogan in the 1930s and 1940s

*It is frequently assumed, not only within dominant representation
but within certain kinds of psychoanalytic discourse, that there are
only two possible subject positions—that occupied on the one hand
by heterosexual men and homosexual women, and that occupied on
the other by heterosexual women and homosexual men. Not only
does this formulation afford a preposterously monolithic reading of
male homosexuality, but it depends upon a radically insufficient
theory of subjectivity.*

Kaja Silverman (339)

Jaime Humberto Hermosillo's 1984 film *Doña Herlinda y su hijo*
(*Doña Herlinda and Her Son*) is one of the most unique films made
in Mexico during the 1980s. There is one long final sequence that
ends with the baptism of Rodolfo's infant child. Surrounded by
his loving wife and adoring mother and accompanied by his
closest friends, Rodolfo (Arturo Meza) presents his son to the
world to the strains of a saccharine melody in praise of motherhood. As she has done throughout the film, Rodolfo's mother,
Doña Herlinda (Guadalupe del Toro), presides with a look of
serene triumph, confident that she has successfully fulfilled her
maternal role of seeing the reproduction of society on into the
next generation. But Doña Herlinda's poise has, as one might expect, a suitable masculine counterpart. Yet, as the film viewer now
knows by this point in this droll film, that masculine counterpart
is not Doña Herlinda's husband (a formulation that would, in
any case, invert the male primacy in the masculinist world that
Rodolfo-son implicitly perpetuates). Rather, Doña Herlinda's counterpart, the individual who stands alongside Rodolfo's wife (Leti-
cia Lupercio), who in one portrait holds the baby, and who moves

back and forth to keep the festivities going, is Ramón (Marco Antonio Treviño), Rodolfo's male lover.

Prior to the concluding minutes to the film, and as Rodolfo's wife begins to experience final birthing contractions, the viewer is called upon to contemplate/cheer/abhor the directly explicit scene of Ramón and Rodolfo leisurely fucking in the private space Doña Herlinda has created for them in a specially renovated wing of her house. Significantly, although Ramón is generally portrayed as assuming the feminized role of the insertee, in this scene and bespeaking the dogged attempt of Hermosillo to defy canonical conjugations of male homosexual bodies, it is Rodolfo, on the verge of assuming the patriarchal role of reproductive father, who is being leisurely serviced by Ramón.

This series of virtually implausible acts, all carried out without the least bit of social and interpersonal tension, marks the problematical utopian space Hermosillo postulates in his film. Transcending the tired clichés of tragic homosexual love (understood as same-sex eroticism dominated by a heterosexist medicolegal codification) to be found in early novels by José Ceballos Maldonado's *Después de todo* (1968) and Miguel Barbachano Ponce's *El diario de José Toledo* (1964) — Barbachano Ponce is the producer of *Doña Herlinda* — or even the rather thinly configured gay identity of Luis Zapata's groundbreaking *Adonias García, el vampiro de la colonia Roma* (1979), Hermosillo's film defies classification in terms of hegemonic homoerotic primes: indeed, it transcends those formulations that, like José Rafael Calva's *Utopía gay* (1983), as interesting as it may be as a radical reinscription of reproductive marriage in Mexican society, can only have meaning if it is clear who the "man" is and who the "woman" (the one who ends up pregnant) is (Foster, 136–39). Hermosillo, however, introduces a significant modification in the Mexican representation of homoeroticism by confusing the issues of male/female identity, even though Rodolfo is generally assigned the male role. For example, in one significant scene in the movie Ramón receives an "anniversary" gift from Rodolfo that includes a container of Nivea, presumably to be used as a lubricant to enhance his performance as the insertee. Conversely, while Ramón plays the jealous lover on those occasions in which, in order to maintain appearances, Rodolfo escorts women in public, it is Ramón who plays the male counterpart to Doña Herlinda in her final orchestration of patriarchal bliss in the baptismal denouement.

But the crucial axis of the film falls to Doña Herlinda herself and the question as to what extent she is a token arbiter in the reduplication in the patriarchal structures of society and the extent to which she actually engages in their subversions, subversions that turn essentially on the refusal to abide by the "epistemology of the closet" (Sedgwick), which involves the definition of homosexuality as a dark, dirty secret that sustains compulsory heterosexuality out of the constant threat of its revelation as the damning identifying mark of the individual. Clearly, Doña Herlinda is a woman who is in full possession of her ability to engineer the social space such that the closet ceases to exist as a site of public scrutiny. It is she who invites Ramón to live in the same house with her son, while at the same time she steers Rodolfo into an engagement with Olga. It is she who undertakes to remodel her house so that Ramón may live in separate quarters, as she will, while Rodolfo and Olga, the apparently happily married Mexican professional couple, occupy with their son the main part of the house. And it is she who is able to balance with equanimity the relationship between Ramón and Olga, fully supporting the latter's desire to have her own career, which will involve a fellowship in Germany: while Ramón will be a companion to Rodolfo, she will be a loyal wife but not dependent and subservient. The fact that the lower-class, provincial Ramón will occupy this slot in the social structure in her stead is one of the possible ideological gaps of the film that remains unexplored: when Ramón's parents come to visit their son in Guadalajara and find him living in Doña Herlinda's house, they are confused and even a bit suspicious, but the ever-attentive Doña Herlinda ends up by winning them over, which is both a measure of her maternal efficiency and also a dimension of the uncertainties surrounding Ramón's social role.

Hermosillo glosses over the question of class differences — those based on economic questions (she is a wealthy widow; Ramón's parents are working-class provincials), professional ones (Rodolfo is a successful pediatrician and Ramón is studying the French horn), and cultural ones (Rodolfo is a big-city sophisticate, whereas Ramón is a relatively humble provincial). The major emphasis of

Doña Herlinda lies elsewhere: Hermosillo addresses the question of public versus private space and the conflicts that cluster around the divergence between social obligation and private needs. Doña Herlinda is once again the pivotal figure here. On the most explicit level, it is she who undertakes to move her son and Ramón out of the sphere of public scrutiny into the privacy of the home. This assumes four stages. In the opening scene of the film, we see her son Rodolfo in front of the early sixteenth-century Guadalajara cathedral, a monument to traditional Catholicism and the rigid moral code of Mexico's second-largest city. This scene exhibits intertextual connections, albeit parodic ones, with examples from classic Mexican films and the master narrative conjunction of mariachi music (which is typical to Guadalajara and which permeates *Doña Herlinda*), machismo (in the style of Pedro Armendáriz), and nationalist sentiment (iconized by the Guadalajara cathedral). Rodolfo's stance evokes Armendáriz's paradigmatic figure of the Mexican macho: Armendáriz is reputed to have countered Luis Buñuel's suggestion that he wear a short-sleeved shirt in a scene with the curt reply, "eso es de maricones"; in this scene, Rodolfo is wearing short sleeves.

Rodolfo is also—in an irony not lost on the cognoscenti—standing in one of the several interconnected squares in downtown Guadalajara that serve as the major cruising areas of the city, where side streets contain several of the city's quasi-gay bars, including the Bar Corona, which appears in the film.[1] In the opening scene, Rodolfo is on his way to meet with Ramón his the room at the boarding house catering to out-of-town students. In a series of comic contretemps, it is evident that this is hardly a trysting place, since the public space of the boarding house, reminiscent of the public space of the plaza, is not at all conducive to intimacy, much less gay intimacy. Even though everyone knows Rodolfo at the boarding house and is appropriately deferential to his social rank, it is clear that he and Ramón cannot pursue their relationship there.

The second stage involves Ramón's moving into the house with Rodolfo and his mother. As I have indicated, this move is engineered by Doña Herlinda, and in a frequently cited scene in the film, after the three have had dinner and the two men have retired to Rodolfo's bedroom and begin to engage in intimacies now protected by the walls of the mother's home, Doña Herlinda settles down in her room to thumb through magazines, looking at pictures of bridal gowns (Berg, 131). A third stage follows Rodolfo's and Olga's marriage. While the newlyweds inhabit their own apartment, Doña Herlinda and Ramón remain back at the house as though they were the proud parents of the newly married couple. In one sequence, they all assemble at the newlyweds' apartment to view the slides of their honeymoon in the United States and Hawaii. Then Doña Herlinda explains to them how she has undertaken a remodeling project at her house that will enable the four of them—and children—to live there comfortably. The fourth stage involves the closing sequence of the film to which I have already alluded, one that juxtaposes the fullness of Ramón's and Rodolfo's protected erotic intimacies in the most explicit sexual scene in the film with the fullness of Rodolfo's and Olga's domestic tranquillity. The beaming Doña Herlinda, having little to say as usual, presides over the events with her face gently fixed in a beatific but knowing smile.

Doña Herlinda is a pivotal figure in another sense. Olga is obviously a key female figure in the film, signaling a modern sophisticate who is able to combine both her career and motherhood—which she is able to do specifically because her husband has a male lover willing to assume parenting responsibilities. It would be inappropriate for any viewer to lament Olga's being shoved to the margins as a wife; to do so would involve seeing the film with social coordinates other than those with which Hermosillo frames his narrative, for Olga is fully aware of the arrangements Doña Herlinda has made. She has become good friends with Ramón and realizes that in the context of Doña Herlinda's world she will be able to fulfill herself both as a wife and as a professional; moreover, she will be able to accept the fellowship in Germany she has been offered, confident that she is abandoning neither her husband nor her child.

Doña Herlinda, therefore, does not overshadow Olga by virtue of the latter's margination, since only a heterosexist and social reactionary standard could see the role she has agreed to fulfill as marginal. Rather, Doña Herlinda is crucial as a woman who binds together both the public and the private. As a wealthy widow, she is able to move comfortably in the public world, in which she is called upon to exemplify maternal discretion. This she does on several occasions, most notably at the beginning of the film when she mediates the initially tense situation between Rodolfo and his two "dates," Olga and Ramón, who have yet to forge an alliance between themselves. But most important, she exemplifies compliance with the social code of compulsory heterosexual monogamous reproductive marriage, a code that she sees to it is fulfilled, at least in regard to critical points of reproductive marriage. Mexico, perhaps more than the United States, is a society in which it is possible to admit the possibility of the conjunction of reproductive marriage and the transgression of the criterion of monogamous heterosexuality in view of the traditional practice of extramarital affairs for men on the one hand, and the way in which varying degrees of homosociality and homoeroticism can be associated with Mexican male bonding on the other. I do not wish to insinuate that male bonding in Mexico is the same as gay sexuality, but rather there is a continuum that stretches from basic *compadrismo* to the possibility of various manifestations of physical intimacy.[2] By contrast, in the United States the concept of "buddyism" is either viewed as a phenomenon of youth that one outgrows with marriage or it is seen to be characteristic of ethnics and other subaltern groups. This is especially so since the "reheterosexualization" of American society in the 1950s, which was in large measure a reaction to the strong male bonding romanticized in cultural productions such as war films, as Kaja Silverman has noted in her chapter "Historical Trauma and Male Subjectivity." Nor do I mean to imply that Mexico in some way is more "morally flexible" than the United States, at least in regard to wandering husbands; rather, there appears to be a level of male-perspective cultural production modeling such opportunities without the aura of sanction that customarily surrounds such narratives in the United States.

Concomitantly, Doña Herlinda exemplifies the private space of Mexican life. As a woman, her realm of power is her home, and therefore to a large degree whatever she does to enhance life within its walls is socially legitimate. Sexual intimacy is a private matter, which is why Mexican and Latin American law in general has been historically less concerned with the nature of acts than with their distribution between the public and the private, as detailed by Lumsden (51ff.) and confirmed by other commentators on the place of male homoeroticism in the Latin American social dynamic (Acevedo; Nuñez Noriega; Trevisan; Murray passim). Transgression involves making private acts public, not the acts themselves, which is why the public display of heterosexual eroticism may be as vigorously defended as homosexual display, both as defiances of public decency. This does not translate into any greater respect in Mexico for gay rights. What it does mean is that the U.S. concept of the long arm of the law reaching into the bedroom of consenting adults is an alien judicial principle in most Hispanic societies. Thus while Doña Herlinda creates within the confines of her own home a love nest for Ramón and Rodolfo, she may be violating some standard of Catholic moral convention but she is also affirming the sanctity of the home and the privileging of her private domain. And, although the film might be decried as immoral by viewers who subscribe to institutional Catholicism, they cannot fault Doña Herlinda for having "rescued" her son from the risks involved in the semipublic display of his sexuality in the boarding house, with its ill-fitting doors, in order to protect it behind the solidly vine-covered walls of her home.

The question has been raised as to whether or not *Doña Herlinda y su hijo* is actually an adequate example of gay liberation or whether it merely reinscribes patriarchal values. I believe this is an inappropriate formulation, because it implies that it is possible somehow to transcend patriarchal values, whatever these precisely may be (e.g., is reproductive sexuality in contemporary society necessarily and always patriarchal, or is modern medical technology really providing an opening for conception and pregnancy that can circumvent patriarchalism and even heterosexuality?). Hermosillo's film might be viewed as utopian in the way in which it supersedes the either/or disjunction—*either* heterosexual marriage for Rodolfo *or* the "gay lifestyle"—in order to model a conjunctive arrangement in which no one is victimized (except for the possible unresolved social subalternity of Ramón). Yet *Doña Herlinda y su hijo* is hardly utopian to the extent that the arrangement figured *is* possible in the real world, rather than being a social fantasy or a science-fiction proposal. Hermosillo's film is micropolitics at its best, the possibility of a gesture of resistance without having to wait for the totally revolutionary restructuring of society in order to make possible the fulfillment of personal needs. It is less a question of reinscribing the patriarchy than of living at cross-purposes to it, less a question of resigning oneself to accepting the impositions of society (Rodolfo seems hardly displeased at becoming a father) than of availing oneself of the gaps or the contradictions in the system in order to construct dimensions of an alternate world (Dollimore). In this case, the criterion of privacy, especially for the professional class, can displace fulfillment of the social code of compulsory heterosexuality. What audiences have identified with in Hermosillo's film—a sort of identification that has been repeated in subsequent films such as María Novaro's *Danzón* (1992)—is the image of personal subversion in what is not exactly a hostile environment, but rather more one that is alienating in a general sort of way. For example, it is not that there is, at least in the universe of the film, any organized persecution of Rodolfo and Ramón, any sense of threat or danger, only the discomfort of the semipublic way in which their meetings take place. Development of the practice of seeking fissures in the social edifice allows for the subversive pursuit of personal needs without becoming a utopian confrontation with the regrettably deeply sunk pillars of that edifice.

I would argue that Hermosillo's film is, rather than either a reinscription of the patriarchy (albeit a singularly defective one) or a utopian imaging of an impossibly polysexual world of alternative family arrangements, an example of what Alexander Doty has described as the queer potential of popular cultural production. According to Doty's formulation, the queer is anything that challenges or subverts the straight, the compulsory heterosexual, either through an ironizing of its limited view of human possibilities or through the overdefiance of its conventions. So-called gay sensibility and its lesbian counterpart are necessarily queer (although lesbians and gays may in some contexts endorse the straight), but queer is something larger than a synonym of gay and lesbian:

> I ultimately use [queerness] to question the cultural
> demarcations between the queer and the straight (made by
> both queers and straights) by pointing out the queerness of
> and in straight couples, as well as that of individuals and

groups who have been told they inhabit the boundaries between the binaries of gender and sexuality: transsexuals, bisexuals, transvestites, and other binary outlaws.

Therefore, when I use the terms "queer" or "queerness" as adjectives or nouns, I do so to suggest a range of nonstraight expression in, or in response to, mass culture. This range includes specifically gay, lesbian, and bisexual expressions; but it also includes all other potential (and potentially unclassifiable) nonstraight positions. This being the case, I like those uses of "queer" that make it more than just an umbrella term in the ways that "homosexual" and "gay" have been used to mean lesbian *or* gay *or* bisexual, because queerness can also be about the intersecting or combining of more than one specific form of nonstraight sexuality. (xv–xvi)

Doty goes on to analyze major popular culture manifestations, finding that such productions are particularly privileged spaces for the elaboration of queer perspectives. Doty does not say whether this is the result of the need for mass culture to be constantly seeking new combinations as part of product consumerism or whether mass culture is only the most public face of a cultural production that is inherently queer because the straight mind has little need for practices built on questioning the given. Such an understanding of the queer may end up by draining it of most of its transgressive value—and indeed many of the examples Doty analyzes, such as *I Love Lucy* or the *Jack Benny Show*, were never viewed as particularly transgressive—and it may also serve to undermine the primacy of alternate sexualities viewed as alternate sexual practices and not just cute gender bending. Nevertheless, Doty's formulations are valuable for defending the notion of queer as a global concept and not just a pejorative synonym of gay and for proposing that the queer be sought beyond the limited confines of the texts of the cognoscenti.

John King describes *Doña Herlinda* as one of Hermosillo's gay divertissements (141), which may not be meant to be dismissive, but which nevertheless gives the impression that it has meaning only for a specifically gay audience. I am proposing, by contrast, that Hermosillo's film be viewed as a significant reinterpretation of clan arrangement possibilities, possibilities that are not utopian in any sort of fantastic way, and possibilities that are legitimated by the full participation of the actors involved. Furthermore, I am suggesting that *Doña Herlinda* be viewed under the purview of Doty's concept of queer culture, as a proposal for subverting the Mexican patriarchy through, significantly, the agency of Doña Herlinda herself, the one figure in the film most charged with defending the heterosexist system. Doña Herlinda "naturalizes" the perversion of the system as, perversely, a way of ensuring its maintenance (in the form of the biological continuance of the newborn, whose baptism at the end of the film is a ritual of his entrance into that system), and a good measure of the success of Hermosillo's film lies in the astuteness of his treatment of the borderlines between inscription and perversion (a "sweet subversion," according to Russo [313]), between legitimacy and transgression.

Notes

1. It should be noted, however, that gay pairs in Guadalajara blend in rather indistinguishably with the traditional all-male clientele of most Mexican non-tourist bars and that some of the bars of the area more known for their legendary Bohemian past blend this past with a specifically gay ambience.

2. Here I have in mind something like a masculine version of Adrienne Rich's lesbian continuum. Rich's proposition is that lesbianism is not a question of yes or no: one is not categorically either a lesbian or straight. Rather, issues of sexual identity, homoerotic feeling and behavior, and gender solidarity extend along a continuum. Different individuals site themselves at different points along the continuum and, more important, individuals may alter their placement along that continuum. For Rich, a lesbian is any woman who essentially defines her life in terms of other women, and not necessarily one who acts, feels, self-identifies, or engages in sex in a specific categorical way.

Works Cited

Acevedo, Zelmar. *Homosexualidad: hacia la destrucción de los mitos.* Buenos Aires: Ediciones Delser, 1985.

Berg, Charles Ramírez. *Cinema of Solitude: A Critical Study of Mexican Film, 1967–1983.* Austin: Univ. of Texas Press, 1992.

Dollimore, Jonathan. *Sexual Dissidence: Augustine to Wilde, Freud to Foucault.* Oxford: Clarendon Press, 1991.

Doty, Alexander. *Making Things Perfectly Queer: Interpreting Mass Culture.* Minneapolis: Univ. of Minnesota Press, 1992.

Foster, David William. *Gay and Lesbian Themes in Latin American Writing.* Austin: Univ. of Texas Press, 1991.

King, John. *Magical Reels: A History of Cinema in Latin America.* London: Verso, 1990.

Lozano Mascarúa, Alicia. "El cine de Jaime Humberto Hermosillo." *fem* 84 (1989): 28–30.

Lumsden, Ian. *Sociedad y estado en México*. Mexico City: Solediciones; Toronto: Canadian Gay Archives, 1991.

Mora, Carl J. *Mexican Cinema: Reflections of a Society 1896–1980*. Berkeley: Univ. of California Press, 1982.

Murray, Stephen O., ed. *Male Homosexuality in Central and South America*. San Francisco: Instituto Obregón; New York: GAU-NY, 1987.

Nuñez Noriega, Guillermo. *Sexo entre varones: poder y resistencia en el campo sexual*. Hermosillo: El Colegio de Sonora, División de Ciencias Sociales, 1994.

Rich, Adrienne. "Compulsory Heterosexuality and Lesbian Existence." In *Blood, Bread, and Poetry: Selected Prose 1979–1985*. New York: W. W. Norton, 1986. 23–75.

Russo, Vito. *The Celluloid Closet: Homosexuality in the Movies*. Rev. ed. New York: Harper and Row, 1987.

Sedgwick, Eve Kosofsky. *Epistemology of the Closet*. Berkeley: Univ. of California Press, 1990.

Silverman, Kaja. *Male Subjectivity at the Margins*. New York: Routledge, 1992.

Trevisan, João S. *Perverts in Paradise*. Trans. Martin Foreman. London: GMP Publications, 1986.

Chapter 12

Will There Be Latin American Cinema in the Year 2000? Visual Culture in a Postnational Era

Néstor García Canclini

(translated by Adriana X. Tatum and Ann Marie Stock)

Who is going to narrate identity? Identity is a construct that is narrated. Founding events—almost always referring to the appropriation of a territory by a group of people or to the independence achieved in confrontations with strangers—are established. Tales accumulate about those inhabitants who defend the territory, solve internal conflicts, and establish ways that differentiate these people from others. Scholarly books and museums, civil rituals and political discourse were for a long time the elements with which the Identity (with a capital "I") was formulated and its rhetorical narrative constructed.

Radio and film contributed to the organization of narratives of identity in national societies during the first half of this century. Both amassed heroic epics and great collective events into a chronicle of daily vicissitudes: common habits and tastes, styles of dress, and dialects that distinguished one place from another. According to the analyses of Carlos Monsiváis and Jesús Martín Barbero, radio programs enabled diverse regional groups—once distant and disconnected—to recognize one another as parts of a whole ("Notas sobre la cultura"; *De los medios*, 180–83). *Noticieros* or newsreels that initiated communication between distant zones made possible new syntheses of this changing national identity, much like the movies that taught migrants how to adapt to city life and deal with intercultural conflicts.

Mexican and Argentine cinema, which situated the narration of identity within visual mass culture in the 1940s and 1950s, reorganized their function in the 1970s when, aligned with the incipient television industry, they structured the imaginary of developing modernization. The mass media were agents of technological innovation; they helped us grow accustomed to relying on electronic appliances in domestic life, and they liberalized our customs with a more cosmopolitan horizon. At the same time they unified consumers under a common national vision. Because these media were supported predominantly by national capital and adhered to an ideology of development that entrusted modernization to each country's substitution of imports and industrialization, even the more internationally recognized actors—television and advertising—encouraged us to buy national products and disseminated information about them.

Up until twenty years ago, part of an artistic and cultural style defined national identities. Even when the early twentieth-century avant-garde movements moved beyond their homelands, they continued to be identified with particular societies: Italian futurism, Russian constructivism, and Mexican muralism. The names associated with many artistic movements in the second half of this century suggest that national profiles continued to define innovation. One talked of Italian neorealism, the French New Wave, and the New German Cinema.

We want to analyze the contradiction between this manner of characterizing artistic movements and the transnational conditions of the 1990s in which art and communication are produced, circulated, and received. What remains of national identities in a time of globalization and interculturalism, of multinational coproduction and the Chain of the Americas, of free trade agreements and regional integration? What remains when information, artists, and capital constantly cross borders?

We live in a time characterized by the intersection of territories and distinct cultural codes. Some films come to mind that address this phenomenon of *multiculturalidad*: for example, Wim Wenders's *The State of Things*, which begins more or less as a metaphysical drama filmed in Europe and culminates as a thriller set in Los Angeles's multiethnic streets. In view of this multinational hybridization, which also blends various genres and techniques, one must ask if—aside from art and mass communication—there exist scenarios of national identity?

Private versus Public: Rediscussing Vices and Virtues

In order to assess the impact of these changes in the relationship of artistic practices to national cultures, one needs to take into account two great transformations related to the private and public spheres that occurred in the same period. First, the relegating of culture to the home, increasing private culture (radio, TV, video) and decreasing attendance at movie houses, theaters, concerts, and other spectacles that rely on the collective use of urban space. Second, the transferring from the state to the private sector of the responsibility for the production, financing, and diffusion of cultural expression. I will outline recent research findings that address these processes in Mexico. Although the information applies to Mexico's situation, I intend to situate the argument within a broader reflection on the future of visual and electronic cultures in Latin America.

The first process, the displacement of cinema from the public arena to the home, involves not only changes in patterns of consumption but also changes in the production and financing of the offering. While movie theaters were closing in large numbers (more than two hundred disappeared in 1992 in Mexico), the purchases of television sets and videocassette recorders increased dramatically. Of 16 million Mexican households, more than 13 million have televisions and more than 5 million own VCRs. Videovisión, the former leader in the field, now linked to Televisa, has already established 722 outlets in the country, primarily in well-populated areas but also in rural villages. There are 674 video stores and 278 shops and supermarkets that reserve store space for video rentals.[1] Thus, the closing of movie theaters and the reduction in box-office receipts do not imply that people watch fewer movies, only that they now watch them at home.

Have ways of looking at cinema changed? Yes, and so have film production and communication. At least three changes should be emphasized in relation to cinema's function in the development of national cultures. First, the importance of films, which are now seen in greater numbers due to the convenience of home viewing, has decreased in the process of becoming linked with a more diverse and far-reaching system of audiovisual programming.

Second, despite Televisa's control over the Mexican video market, the vast majority of material offered through rental and purchasing centers comes from Hollywood Pictures, Paramount, RCA, Columbia, Touchstone, Turner, Universal, and Walt Disney; Mexican films take up very little catalog space and Latin American and European titles are absent altogether, unless they happen to be distributed by a U.S. company. In a survey of moviegoers conducted in Mexico City, 57.6 percent of those interviewed said they generally watch movies on TV or on video. This percentage will increase, taking into account the age of the population; the historical tendency is for a constant increase in the viewing of films in the domestic environment. This preference for watching movies at home is in direct contrast with the limited availability of Mexican films on video. When asked where they had seen the movies they considered to be the most important, 33.8 percent responded in the cinema, 37.4 percent answered on television, and only 2.1 percent said on the VCR. The low usage of video in the national film industry explains in part the scant offerings of Mexican movies in video stores. The difficulty of access to national cinema is compounded if one considers that the period least represented in video catalogs, the 1940s and 1950s, is the one preferred by the majority of those surveyed (García Canclini and Módena).

Third, the radical change in supply and demand is accompanied by a radical change in investment and financial strategies for film production. Whereas thirty years ago a film attempted to recover its costs through national and international screenings, it must now negotiate a range of channels: public and especially private television, other national networks, cable television services, video satellites, laser disc, and so on. It is no secret that in these avenues of advanced technology, financial and programming control rests in the hands of large transnational enterprises. The ability of national film, television, and video production decreases as the complexity and innovation of technology increases.

Mexico, like most Latin American countries, does not have a mechanism in place for regular investment in up-to-date innovations in the exchange of information, nor in the training of national personnel to effectively manage such equipment. We import from the United States almost all the electronic equipment used for cable television: signal codifiers and decodifiers; converters for VHF channels; specialized equipment to control signals purchased by subscribers; computing equipment specialized to control services and subscriptions; equipment for video recording, copying, editing, monitors, cassettes, and so on.

These tendencies—combined with the transnationalization of cinematographic offerings and the privatization of their consumption—are accentuated by the state's reduced role in culture industries and mass communication. The Latin American states, which through neoliberal politics have impoverished culture budgets, still maintain a greater presence in the administration of those forms of culture bound to territorial identity: archaeological sites, museums, the promotion of arts and national crafts. The audiovisual industry is relegated to the private sector. In other words, the most dynamic sectors of cultural expression, which produce the most innovative work, suffer the greatest repercussions. The private sphere, where transnationalization and deterritorialization prevail, has almost exclusive control over the voices and images.

What will happen to national cultures if television, video, and other related forms of technoculture are left in the hands of those with commercial and transnational objectives? How to avoid increasing dependency on foreign communication while television channels continue to merge and no policy for acquiring cultural technologies exists? In the case of Mexico, facilitating the investment and expansion of foreign enterprises may reduce Televisa's monopoly, thereby encouraging, through competition, the improvement of quality. Nevertheless, the expansion of television offerings by means of the arrival of Multivisión—a Turner channel—opens the industry only to U.S. programming and reduces the matter to one of marketing alone. This would not help to diversify or promote the cultural enrichment of our national screens.

It is true that Mexican cinema seems to be recuperating, and that other announced actions—such as dedicating channel 22 to independent culture and information—give reason to hope. Yet, what is the good of an isolated impulse toward national cinema if the vast majority of audiovisual space continues to be considered only a collection of settings that permit large corporations to hunt for clients? There is no reason to expect that the most powerful media will enable us to look at ourselves and to recognize our own cultural and regional diversity in order to consider our identity.

These recent changes, and their foreseeable escalation by NAFTA, provide another perspective for questions crucial to the identity debate—for example, the confrontation between tradition and modernity. The principal problem is no longer whether we should opt for one or the other; rather, it involves knowing if, with this most recent modernizing impulse, NAFTA, the key zones of cultural development—both traditional and modern—will be reorganized in terms of market value only.

It is common knowledge that the most dynamic and influential cultural activities require high investments, so private enterprises logically occupy that space and reap the financial benefits. But the question remains as to whether a society's sociocultural sense of itself can be produced like merchandise and accumulated like capital. Isn't supporting certain areas of culture and social welfare also a triumph of modern cultural development? Human rights, aesthetic innovation, scientific investigation, and the collective construction of a sense of history—being in the public interest—cannot be privatized or subjected to the rules of pragmatism and economic gain.

If we do not wish to renounce this, we must revise the state's function in and responsibility for education and culture. This does not involve a return to the state's idealized perception of itself as the seat of telluric nationalism, or as an agent of populist donations. (Television and video programming performance indicates that there is no reason to confer exclusive control to private enterprises.) What it does involve is to reconsider the state as a locus of public interest, as arbiter or guarantor of the collective need for information, recreation, and innovation, and not to subordinate these needs under commercial viability. In this scenario, the state or collaborative groups involving the government, private foundations, and independent associations must continue to subsidize many programs—public education, libraries, museums, regional and national television, experimental and cultural programming—to prevent the subordination of public interests to market forces.[2]

Rethinking national identities today supposes a questioning of the ways the state represents these identities. At the same time it is necessary to refute the neoliberals' swift transfer of the responsibility for narrating history and identity to enterprising monopolies and reducing the circulation of those narratives to consumption in homes. The weakening of the nation-state should open up the possibility for diverse voices and images—both local and transnational—to create many public scenarios in order to discuss the ways in which we wish to change and the directions for achieving that: radio stations, television channels, and independent video circuits that are able to compete for public funding, with the only conditions being the quality and collective interest or aesthetic experimentation of their programming.

From Cinema, TV, and Video to Audiovisual Space

If we consider the four principal cinema industries in Latin America—those of Argentina, Brazil, Cuba, and Mexico—we find that the first three have suffered a production decline of 60 to 90 percent in recent years. In Mexico, state-supported films, which represented 26.5 percent of the country's film production between 1971 and 1976, dropped to 7 percent between 1985 and 1988. From 1989 until the present, there has been a slight turnaround. The rejuvenation of cinema is very precarious, however, in that it does not extend to video stores or find an outlet in Televisa's channels, which cater to 88 percent of TV audiences (García Canclini and Piccini).[3]

The shift in spectators' preference from public theaters to their homes accounts for only part of the increasing difficulties of the Latin American film industry. One must also consider the disabling of cinema's industrial infrastructure in our countries, the lack of investment in technology for film production and even for the maintenance of auditoriums. The deterioration of the quality of films and their projections coupled with the rapid improvement of video quality and the televisual image (which will be boosted even more with the expansion of high-resolution television) increases the comparative advantages of the "cultura al domicilio" or "at-home culture."

In many European countries, and to a lesser extent in the United States and Canada, cinema is attempting to save itself by drawing upon television and video techniques so as to lower production costs. In the process of European integration, these diverse media — cinema, TV, video — are conceived as part of a similar paradigm under the rubric of audiovisual space. This unified perception of the diverse media is justified as much by the integration of production techniques in the three systems as by their aesthetic and cultural interrelations, and also because consumers tend to consider them together.

How do we situate ourselves in this process? In a study carried out recently on the possible effects that NAFTA will have on Mexican cinema and on foreign films projected in Mexico, we found few foreseeable changes in *production*. Few Mexican movies are filmed in the United States. As for foreign producers who want to film in Mexico, they may import almost everything they use (animals, film, cosmetics, and even technical equipment) without paying taxes. Equipment considered nonessential, currently assessed a 20 percent duty, may be freed from this stipulation by NAFTA. With respect to *distribution*, the changes under NAFTA will benefit the U.S. more than Mexico. Presently there are no duties on exports of foreign films to the United States; they do exist in Mexico but they will be abolished by the agreement so U.S. films will enter more easily. A recent estimate by the Instituto Mexicano de Cinematografía (Mexican Film Institute) indicates that U.S. cinema accounts for 62 percent of the films released in Mexico: some cineasts and critics predict that the number will soon reach 80 percent. Mexico's Ley de Cinematografía (cinema law) until recently required that Mexican films hand over 50 percent of all screen earnings. (Compañía Operadora de Teatros, S.A., the only company that has complied with the policy in the last few years, is now in the process of privatizing.) The elimination of this requirement will also contribute to an increased proportion of U.S. films.

Upcoming changes to international distribution and exhibition must be added to the conditions already mentioned. When U.S. chains begin in three or four years to transmit movies via satellite to the entire continent—projecting them on large hi-fi video screens installed in medium-sized viewing rooms—they will benefit from reduced circulation and exhibition costs.

Such changes confirm the need for global policies that integrate solutions for the film industry with those aimed at television and video. Within this framework, the NAFTA agreement will facilitate the generation of better facilities for the entry of U.S. and, to a lesser extent, Canadian filmmaking groups that want to use Mexican landscapes and historical monuments. But it can only happen by acknowledging the reconfiguration of the audiovisual market that has been taking place over the past few decades; in not assessing these changes, Mexican and Latin American cultural industries have fallen behind.

From this perspective, the question as to who will narrate our identity does not seem to offer a globalized response. A look to the forseeable future of Latin American electronic and audiovisual production, or even just a glance at the list of film and video advertisements in our cities, reveals that more than moving from the national to the global, there is an increasing dependence on a single country. A transformation imagined by a group of comedians seems appropriate to this discussion. In conjecturing as to what history books would say about Mexico in the twenty-first century: "Mexico is bordered on the north by the U.S., on the south by the U.S., on the east and west by the U.S., and even on the inside, by the U.S."

From the Last Film to the Last Polemic

Perhaps the future is not quite so bleak if we consider some recent European debates about the future of cinema and about audiovisual spaces. There exist, on the one hand, those who promote a Hollywood-style tactic that would consist of dislocating the production toward countries where the costs are lower and the markets are less saturated. Such new "Hollywood countries," including Singapore, Hong Kong, India, Mexico, and Egypt, could furnish locations, cheap labor, and untapped publics (Michelet, 156–61). On the other hand, there are those who forsee a *cinemundo* or "cinema world" that would purportedly strive to use more sophisticated technology and marketing strategies in order to become incorporated into a world-scale market. Coppola, Spielberg, and Lucas, for example, construct spectacular narratives independent of culture, level of education, national history, economic development, or political regime. *Cinemundo,* says Charles-Albert Michelet, "is closer to Claude Lévi-Strauss than to John Ford" (159). It deals with fabricating a spectacle dazzling enough to persuade television viewers that once or twice a year it is worth leaving the sofa at home in order to occupy a less comfortable seat in the dark theater.

Can these tactics arrest the decline of cinema? Neither the neo-Hollywood nor the *cinemundo* model occasions innovations that renew the language or the social and narrative role of cinema. It is difficult to conceive of how cinema will sustain itself—not to mention resolve the crisis—without artistic innovation that transcends the occasional dazzle of special effects.

Perhaps it would be easier, Michelet suggests, to change the conception of cinema from being a distraction to being an instrument of a mass media that today organizes the communication industry. In the past it produced terminal benefits, but in the future it should generate intermediate benefits, programs for the networks, and serve as an industry subcontractor. Although it would lose in creative independence, it would gain in security of serving the needs of the television programmers and video distributors. Of course, cinema must adapt itself to the more frivolous tastes of television audiences; there will remain very few movie houses for those nostalgia buffs interested in history, national identity, and ethnicity.[4]

It pays to ask, however, whether a product as culturally complex and fertile as cinema plays with its destiny only under the rules of standardization and globalization of the economic rationale. Some recent Latin American films with considerable public and critical success or with a short-term repercussion in television and in video would not enter easily in an apocalyptic vision. Brazilian cinema of the 1970s and the first half of the 1980s, which, thanks to the combination of testimony about identity and the internationalization of the culture in that country with an imaginative and parodic representation style, seduced audiences inside and outside of Brazil: from *Macunaíma* to *Doña Flor and Her Two Husbands* to *Xica da Silva*. I am thinking of the rereadings between *policiacas* and politics in Argentine history made by Adolfo Aristaráin; in the narrations of the history of daily intimacy proposed in Mexico by *Rojo amanecer* (*Red Dawn*) and *Como agua para chocolate* (*Like Water for Chocolate*). This last film, viewed by more than 1.5 million spectators in Mexico in just a few months, may seem to be nothing more than a *telenovela*, perhaps better made than most. Yet, it is connected to other less conventional Mexican films — *La tarea* (*The Homework*), *La mujer de Benjamin* (*Benjamin's Woman*), *El bulto* — that rework the crisis of personal identity and political projects with irony and irreverence and without complacent nostalgia.

These and other films, well received by heterogeneous publics, reveal that identity and history — including local and national identities — fit in the cultural industries even with their need for high financial yield. Along with the deterritorialization of the arts, there are strong movements of reterritorialization. These are represented by social movements that affirm the local, and also by mass-media processes such as regional radio and television, and the creation of micromarkets of music and folk elements; the "demassification" and *mestización* of consumption engenders difference and diverse forms of local rootedness.[5]

Nations and ethnicities continue to exist. The key problem seems not to be the risk that globalization will erase them but rather to understand how ethnic, regional, and national identities reconstitute themselves through processes of intercultural hybridization. If we conceive of nations as multidetermined scenarios, where diverse symbolic systems intersect and interpenetrate, the question is what kind of cinema and television narrates heterogeneity and the coexistence of various codes in a single group, and even in a single subject.

We need an electronic iconology that corresponds to the current redefinition of identity. By constituting itself not only in relation to a territory but also in the middle of international webs of information, we must work with a definition of identity that is not only *sociospatial* but *sociocommunicational* as well; that is, a definition that articulates the local, national, and postnational cultures that play an increasingly significant role in configuring identities everywhere and in restructuring the significance of local or regional qualities emanating from distinct territorial experiences.

If identity conforms in relation to multiple contexts, then the mass media associated with the transcultural relocation of communication, including cinema, will not be ill prepared to act.

Multimedia and multicontextuality are two key notions for redefining the social role of cinema and other communication systems. The extent to which cinema is revived depends on our relocation of it in a multimedia audiovisual space; national and local identities can persist if we resituate them in a communication that is multicontextual. Identity, made more dynamic through this process, will not be only a ritualized narration, the monotonous repetition of outmoded principles. Identity, as a narrative we constantly reconstruct with others, is also a coproduction.

Notes

This essay first appeared in Mexico City in Spanish, published in "La jornada," *Nueva Epoca* 193 (21 February 1993): 27–33.

1. Report by Deborah Holtz for research in the course "Cinema, Television and Video: Habits of Audiovisual Consumption in Mexico," carried out under the auspices of the Instituto Mexicano de Cinematografía" under the coordination of Néstor García Canclini, Ella F. Quintal, Enrique Sánchez Ruíz, and José Manuel Valenzuela Arce. The total number of cinema closings and the increase of televisions and videocassette recorders correspond to the year 1992.

2. For a more fully developed discussion of this point, see Gilberto Guevara Niebla and Néstor García Canclini (coordinators), *La educación y la cultura ante el Tratado de Libre Comercio* (Mexico City: Nueva Imagen, 1992), especially in the chapters of María y Campos, García Canclini, and Carlos Monsiváis.

3. The figure of 88 percent of the audience tuning in to Televisa channels corresponds to our 1989 survey of cultural consumption carried out in Mexico City. Given the reduced coverage of the other channels in the country, we suppose that national statistics would give a greater rating to Televisa.

4. Bernardo Miege treats the related debate in his article "L'industrialisation de l'audiovisuel," in *CinemAction* (1988): 162–65.

5. Two critics have recently addressed this question: Armand Mattelart ("La communication-monde" [Paris: La Découverte, 1992]) and Stuart Hall ("The Local and the Global: Globalization and Ethnicity," in Anthony D. King, ed., *Culture, Globalization and the World System* [Binghamton: State Univ. of New York, 1991]).

Works Cited

Barbero, Jesús Martín. *De los medios a las meditaciones.* Mexico City: Gustavo Gilli, 1987. 180–83.

García Canclini, Néstor, and Mabel Piccini. "Culturas de la ciudad de México: símbolos colectivos y usos del espacio urbano." In *El consumo cultural en México.* Mexico City: CNCA, in press.

García Canclini, Néstor, and María Eugenia Módena. *El cine mexicano y sus públicos.* Mexico City: Instituto Mexicano de Cinematografía, 1995.

Michelet, Charles-Albert. "Réflexions sur le drôle de drame du cinéma mondial." *CinemAction* (1988): 156–61.

Monsiváis, Carlos. "Notas sobre la cultura mexicana en el siglo XX." *Historia general de México,* vol. 4. Mexico City: El Colegio de México, 1976.

Contributors

José Carlos Avellar is a film critic. He is the author of five books on Brazilian and Latin American cinema: *Imagen e som, imagem e açao, imaginaçao* (1982), *O cinema dilacerado* (1986), *O chão da palavra, Brazilian cinema and literature* (1994), *Deus e o diabo: a linha reta, o melaço de cana e o retrato do artista quando jovem,* an essay on Rocha's *Black God, White Devil* (1995), and *A ponte clandestina,* essays on Latin American film theory (1995). His essays have appeared in *Le cinéma brésilien* (Paris: Centre Georges-Pompidou, 1987), and *Hojas de cine* (Mexico City: Univ. Autónoma Metropolitana, 1986).

Beat Borter is the president of Filmpodium in Biel-Bienne, Switzerland. He regularly attends the International Festival of New Latin American Cinema in Havana, selecting films for the Fribourg Festival and for other film events in Switzerland. He recently organized a retrospective of Tomás Gutiérrez Alea's work.

Julianne Burton-Carvajal is founding director of the CineMedia Project at the University of California, Santa Cruz. The editor of *Cinema and Social Change in Latin America: Conversations with Film- makers* and *The Social Documentary in Latin America,* she is currently assembling an anthology, *Mexican Movie Melodrama: New Critical Directions*, and compiling *Three Lives in Film: An Illustrated Memoir of the Improbable Careers of Mexico's Matilde Landeta, Venezuela's Margot Benacerraf, and Argentina's María Luisa Bemberg.*

Ambrosio Fornet presides over the editorial board of the Cuban Writer's Union (Unión de Escritores Cubanos [UNEAC]) and has served as literary adviser to the Cuban film institute (Instituto Cubano de Arte e Industria Cinematográficos [ICAIC]). Essayist, editor, literary critic, and screenwriter, Fornet's most recent book is *El libro en Cuba: Siglos XVIII y XIX* (Havana: Letras Cubanas, 1994).

David William Foster is Regents' Professor of Spanish and Women's Studies at Arizona State University. He has written and edited numerous books on Latin American literature and cinema, including *Gay and Lesbian Issues in Latin American Literature, Latin American Writers on Gay and Lesbian Themes: A Bio-Critical Sourcebook,* and *Contemporary Argentine Cinema.*

Néstor García Canclini is a professor in the anthropology department at the Universidad Autónoma Metropolitana in Mexico City. His recent books include *Los nuevos espectadores: Cine, televisión y video en México* and *Hybrid Cultures: Strategies for Entering and Leaving Modernity* (Minnesota, 1995).

Ilene S. Goldman has curated a collection of Latin American and U.S. Latin video art available for distribution through the Video Data Bank at the School of the Art Institute of Chicago. She teaches film studies in the Chicago area.

Gilberto Gómez Ocampo, born in Armenia, Colombia, teaches Spanish at Wabash College in Indiana. His works include *Entre María y La vorágine: la literatura colombiana finisecular* as well as numerous articles about nineteenth- and twentieth-century Latin American narrative.

Teresa Longo is an associate professor in the Department of Modern Languages and Literatures at the College of William and Mary in Virginia. Her research focuses on Central American revolutionary discourse and the intersections between literary language and the visual arts. Longo's recent scholarship appears in the *Latin American Literary Review*, the *Journal of Interdisciplinary Literary Studies*, and *Teaching and Testimony*.

John Mraz describes himself as a "graphic historian." A senior researcher in the Instituto de Ciencias Sociales y Humanidades of the Universidad Autónoma de Puebla (Mexico), he has published widely on Latin American history as recounted through photography, cinema, and video. His books include *La mirada inquieta: Nuevo fotoperiodismo mexicano, 1976–1996* (Mexico City: Centro de la Imagen/UAP, 1996) and *Uprooted: Braceros Photographed by the Hermanos Mayo* (Houston: Arte Público Press, 1996). He has directed award-winning documentary videotapes, and has curated international photographic expositions.

Paulo Antonio Paranaguá, film critic and historian, is a specialist in Latin American audiovisual production. Among his recent books are *Le cinéma cubain* (1990), *A la découverte de l'Amérique Latine: Petite anthologie d'une école documentaire méconnue* (1992), and *Le cinéma mexicain* (1992), all published by the Centre-Georges-Pompidou in Paris. The British Film Institute has translated Paranaguá's work on Mexico, which is now available under the title *Mexican Cinema*.

Laura Podalsky is an assistant professor of Romance languages at Bowling Green State University, where she teaches Latin American cinema and culture. Her work has been published in *Mediating Two Worlds: Cinematic Encounters in the Americas*, *Velvet Light Trap*, and *Studies in Latin American Popular Culture*. Her doctoral dissertation is titled "Urban Negotiations: Buenos Aires and the Articulation of Hegemonic Discourses in the 1950s and 1960s."

Patricia Santoro teaches Spanish at Montclair-Kimberley Academy in Montclair, New Jersey. She is the author of *Novel into Film: The Case of* La familia de Pascual Duarte *and* Los santos inocentes.

Ann Marie Stock, assistant professor at the College of William and Mary, teaches Hispanic cinema and literature, and cultural studies. Her recent research has been published in *Marges, Revista Canadiense de Estudios Hispánicos,* and *Historia general del cine mundial.* With a Fulbright Lecture-Research Award, Stock taught at the University of Costa Rica and collaborated with the Centro de Cine in San José to investigate the compiling of a reference guide to Central American and Caribbean cinema.

◆ Index